THE GOLDEN CORD
The Alchemy of the Lord's Prayer
Adonijah O. Ogbonnaya, Ph. D.

The Golden Cord: The Alchemy of the Lord's Prayer
Publications Copyright © 2009, literature arm of AACTEV8 International
(Apostolic Activation Network)
Aactev8 International 1020 Victoria Ave. Venice, CA 90291

www.aactev8.com

Published by Seraph Creative
Third Edition
ISBN: 978-0-9946974-4-8

Library of Congress data

Alchemy, prayer, provisions, personal growth, spirituality. The Lord's Prayer, Will, will of man, will of God, Kingdom of God, heaven, forgiveness, temptation, spiritual power, transformation, Bible study.

No part of this book may be reproduced, stored in retrieval system, or transmitted in any form or by any means, electronic, mechanical, photocopy, recording or otherwise except for brief quotation in print review without prior permission from the holder of the copyright.

Scripture quotations from the New American Standard Bible, unless otherwise stated.

ESV, NIV, NKJV, KJV

Cover art by Taylor Remington

Typesetting, Illustration & Layout by Feline
www.felinegraphics.com

Table of Contents

Acknowledgments — 5
Introduction — 7

Part I: The Meaning of Prayer — 13

1. The Meaning of Prayer — 15
2. Prayer and Human Emotion — 29
3. Praying in the Spirit — 37
4. Varieties of Prayer — 45
5. Methods of Prayer — 69
6. Atmospheres of Effective Prayer — 77

Part II: The Golden Cord — The Alchemy of the Lord's Prayer — 85

7. Key 1: Relationship — 87
8. Key 2: Heavens — 97
9. Key 3: Hallow the Name — 103
10. Key 4: Call Forth the Kingdom — 113
11. Key 5: Aligning Will to WILL — 127
12. Key 6: Access to Provision — 165
13. Key: 7: Forgive — 177
14. Key 8: Follow the Leader — 185
15. Key 9: Call for Backup — Deliverance — 203
16. Key 10: Release All to the All — 215
17. Amen — 233

Bibliography — 236
About the Author — 238

ACKNOWLEDGEMENTS

Since Christmas 1970 when I returned to Nigeria (a few weeks after an encounter on the road to a farm), God has placed many people in my life who have helped me.

Mr. Josiah Ikedi trained and mentored me in business, as is the custom of our people, and encouraged me to go to school. I still remember Bishop Edward Ezenwafor's fiery preaching on the streets of Onitsha in 1971. A. A. Nwodika, who baptized me in the Nkisi River, helped me to stop going up repeatedly to altar calls for salvation! Rev. N. C. Thompson, who is truly my Father in the ministry. He turned me to a passion for study that still bears fruit today. He sent me to Jalingo in Northern Nigeria as a young pastor of fifteen years old. There, by the help of Rev. Alfred and Marianne Bohr, who were missionaries to Nigeria, I came to Canada and then onto the USA. To the Bohrs, "Mom and Dad," words cannot express how much I love you.

Thanks to my dear brother and friend and his lovely family, Bishop Freddie Steele, my "twin." Only heaven knows how much you have done to encourage me.

Bishop Ruddel and Audrey Bloomfield, a man with a father's heart and woman with a mother's heart, thank you. I am grateful to Apostle H. Daniel Wilson for your encouragement. I also want to express my gratitude to Dr. Arvid J. Lindley, the former president of Hillcrest Christian College, who took a chance on an African pastor and opened the door of education to me.

Overall, I must thank my wife and great friend, Benedicta Chinyere, for her love, encouragement, and support. She has continued to support the work of the Kingdom, even when it has not been easy. Her joy, even in the face of hardship, continues to be an inspiration.

I thank God for all my children and what they have done to educate me as much as I have educated them.

Wherever you are, may the Lord bless you and your generations.

Dr. O

Introduction

This is a book on prayer. One cannot be theoretical about prayer. It would lack authenticity. Therefore, I will introduce this book by giving you a sneak peek into one of the major experiences of my life.

I am often reticent about autobiographical stories in public preaching and lectures. But I find no other way of exploring the subject of prayer and maintaining authenticity without sharing from my life.

My prayer life is greatly influenced by the Hebrew system found among the old Igbos (my people in Nigeria) and later on by the Siddur (Jewish prayer book).

I also learned much while attending Christian schools run by missionaries. In reading the New Testament and attending missionary schools, what especially caught my imagination was the prayer taught by Jesus and the prayers he prayed. When the disciples said "teach us to pray," He prayed what we call today the Lord's Prayer. Every day, as we recited the Lord's Prayer at my grade school, it took on a deeper meaning for me. Several times while praying the Psalms and reciting the Lord's Prayer, I had a vision of the Lord. On one of those occasions, I received the call to preach but paid no attention to it!

From 1968 to 1970, I secretly attended a small 'full gospel' church led by an elder called Mr. Oko. My father was not very keen on my going to this church. He believed it would remove me completely from our tradition. In 1969, Mr. Oko had taken us to a convention. There I was filled with the Holy Spirit and began to speak in tongues, though I was not yet baptized in water. There I had visions of another world. I must have spent over three hours at the altar. When I came back home, my father was not happy. He stopped me from going to this "crazy people church," but the die was cast. I prayed continuously in my newly found language as I walked and meditated on the experience of being caught up in the spirit. My spirit was filled with sweet ecstasy. In fact, I was having so many visions that my father and some of his friends

began to come to me for answers to certain troubling issues. During my stay in the small church, the leader gave me opportunities to preach and to teach though I was the youngest there.

THE ENCOUNTER

In September of 1970, on the way to a farm, I began to say the Lord's Prayer. "Our Father who art in heaven, hallowed be thy name, thy kingdom come, they will be done on Earth as it is in Heaven." As these lines flowed from my lips, I knew something was happening to me. It was as though someone else was speaking through me. I could not resist. I kept speaking. I could hear myself saying, "Give us this day our daily bread," and the rest that follows, as the whole landscape melted away. The trees, the fields and the hills in that moment began to move as if they were liquid oil reflecting light. Powerful lights shone through. I could still hear myself in the distance, faintly whispering the Lord's Prayer. My whole being was passing through dimensions that, until this day, I can hardly find words to describe. I stood before a vast stream of indescribable light, rivers of golden fire, and waves of blue flame - as one finds towards the end of a burning candle, but infinitely larger in dimensions.

The streams of light and fire gave forth sounds of great harmony. I saw men and women clothed with garments, reflecting various colors of light that mimicked the rainbow. I beheld creatures the like of which I have never seen. I heard my inner man speaking the name of the Lord in Hebrew. I spoke the name of Jesus, the Messiah - "Yeshua HaMeshiac." The sound of my voice was like a song from a myriad of voices. Sound poured out from every pore of my body; my whole being was a harmony of praise. My body was not my body; it became transparent light. I could see through my body. I remember hearing the question, "Do you believe?" Without hesitation, I responded, "Yes, I believe." In that one moment, I experienced the God of Abraham, Isaac, and Jacob in His great love, beauty, and terror - all at once!

Since then, the Lord's Prayer has held a supernatural fascination for me. That moment with the Lord's Prayer opened up for me the vistas of the Heavenly dimensions. The pattern and process of this prayer were the magma that formed the stone of my prayer life. Of the numerous spiritual experiences I have had through the years, this one was so indelibly imprinted into the depth of my soul that I find myself returning to the Lord's Prayer in times of confusion. This meditation has never failed to yield fruit.

The experience with the Lord's Prayer affirmed my faith in Jesus Christ as the Way, the door into that eternal realm. Jesus did not just teach the prayer to recite by rote or to turn into mere traditional. The prayer came to represent for me a glory cipher, a kingdom code, a power formula. The Lord's Prayer holds, within its sentences, gates, and channels of deep spiritual terrain through which our souls can traverse in God our Father. It contains keys that can unlock the spiritual possibilities in our body, soul, and spirit, and launch us into deeper spiritual experiences. This prayer is for me the "Golden Cord" which threads from this temporal dimension into eternity.

I know by experience that, when we pray, we open up gates and channels for traveling in spiritual dimensions. I have spent hours meditating on the Lord's Prayer, resulting in numerous spiritual journeys, visions, and dreams. It is a door for entering into the worlds, desired by the Father, for the disciple of Jesus Christ. This is just the beginning of the lessons I have learned from this prayer in the past forty years.

I consider the Lord's Prayer to be the 'golden cord' of prayer to pierce through dimensions. Here, we can hang our prayer life in our pilgrimage upon this Earth and seek to enter our mansions in the Heavens.

I write as an apprentice who is still learning from the Master. In matters of spirituality, it is the personal inner experiences that are often paramount to me, but not without reference to objective reality. In a sense, I am an 'empiricist,' giving more importance to my direct, inner experiences of God than to the dogmatic traditions and formula of man.

How To Read This Book

This book is written to help you with your spiritual life, especially in the area of prayer. These days there is so much put forward as spirituality that is not biblically based (and may even go against Judeo-Christian perspectives!) that many honest men and women have given up on spiritual processes. They have become suspicious of anything that speaks of mystery. Some have developed the fear that being spiritual may make them susceptible to all sorts of deceptions and devils. It does not help that much of what we hear focuses on dealing with demons or the Devil. This undermines the completed work of Jesus Christ!

There is no question that prayer plays a strong role in the development of authentic Christian spirituality. Prayer can work in all sorts of practical ways in your life.

In this book, I will provide you with a guide to enter into prayer and tap into the supernatural realm. I will describe straightforward ways to understand and practice your spirituality. You will encounter interpretations and principles that have been proven in my life and the lives of many throughout the world. The teachings and

ideas contained in this book will help you transcend some of the spiritual constructs that have limited your ability to overcome certain obstacles. You will discover that, through prayer, you can access a life of miracles and joy. Prayer has been given as a key to help you make quantum leaps into new territories and spheres of wellbeing and wholeness. There was a great inner current of power placed in you when you became God's child through Jesus Christ! It is not necessary to die with it still stuck inside of you. You do not need to keep wandering in the wilderness of powerlessness.

In this book, you will tap into language and process that will help unleash that inner power of Christ in you. Power for a whole life transformation! The language of prayer, especially as we find in the Lord's Prayer, is for releasing miracles directly into your life and world.

The first part of this book, chapters one through six, deals with the meaning of prayer, the Holy Spirit, human emotions, varieties of prayers, methods of prayers and atmosphere for effective prayer. The second part concentrates directly on the Lord's Prayer.

Get ready!

The Lord's Prayer

Jesus said when you pray, say:

Our Father

Who is in heaven,

Hallowed be Your name.

Your Kingdom come.

Your will be done on earth

As it is in heaven.

Give us this day our daily bread,

And forgive us our debts,

As we forgive our debtors.

And do not lead us into temptation,

But deliver us from the evil one.

For Yours is the kingdom,

The Power

And the Glory,

Forever. Amen.

Matthew 6:9–13

PART I

THE MEANING OF PRAYER

CHAPTER 1

The Meaning of Prayer

Prayer is a meditational harmonizing of our being with the nature and purpose of God. It is the concerted effort of our whole being to become attuned to the creative Spirit of the Creator. Prayer can be done collectively or individually. Prayer can be thought, emotions or even attitude. It can be quiet serenity or boisterous sound and movements. Prayer is mighty.

Attitudes, Thought And Action

The power of prayer is often affected by our attitude to God and our attitude regarding ourselves and others. In relating to God, we must have a position of faith, "And without faith it is impossible to please Him, for he who comes to God must believe that He is and that He is a rewarder of those who seek Him." (Hebrews 11:6). In relating to others, we must express love and forgiveness because God measures back to us the measure we use with others. In relating to ourselves, we must express acceptance and grace because self-hatred is the root of unbelief and lack of forgiveness.

> How deep we can go into God and this power depends on how much we are willing to let go of the wounds and inner pain we harbor - either against God, others or ourselves.

These are catalysts for the power of prayer. How deep we can go into God and this power depends on how much we are willing to let go of the wounds and inner pain we harbor - either against God, others or ourselves. The prayer which the Lord Jesus taught us to pray, commonly called "The Lord's Prayer," calls us to live as we pray and to pray as we live. In other words, our daily thoughts, actions, and beliefs must strive for the same level of harmony with God that we seek in prayer.

Thoughts and ideas have a powerful impact on prayers. It can be argued that our every thought has the same impact as a prayer. The longer one holds a thought in one's mind, the more power it possesses. The New Testament views the mind as a

builder that contributes to help or harm, bless or curse every individual that we hold in our thoughts or spoken prayers.

> *Blessed are the pure in heart (thought), for they shall see God. (Matthew 5:8).* *Sight + purity*

In tuning our being to what I term "the God wave," it also helps to foster our relationship with the Divine in all His forms. Whether we are praying for ourselves or others, our thoughts are important. If people have asked for prayer, it is important that we surround them with intentional, thoughtful concern. It is important as people of faith that we saturate the world with thoughts of divine compassion and love. The pulse of our thought reaches out and affects even those who have not asked specifically for our prayer help. This is our likeness to God. This is why Paul insisted in Philippians 4:8

Thoughts empower existence

> *Finally, brethren, whatever is true, whatever is honorable, whatever is right, whatever is pure, whatever is lovely, whatever is of good repute, if there is any excellence and if anything worthy of praise,* **dwell (think) on these things.** *(emphasis added)*

Divine Energy

I believe that the power of prayer travels through thought and mood. When done effectively, prayer is the light of Christ's nature traveling through our **thought** and words to the dimensions, locations, situations or persons for which we are praying. Now, prayer is not "telling God what to do." Instead, prayer is the creation of a tabernacle of thoughts, ideas, and words in which the Glory of the Lord may travel and dwell. If we can align thoughts, ideas, and words with the Word of God, our prayer can be the means for manifesting the perfect Will of God in any earthly situation - on Earth as it is already in Heaven!

> *When we pray, we crash the false walls of our rationalism and are carried on the wings of grace, answering the inner longing of our will.*

When prayer is effective, God releases glory and energy that radiates its content to whatever dimension our thought is willing to carry it. Thus we read in Ephesians 3:20, *"Now to Him who is able to do far more abundantly beyond all that we* **ask or think,** *according to the power that works within us,"* (emphasis added). This power

Asking + thinking create

that works within us is the Holy Spirit of Christ, impregnating our thought and will in such a way that God works in us and through us to transform the world. If the power that works in us is God Himself, then our very prayer is the interweaving movement of the Divine energy. This energy is moving

16   1 - The Meaning Of Prayer

from within us to God, returning to Him so that He is "all in all" in our prayers.

The basis of the movement of God's power (or Divine energy) in a human being is the commitment of thought, imagination, and speech to God.

Prayers, as expressions of the deepest desire of man, can carry not only the positive power of God but also the negative influence of the demonic! Prayer, not aligned with God, can carry negative qualities, taking whatever we ask or think and multiplying it by God or the demonic. Given this power, there is the need for purification of our desire for prayer to be effective and righteous. True prayer moves beyond the principle of asking and even supersedes the human conscious thought process. This is the mystery of prayer: God can answer unformed thought and that which is beyond words. In fact, we read in Isaiah 65:24, "It will also come to pass that before they call, I will answer; and while they are still speaking, I will hear."

The Supernatural Sphere

Prayer is the feet by which we walk the way of divinity and enter the door of eternity. It is the vehicle, whose engine is Christ, leading us from the Judgment Seat to the Mercy Seat - wherein shines the sacred flame burning over the hidden manna, the ever living rod of Aaron and the words engraved upon clay of tablets by the finger of YHWH (Jehovah) ELHM. In prayer, we turn our full attention to the Mercy Seat as we gaze intently at the sacred flame of faith and envision hope, even in the wilderness. Prayer is a divine love language, whose wondrous lyrics are joyfully tuned by notes of worship, adoration, thanksgiving, praise and jubilant dance before the One who sits within the flame - the Son of God. It is the sacred flame of eternity, breathed upon our temporality.

When we pray, we activate the instrument for crossing over with the Lord Jesus Christ through the storm-tossed sea of life. As we pray, we instigate the purification of the emotions, thoughts, and feelings in body, spirit, and soul. This process permits us to pass over to the supernatural sphere and to enter into these mysteries, hidden behind the flame, into the Ark of the Covenant. For this to happen, we must, as Paul tells us, "*With all prayer and petition pray at all times in the Spirit, and with this in view, be on the alert with all perseverance and petition for all the saints,*" (Ephesians 6:18).

Prayer that releases the supernatural and suspends natural boundaries must itself be from the Spirit of God. It is when prayer flows from the very heart of the Holy Spirit that it can transform all carnal operation of the flesh and mind. We can be transported directly into the presence and throne of God! In prayer, we enter into the sacred mystery of which Paul speaks when he says, "*For one who speaks in a*

tongue does not speak to men but to God; for no one understands, but in his spirit he speaks mysteries." (1 Corinthians 14:2).

The Mystical Gate of Fellowship

As children of God, our prayers must flow from a heart fully surrendered to the Spirit of Christ, directed by the inner longing of the spirit within. The Holy Spirit empowers and nudges us to become more intimate with God our Father. As we develop a life of effectual prayer, we can go through this mystical gate of fellowship, not only by a one-time infilling of the Holy Spirit but a constant in-flow of the Spirit of Christ.

When we pray, we crash the false walls of our rationalism and are carried on the wings of grace, answering the inner longing of our will. We reach into our subconscious as we groan with sighs of anticipation for the refreshing that comes from the Lord Jesus Christ. Like the bridegroom longing for the bride, God in man reaches through the darkness and looks, face to face, upon Himself with the frailty of our human eyes. We speak mouth to mouth with our stammering tongue of clay. Prayer is holy fire, burning in the soul toward God. The glowing fervency for God and love for Him sounds a harmonious chord. Prayer tunes our souls as musical instruments to the God-sphere. Through prayer, let us enter into the Holy of Holies. Let us die to the natural that we might live supernaturally. Let us burn the flame that we might overcome the darkness that surrounds us and be raised by the crucified Christ, who is that Light, to new life.

Prayer Protects the Human World

The relevance of prayer for human life cannot be overstated. Even the skeptics of the secular world are now buying into the potency of prayer. Prayer is among the acts known to ground a human person while simultaneously thrusting them into transcendence! Prayer is a creative principle within man, far exceeding what the mind has even dared to grasp in its fallen nature and frailty. When eternity completely swallows time, and the influence of prayer upon the universe and human affairs is unveiled, we will realize a powerful truth - prayer has kept the world from the grasp of the abyss and held it from plunging headlong into the precipice of a personal and social demonic black hole! Prayer resists the oppressive power of the demonic that strives to take over our personal and communal world.

In prayer, human beings soar upward into unfathomable mystery. We fall upward into the heart of God, and God comes "downward" into our humanity[1]. Prayer is the spiritual practice that the Holy Spirit uses to release us from carnality into true spiritual friendship with God. By its sweet communion, we gain the deeper knowledge of God. It is the key given to us to unlock mysteries of the inner sanctuary of the heavens. The Bible calls us to pray without ceasing. It is an act for all seasons which releases us into divine righteousness and pleasure - which is the life of Christ. Here in prayer is the secret of the believer's subjective intimacy with the objective God. He is the object of his/her supreme devotion.

Through this divine focus on the God who has come to live in the intimate center of our being, we transcend the bondage of the mundane and are drawn into divinity. The mundane becomes sanctified reality! Now and then, the believer must consciously enter that inner sanctum and travel the path called Jesus, to the truth and the life that He is.

By constant prayer, and tuning of the heart to the rhythm of divinity, the daily life of the child of God is filled with new courage and strength to face the ungodly forces of the universe that array themselves against them. Here, in the intimacy of Father and child, the long process of glorification initiated by God in the garden, confirmed by the call of Israel, reinforced by the covenant of blood, and set ablaze upon the altar of fire, is now established at the altar of the blood and body of the Lamb. In prayer, we return to the primal purpose of the Divine creative image and likeness - in which we are made a little lower than Elohim (Psalm 8:5). What is the chariot of wind by which we fly into that realm of the angels and become a radiating image of our Father? Prayer, I say!

Prayer is where we pass beyond the veil, through the luminous darkness (Howard Thurman) into the supernal light[2], bypassing the flaming sword, clothed by the love of God in His Christ, and then proceed to eat of the fruit of the Tree of Life.

> In prayer, human beings soar upward into unfathomable mystery. We fall upward into the heart of God and God comes "downward" into our humanity. Prayer is the spiritual practice that the Holy Spirit uses to release us from carnality into true spiritual friendship with God.

Intimacy And Lack Of Prayer

Prayer provides a solid ground for growth and intimacy with God. We can make choices based on the influence of the Holy Spirit (who knows the innermost thought of God) and not based on our desire or thoughts derived from worldly patterns or processes. By prayer, our will becomes aligned with our Heavenly Father. Our spirit tunes to the highest harmony of truth and righteousness with Christ and He makes our lives music for the Divine dance.

Our actions and plans in life, if not seasoned with prayer, become ineffective and out-of-sync with divinity. A lack of prayer results in a lack of spiritual concentration. It robs us of a focused vision on God, who alone is capable of setting our affections in order for His righteous priorities. Prayer is a most significant undertaking. It

demands the commitment of all our being and provides perspective from the eternal on the spectrum of our entire life. Lack of prayer is not merely regrettable; it allows a destructive inflow of negativity into our being that cuts us from true life.

Lack of prayer is a drainer of spiritual energy and causes most of the disintegrative chaos within the believer and their communion with God. It is at the heart of much disunity and failure of resolve into which great men and women of faith sometimes fall. Somewhere at the root is dismissal, or even worse, the complete neglect of genuine prayer.

Again, I must reiterate that prayer, in this sense, is not me working to be accepted by God. It is my falling unrestrained into communion with my Lord and my God so that I, in communion, feed on God's eternal presence. Where the circle of prayer is broken, power begins to wane, and the elegantly woven thread of genuine fellowship starts to pull apart. Lack of prayer often leads to self-justification and prideful resistance to the Holy Spirit. I see much of this as a pastor - where people who refuse intimacy with God want to make decisions affecting the flow of God's Kingdom. May God help us! When prayer is lacking, because one is no longer looking steadily into the heart of God, one becomes self-focused.

> Through this divine focus on the God who has come to live in the intimate center of our being, we transcend the bondage of the mundane and are drawn into divinity. The mundane becomes sanctified reality!

Prayer is a mighty weapon for effectiveness. Conversely, its lack is a potent weapon in the hand of our carnality and whatever enemy that seeks our downfall. Unfortunately, this is especially true in ministers. Its lack can be devastating to the people they tend because it keeps them out of touch with the inner realities of their own lives. Lack of personal prayer in ministers may often lead to rationalization of the spiritual inadequacy in their lives and ministry or a legalistic conformism - from which God is absent. Both of these often parade themselves as holiness and may keep us from discovering the truth about ourselves. Thus, we end up ministering from a false center.

False Prayer

Prayerlessness may be terrible, but a false kind of prayer or ungodly prayer is destructive in and of itself. This false kind of prayer ignores the Word of the Lord Jesus, focuses on the emotional despair of the people, and works on their desires. Its focus is often upon the devil and his plans, not Christ. It is answered, but never by God. It can often create a negative atmosphere that can bring into manifestation the inner pain of the one who is praying. An effective spirituality requires a prayerful life.

The Prayerful Life

A prayerful life:

- helps you identify divine priorities for your life
- leads you to transformative actions
- activates and encourages an atmosphere of mutuality between believers
- opens us up to the flow of Divine life
- produces true humility

Close contemplation of prayer will cause awe at God's Grace, which brings us, with all our inadequacies and lack of worth, close to such a Holy God. The person who prays often becomes overcome with the depth of God's Mercy and Grace. This prayer-consciousness will silence the pride of life as one is filled with the Glory of the Lord. It will hush the lust of the flesh as one is filled with Godly love and it will wash the lust of the eyes as one gazes intently on the beauty of Jesus Christ.

Relationship, by its very nature, demands communication. Our relationship with God requires that the inner spring of prayerful communion with God flow continually. This spring of prayer waters the garden of our communion with Christ.

Jesus the Messiah often went off alone to drink from this spring. Out of this fountain of prayer flowed miracles, signs and wonders, wisdom, knowledge and revelation (Matthew 14:23ff, Mark 6:46-47). The Spirit of the Lord which came upon Jesus was the Spirit of prayer and intercession. If we follow Jesus in this regard, prayer will be the hallmark of our lives. Every spiritual person is truly a person of prayer. As water is to fish, so prayer is to the spiritual person. Entrance into the inner sanctum, the Holy of Holies, the Ark, the Mercy Seat and the piercing blue flame between the cherubs are accessed only through prayerful communion with our Heavenly Father. As children of God, our n*ephesh* (our normal soul), n*eschemah* (our higher soul), r*uach* (our spirit) and even our physical body often longs for the Heavenly Father's embrace.

In prayer as deep communion with God, this longing is filled. Our love is set ablaze, our hunger satisfied and our thirst quenched as we enter into the chamber of divine love through prayer. Often we will find ourselves drawn away from the hustle and bustle of life into the Holy of Holies where the Father and the lover of our souls wait to overflow our being with love and mercy. If the Lord God is the highest love of our being, we will seek to join our being to His Being, our spirit to His Spirit, our heart to His Heart, our mind to His Mind, our will to His Will and, yes, our body to His Body. In prayer, we share in the fullness of God-life. We then move into our world with Him as we embrace her hurting, dying and hungry - those who truly need the life we have touched in prayer.

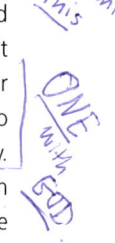

THE GOLDEN CORD

The Blessing of Our Finite Nature

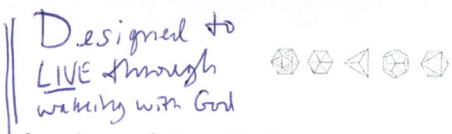

Our earthly life, with all its attendant needs, demands prayerful communion with the Creator. "God creates us to exhaust ourselves" (Rufus Jones, the Quaker mystic). Our energy dissipates, our strength fails, our resources run dry and we must go to God, the source of our life, in prayer. Our wisely crafted solutions to our unmanageable problems shatter like worn out crystal. All of these are God's ways of assuring our flight to the refuge of prayer[3]. To find our way we must plunge into the heart of God.

Our finite nature, as Jacque Ellul says[4], is the crucible in which our Heaven piercing prayers are forged. God gave prayer as a way of replenishing our spiritual, psychological and physical supplies. By prayer, we acknowledge our total dependence upon the Lord. We can do nothing by ourselves. Absolutely nothing. If we go on our own, we lose our way. If we speak on our own, we lose our words. If we fly alone, we fall. **Therefore, we pray**. I flee to the chamber of prayer within my heart so my God may truly be the one that speaks, does, moves and has his being within me.

Prayer is probably the most vital way of replenishing the earth. By it, we subdue. Through it, we receive the capacity for continuous dominion. In practicing it, we become more like our Lord through whom and with whom we communicate. Through prayer, the trees of our lives grow more fruitful and our seeds are watered for multiplication. Because the source of all these is not ourselves but God (for the excellence of the power is of God and not of us), prayer becomes necessary.

If we would remove the poisonous effect of the carnal self, so poisoned by the old serpent, **we must pray**. Jesus said, "pray that you enter not into temptation." Prayer serves as a covering from the tempter's snare. It does not mean that we are not tempted but, because we are focused on God and radiated by Him, we can withstand. If we fall, we will not stay fallen.

Becoming Prayer

Whoever we communicate with, we bear their fruit in our thought and actions. Lack of communication with God is communication with self, world, and Satan, which leads to falling away from God and into temptation. If we do not pray and communicate with God, it means that we are sharing our love with someone else. Our expectation has moved from God to self, the world or the Devil. It is imperative that human beings share their need with Heaven's heart. Prayer moves the need of the world Heavenward. By it, we traverse the storehouse of Heaven, releasing its supplies into the atmosphere of Earth's open fields. Prayer is more important and of greater power than preaching and teaching. Preaching and teaching need to flow from prayer to be able to touch the human heart with the love of Christ.

It is therefore not only important that we commence, continue and consummate all our acts as children of God in prayer - but that we become prayer! As we delight in His glorious presence and live consciously in it every day, we will begin to greet the day in response to our prayer of His presence. The manifestation of the glory and its continuous abiding will come when we engage in this type of prayer.

Effective Prayer

How is prayer to be effective? What makes prayer avail much? For Christian prayer, four things must happen. Prayer must be:

- God-focused
- Christ-informed and centered
- Holy Spirit-enlivened and directed
- other-concerned

The Father of light must stand at the center of the circle of our prayers. Unless God is at the center, we lose the life of prayer and our prayer life fails. That is, God-focused - not man-focused or need-focused. All the prayers of Jesus were God-focused. John 17 and other recorded prayers of Jesus were God-focused and informed by His relationship with the Father. He also was other-concerned in His prayer. But that concern for other flowed from what He heard from the Father's heartbeat. Effective prayer depends more on time listening to the heart of the Father than telling Him what to do.

Effective prayer is grounded in righteousness. Righteousness is not always right action but the state of the heart and its intent - which must be love. There is no law against love. Where love is foundational, there is no sin. It springs forth into its own streams and, even though some dirt may fall upon it, it remains pure and clean, for God is love and love is of God. The righteousness from which prayer must flow to be true and effective is God Himself, expressed lovingly toward God, neighbor, and self. Effective and availing prayer flows in vertical and horizontal love.

Prayer that releases the supernatural and suspends natural boundaries must itself be from the Spirit of God. It is when prayer flows from the very heart of the Holy Spirit that it can transform all carnal operation of the flesh and mind.

When prayer is true, one can pan the silver of true doctrine and find where the gold of knowledge is refined. By it, one enters into the secret chambers of the earth and releases the treasures of darkness. Only in prayer as entrance into the divinity does one put an end to darkness. With that Light, one searches the deep recesses of the kingdom storehouse and finds

treasure. With prayer, we take hold of the God who is Light and so can find our way in the thickest darkness.

A man of prayer cuts into the place forgotten by men of lesser consciousness, men who have been enchanted with fleeting values of the age. He often removes himself from the noise of the world and his head and ties himself to the crimson thread, dangling and swaying, until Heaven finds him and pulls him into its bosom. He transforms the ordinary means of the Earth into the extraordinary highways of holiness. By the fire of his hunger, even his breath becomes flight into divinity. His word becomes the seed of God planted in the heart of the world. By prayer, the rocks that are often men's hearts become burning sapphire, and the dust transforms into gold nuggets. By prayer, the man or woman of God assaults the rock-hardened heart of the sons and daughters of Adam and lays them bare without lifting up a finger or voice of vengeance. The praying man or woman tunnels through the walls, built up by fear and doubt. They see by the eyes of the Divine Spirit the treasures hidden in the people's soul. The prayer warrior, though praying in the dark closet, radiates the light of God to the furthest reaches of God's creation.

A Personal Experience

One day as I was praying I got caught up into another realm. I suddenly realized that, in *"this place of prayer, no bird of prey knows the hidden path and the enemy's eyes do not peer through. No evil demon abides there and the false lion does not prowl there,"* (Job 28:7). That is why he seeks so much to pull me down and away from Divine intimacy and to uncover me from this secret place. For in that secret place I know the intimate embrace of my Shepherd. I lay there by the still gentle waters of my Shepherd's gentle stream, listening to the whispering melody of His voice to the depth of my depth. I am brought into the inner chambers of my Lord. I see the keepers of His rainbow, revelations of beings, creatures fearful and awesome, radiant and beautiful. *"O my Lord! What a wonderful beauty I see in this place. I do not want to leave. I want to stay!"* He gently nudges me back and, on the wings of grace, I glide back gently here. I emerge, only to feel chills of fear and tears for the sons and daughters of my Father, my brethren among whom the enemy has set camp. I look up, I breathe deeply and I smile and take courage. I have been with the Lion of my Tribe. My heart is submerged in praise and adoration, radiating all over me. Glory be to my Beloved for His love. It is well!

> Effective prayer is grounded in righteousness. Righteousness is not always right action but the state of the heart and its intent. This must be love.

Transformative Prayer

The prayer of the believer flows from pure emotional delight, combined with the force of the divine intellect. From such prayer emanates sanctified imagination, that works itself into transformative reality. This is what I believe is communicated by 2 Chronicles 7:14: [5]

> וְיִכָּנְע֨וּ עַמִּ֜י אֲשֶׁ֧ר נִקְרָא־שְׁמִ֣י עֲלֵיהֶ֗ם וְיִֽתְפַּֽלְלוּ֙ וִֽיבַקְשׁ֣וּ פָנַ֔י וְיָשֻׁ֖בוּ מִדַּרְכֵיהֶ֣ם הָרָעִ֑ים וַאֲנִי֙ אֶשְׁמַ֣ע מִן־הַשָּׁמַ֔יִם וְאֶסְלַח֙ לְחַטָּאתָ֔ם וְאֶרְפָּ֖א אֶת־אַרְצָֽם׃

> *"and My people who are called by My name humble themselves and pray and seek My face and turn from their wicked ways, then I will hear from heaven, will forgive their sin and will heal their land."*

As per this powerful verse, when authentic prayer flows from the divine spring of life it is:

1. Transformative – wherever its river flows it brings healing and life. Its transformative balm comes from the fact that it is embedded in the consciousness of God's absolute rule over God's people. God can make and remake because God is the zero point from which all proceeds and to which all must go. At "God-Point," any change is possible. Since they are "My people," they are in fact at the "God Point." They are the ones who need transformation ("if my people").

2. Devotional – it flows from a deep devotion to the Master. The concept כָּנְעוּ (kav-nah') in the Hebrew evokes the idea of a man on bended knee. He is not vanquished by the enemy, but by forceful devotion to that which he sees as being infinitely greater than his mind can grasp. This sense of awe brings him down to touch the root, symbolized by the kissing of the feet and coming into subjection. He lets himself be subdued by its radiating and loving presence. This humility is the essential process of Divine/human combination, creating an atmosphere for an expanding life. It opens the frontiers of human consciousness. By prayer, the unmapped areas of our innermost being open to the exploration.

3. Kenotic – kenosis is the 'self-emptying' of one's own will and becoming entirely receptive to God's divine will. Prayer is the self-emptying embodiment of humility. In the Chronicles passage, God requires humility as part of the process of prayer. Humility is kenotic. Kenosis is a requirement for the meeting of eternity and time as we see in the Lord Jesus Christ (Philippians 2).

4. "Pressing in" – is what I understand the word translated "seek" to mean. The

> *By prayer, the man or woman of God assaults the rock-hardened heart of the sons and daughters of Adam and lays them bare without lifting up a finger or voice of vengeance.*

Hebrew word בַּקֵּשׁוּ (baw-kash') is to speak to the primal rooted search of the soul for its bridegroom. It is a mode of worship whereby one presses with one's whole being after someone or something - in this case, God. We press into the glory. We press into the presence to experience its fullness. We press until we break through or until the Divine breaks upon us with His flood of grace and mercy. It is not just that we beg or beseech God for something or that our desire is for Him not merely to procure a thing. God, as God, is the focus of our pressing in.

5. Turning/whirring – is the sense of the word "turn" שׁוּבוּ ("shuwb" or "shoob") used in this Chronicles passage. It is the idea of repentance. This is not merely a single act of turning; at its root, שׁוּב involves the disposition and willingness to turn back away from a particular act or way of life. It is also the turning or a transition, from one state of being and doing to another. As used here it does not mean to return to where one started but to where one veered off the right track and to rebuild the broken breach. By this turning, we reopen the wells that have been covered by dirt. In praying, it is to bring the heart back home again. This can be done in the mind or the recess of the soul.

Prayer also allows us to cease from certain acts or behaviors that may have overtaken us. We continually experience deliverance over and over again. Thus, when I pray, I fetch my thoughts, emotions, imaginations, intellectual processes, and bring them back home again. It is also the idea of recovery, refreshing, relief and rescue. Through prayer, restoration occurs and often there is a reversal of adverse conditions. In prayer, I can retrace my steps and take corrective measure that erases certain bad choices.

References

1 Harry Emerson Fosdick ed. Rufus Jones Speaks to Our Time (New York: Macmillan Company, 1951), p. 157.

2 Howard Thurman, The Luminous Darkness: A Personal Interpretation of the Anatomy of Segregation and the Ground of Hope (New York: Harper and Row, 1965). I borrowed this term from his book. This was among the first books I read when I arrived in Canada to go to school. His Quaker spirituality impacted my life and fitted into what had been going on in my life.

3 Harry Emerson, Fosdick, ed. Rufus Jones Speaks to Our Time (New York: Macmillan, 1951), p. 160ff.

4 Jacques Ellul, L'impossible Prière (Paris: Centurion, 1977), p. 82.

5 2 Chronicles 7:13-14, Interlinear Transliterated Bible. Copyright (c) 1994 by Bible Soft.

Chapter Two
Prayer and Human Emotion

Defining human emotion is rather difficult, so I am just going to focus on emotions as the human capacity to translate experiences through feelings. Emotions may be deeper than feelings, but they are so intertwined that no one has been able to separate them. **"Emotions are those processes that both engage us in the world in a way that promotes well-being, and that signal to us and to others how these interactions are going, that is to say whether we are or are not flourishing."** [6]

Fruit and Works

The Bible ties emotions to the works of the flesh and the fruit of the Holy Spirit. They are connected in the core to ingredients that form our spirituality. When we see the connection of our emotions to the Holy Spirit, they help us relate to each other in a meaningful way, but when they are tied to the flesh, they lead us to produce "the works of the flesh (Galatians 5:19)." If we emote anger, this births rage, wrath, strife, and violence. When our emotion is of hatred, this does the same thing and results in violence, war, and strife. If greed is the emotion of being, it leads to emulation, covetousness, and bitterness. When prayer grows out of the emotions of fear, anger, and envy, it leads to witchcraft, idolatry, and superstitions. Revenge is not emotion; it is an act resulting from an emotion filed through the feelings of anger or hate. Lust is an emotion which can influence prayer and make it less effective or keep even good prayers from being answered. Fear, hatred, anger, greed, lust, and envy are foundational to the works of the flesh. Prayer can indeed grow from these emotional centers, but they are hedge breakers and serpent releasers.

The other groups of emotions which we find together in the New Testament are love, joy, and peace. To me, these three emotions have the greatest impact on prayer, as they are of the Holy Spirit from which patience, kindness, goodness, faithfulness, gentleness, self-control and faith flow. I cannot accept the psychological idea that

faith is feeling or an emotion. That is not to say it does not affect the emotion. Rather, faith is usually contrary to the immediate emotion or mindset of the believer. The Holy Spirit travels on the wings of love, joy, and peace to make our prayers more effective. These emotions, when they are present, evoke faith and allow the Holy Spirit to work toward the transformation of the six negative emotions, at least for a moment. We need then to learn how to harness the positive emotions for prayers, especially if they will build up our spirit and prepare us to act like God our Father. This is why we must be filled with the Spirit.

Exercises for Emotion

How do we deal with emotion and use it effectively in prayer? First, we learn how to breathe by using the Word of God. This may be done by intentional breathing in between a short whisper of a passage of Scripture that speaks to the inward person. For example:

- Breathe in deeply in for four counts and say, "The Lord is my shepherd" as you gently breathe out.
- You may do the same with short phrases that describe who the Lord is to you. Breathe in, 1- 2 - 3 - 4, and breathe out while saying, "The Lord is my light." Breathe in, 1- 2 - 3 - 4, and breathe out while saying, "The Lord is my Salvation," and so on.
- You can do the same with verses that affirm your identity in Christ.

Another way of aligning your emotions with a positive prayer process is to quote Scriptures that speak directly to your feelings.

Emotions are Essential to Prayer

The heart is said to give emotions their potency in prayer. "The emotion is the impulse by which the soul is drawn to a thing," (Thomas Aquinas). It follows then that an emotion is also an instrument by which we are drawn to the highest object of the human spirit which is God. Emotion also involves the instrument of repulsion that causes us to flee from an object of terror. The person being drawn to God involves their emotions in the process. One religious scholar, Rudolph Otto, said that God is *"mysterium tremendum et fascinans."* God is both an object of fear and fascination. In prayer, not only are emotions key to our passionate seeking and holding onto God, but they are also the key to our physical equilibrium. Our emotions are never silenced as long as there is a desire to take hold of God. No matter what prayer it is, it must tap into emotions and channel

> Prayers arising out of purified emotions are a means to draw the power of the Divine into the circumstances of our lives.

them to the object or subject of desire.

To say that prayer should not be emotional is to say that the body should not be involved in prayer. We have been taught to fight passions since the days of the Stoics. The goal was to attain *"apatheia"* - a state undisturbed by our passions. The church even came to teach that the absence of passion was the qualification for receiving from God. In prayer, we were told that we were to use emotion without being emotional. We were to have joy without enjoying it, to be angry without feeling it. We are to be enthused without becoming enthusiastic. We were to be excited without being excitable. We were, in fact, to have feeling without feeling it! In all these was the assumption that it is possible to separate the emotional from the rational. People were instilled with fear of emotion. I must say that prayer lost much of its fervor when passion was sent packing. However you understand emotion, the human person will be incomplete for not being in touch with it and prayer will lose much of its zest without it.

Our Emotions Reveal Us

Our emotions are connected to our beliefs, desires, values, and thought processes. Our emotions are more than a mix of beliefs and desires and are not separable from us. An emotion has instinct, intuition, intention and interactive force. Instinctively it ties to our basic need for survival. Emotions deal with our participation in the real world. An emotion is attuned to your need for relationship and care. It can measure to a large extent the authenticity and inauthenticity of an act, speech or gesture to or for us. Emotions are part of us, attached to our beliefs about our world, self, and others - even negative emotions which do not serve to attune us to our environment. For example, anxiety may lead a Christian to prayer. A feeling of anger may attune us to the vibration of things we do not like. Fear may cause us to veer away from danger.

Scripture Promotes Emotion

Many Christian mystics and teachers seem to be calling for abolishing emotion from the sphere of prayer. I find no such support in Scripture. There is no call to forgo emotion in prayer. Rather, there seems to be a call for the purification of prayer and an encouragement to pursue prayer with holy intensiveness and fervor. This intensiveness cannot exist if emotions are left out. Emotion is a crucial aspect of people. Some say things like "joy is not an emotion" or "happiness is not an emotion." That is a lie. All the fruits of the Holy Spirit call on the emotions and are intricately connected with human emotions, purified by the Holy Spirit.

*Therefore I say unto you, what things so ever **ye desire**, when ye pray,*

believe that ye receive them, and ye shall have them. And when ye stand praying, forgive, if ye ought against any: that your Father also which is in heaven may forgive you your trespasses. But if ye do not forgive, neither will your Father which is in heaven forgive your trespasses. (Mark 11:24-26 KJV, emphasis added)

This passage of Scripture, in which Jesus deals with prayer, is directed to human emotion. Desire, belief, the feeling of joy at the reception of good news. It is easy to dismiss emotion and denigrate its importance for the spiritual life, but emotions with all their problems are necessary for our spiritual well-being. Pure and positive emotion adds to the power of prayer and improves the outcome of prayer. When praying, our thought process regarding the events of our life can positively or negatively affect the meaningfulness and effectiveness.

Power of A Pure Heart

This process of heart-filled purity is something that causes a breakthrough in prayer or brings hindrance to our efforts. The focus of your thought processes, feelings being processed and the images stored within you before, during and after prayer can improve the power of your human spirit in its interaction with God. Prayers arising out of purified emotions are a means to draw the power of the Divine into the circumstances of our lives. Emotion amplifies the force of whatever it does and, in prayer, it gives more power than one can ever imagine. Emotions have a reservoir of force available to them for the lifting up of the person who can harness them. Purifying and focusing emotion in prayer taps into that reservoir and quickens you as someone with confidence and increases receptivity from the Heavens. By this I am not talking about emotionalism and vain repetition. I am referring to the speaking of the language embedded by God in human beings for effective navigation of the universe He created for them.

Rabbi Kook in his notes points out that the Hebrew verb *"lehitpalel"* (to pray) is in the reflexive tense - an action you take upon yourself. This emphasizes the aspect of prayer's spirituality as intricately connected to emotion and its impact on the whole person. The state of contemplation brings out an outpouring of directed emotion, beyond the soul's normal range. Prayer bathed in passionate emotion has the power to fulfill desires because there is a power in the world which is greater than the sum total of the problems. That power comes to reside in any human through Jesus Christ. *"But as many as received Him, to them He gave the right to become children of God, even to those who believe in His name,"* (John 1:12). The diminished effectiveness of so many prayers throughout this century has to do with the removal of the legitimacy of human emotion. But emotion is the chariot wing of prayer which passionately ignites the fuel of the soul, sets it ablaze by the power of God and its vibratory pitch chases the night of despair and the evil beast away. When directed by the positive vibration of the Holy Spirit's presence, prayers that flow from pure emotion release power and force for the saturation of the supernatural into the atmosphere.

The power of prayer, charged with emotional intensity and informed by purity, supersedes routine prayer in its ability to release others. This may explain why the Lord Jesus Christ insisted that we forgive our enemies and love them - so that the force of prayer flows in emotional purity, benefitting those for whom we pray and us. For we read, *"Blessed are the pure in heart for they shall see God"* (Matthew 5:8). Because of the possibility of an emotion to be a hindrance to our prayer, we must bring the prayer to the fiery center of the Shekinah. Most people do not know this and tend to pray only for themselves and those whom they know and like and avoid praying for those who may have hurt them. Christian prayer is the training of emotion to vibrate at the level of Divinity. Praying for others, especially those whom you do not know, especially those who may be at odds with you, releases a powerful force from the unconscious that benefits you as well. Praying for others helps to purify your emotion for effective intercession.

Emotions Connect You

Prayer deals at the most primitive level of our being. For example, when we are "caught up in the spirit" we return to the primordial language of hidden and pent-up emotionality - whose only sounds are groaning that cannot be articulated in conventional languages.

> Emotion amplifies the force of whatever it does and, in prayer, it gives more power than one can ever imagine.

Different types of prayer call forth different emotional states. The emotion that attains prophetic prayer is not the same as those which attain intercessory prayer. That which attends confessional contrition is not that which attends prayers of exuberant praise, thanksgiving or glorification. Some prayers are labor intensive; others are not. The emotion in prayer produces changes based on experience and need. There is no way that we can come to a place of emotionless prayer - especially when we see Christ face to face. The very longing of our heart to be united with our Father causes our soul to cry out. Most Christian prayers, unlike other religions, grow from our deep compassion for the world. When we see the world in its current state and far removed from the intended ideal of the Heavenly Father, our heart moans in prayer. When we see the sick, when we see the oppressed, the abused or the lost, our hearts cry out with a passionate plea for their salvation. When they are saved, we release our emotions in joyful praise. We could never logically reach the

threshold of the heart of Christ and the Father if our emotions have been shut off in prayer. To understand this, we see how many times Jesus shed tears or grieved in the spirit for His people.

There is a passage in Scripture which shows that God intends to elicit our emotions in our relationship with Him:

> For we do not have a High Priest who cannot sympathize with our weaknesses, but One who has been tempted in all things as we are, yet without sin. Therefore let us draw near with confidence to the throne of grace, that we may receive mercy and may find grace to help in time of need. (Hebrews 4:15-16)

Feelings do not sum up emotions. Rather, they form a small part of our emotional experience. So then prayer is not about how one feels, though feelings do play some role. All kinds of feelings are often manifested in prayer depending on what the praying person is going through and how the person seeks to enter into the heart of God or deal with the problem. Depending on what the prayer is, joy is an appropriate expression as much as sorrow, sadness, exuberance, guilt, etc. So do not confuse a particular feeling as a sign of effective prayer. It is the momentary signature of the situation in which you are going through upon your body. One feeling can be used to silence the other in a flash of thought and focus.

Sanctified Emotion Amplifies Prayer and Protects Hearts

Emotion in prayer helps one to discern the mind of the spirit in issues of justice and equity. It can also attune the heart to compassion and mercy as it flows from the Lord. Emotion links us to the intuitive subconscious location of the Divine voice. In Deuteronomy 6:5 (KJV) we read: "*And thou shalt love the LORD thy God with all thine heart, and with all thy soul, and with all thy might.*" This command is repeated in Mark 12:30 (NIV): "Love the Lord your God with all your heart and with all your soul and with all your mind and with all your strength."

> *Christian prayer is the training of emotion to vibrate at the level of Divinity. Praying for others, especially those whom you do not know, especially those who may be at odds with you, releases a powerful force from the unconscious that benefits you as well.*

Prayer is not just talking with God. Prayer involves the assessing, valuing and empathic consideration of decisions and choices in light of Divine nature. In prayerful emotion, our being learns to align itself with the beauty of the Lord and we may sometimes sense His displeasure when we showed lack of discipline. It is our emotion that cautions us to approach God with reverence and not with arrogance and rudeness (which often tends to be confused with faith). If we can bring the force of our emotions to bear positively on prayer, we can change the vibratory resonance of any atmosphere. This atmosphere will be conducive for our prayer and for reception of what is birthed as a result.

Because of the capacity of emotions to confuse our motivation and lead us into spiritual quicksand, we need the Holy Spirit. When we get to the edge of control over our emotions, we tend to lose focus and become confused. Sometimes we do not know what to do. This capacity of emotion to mislead means that we need the Holy Spirit to make sure that our emotions do not set up idols which may end up displacing the purpose of God in our lives. This means that while emotions are vital to prayer, if they are not honed by the Spirit of God and channeled through God's will as sanctified by the Holy Spirit, our emotions may compel us to set up idols or spirits whose primary function is to flatter our wishes to our destruction. So God gives the Holy Spirit to protect us from ourselves most especially as this relates to our prayer lives. Why this divine protection as it relates to prayer? Because in prayer we are more likely to meet various entities who seek to distort our goals and offer us false images which are not in submission to the image of God or ourselves.

References

6 K. Oatley and E. Duncan (1994). The experience of emotions in everyday life. Cognition and Emotion, 8, 369-381.

CHAPTER THREE
Praying in the Spirit

Because of the possibility of emotional distortion, we must pray in the Spirit. If only to communicate with Divinity without the noise and static of our prejudices, praying in the spirit is worth it. Paul makes this clear when he says in Romans 8:26-27 (emphasis added):

> *Likewise, the Spirit also **helps in our weaknesses**. For we do not know what we should pray for as we ought, but the Spirit Himself makes intercession for us with **groanings which cannot be uttered**. Now He who searches the hearts knows what the mind of the Spirit is, because He makes intercession for the saints according to the will of God. (NKJV)*

Our weakness is from our ignorance of the divine method to approach the throne of God. Language this side of Babel also limits us. We do not know how to form the words in our barbaric, sinful language that can penetrate the fiery veil of the Heavens. When we approach the gate, the cherubs with their flaming sword await our stammering tongue and stand in the way. There we cannot speak the password. The only password of the initiate here is the name of the one who said, "I am the door."

> *So Jesus said to them again, "Truly, truly, I say to you, I am the door of the sheep. All who came before Me are thieves and robbers, but the sheep did not hear them.*
> *(John 10:7-8)*

We know that whatever we ask the Father in the name of Jesus, He does it. We also know that if we ask Jesus for something because we are "in His name" He will do it for us. But there is an infirmity deep within our souls, something deeper than just saying the name of Jesus. Our intellect gets in the way of our ability to speak to Heaven in a way that conforms to the Will of God. We are often in trouble because we confuse our present desire with the Will of God and our prayer language becomes the language of self. Note that Romans 8:26 does not say, "we know not how to pray"; the passage says, "we know not what to pray." It is "what" to pray not "who" to pray to or "how" to pray that is our problem. What refers to "things" or outcomes that we desire in our pursuit. The breaking out of the Spirit upon our apathy and materialistic world is what helps us in the quest for the "what" that is pleasing to God.

A Specific Language

The passage in Romans implies that there is a way we ought to pray for "what." Everything we desire has a specific language which it will listen to and hear. There is a language for everything which is the object of our desire - but we do not necessarily know the language for it. It is true that whatsoever we ask the Father in the name of Jesus, He gives it to us. This means that the problem is not that our prayers have not been answered but we have not yet spoken the language of that which has been given to us. How can we speak to the 'what'? The Spirit is the one with the linguistic capacity to speak to the things which have been released from the mind of the Creator by their own language to cause them to come into manifestation.

Our linguistic infirmity is the result of Babel. For at Babel it is not just man's language that was confused. Our ability to speak the language of things that have been freely given to us by God has been closed up. At Babel, there was also a confusion of our ability to hear God and the universe in which we live. If the Holy Spirit does not check the emotions we can become victims of the nine confusions of Babel:

- Confusion of hearing
- Confusion of speech
- Confusion of communion with physical structure
- Confusion of love with lust
- Confusion of spirituality with materiality
- Confusion of noise with voice
- Confusion of man with God
- Confusion of grace with human works
- Confusion of murder with sacrifice

All these are healed with the coming of the Holy Spirit which brings these miracles:

- Hearing
- Speech
- True communion
- Love

- Voice
- Spiritualization
- Grace
- Sacrificial activation of divinity

The Spirit Overcomes Our Weaknesses and Infirmity

The Spirit helps us by speaking the language of the manifestation of what we have been given, cutting short the interruption in the Heavenlies and causing that for which we have prayed and which according to the promise of the Master has been given to us to flow joyfully into our lives. Our infirmity, in this case, is not the removal of apathy but the use of irrelevant language. But through the Spirit prayer becomes the decisive instrument to uplift us and cause us to plunder and make manifest what the enemy is holding captive in the ethereal sphere. It is here that the Spirit must move beyond all human thought and philosophy. In fact, by the definition of prayer as that which the Spirit does with us and sometimes for us (because we lack the language of manifestation), we can say that modern man does not know how to pray.

This infirmity cuts even deeper to the illegal enthronement of rationalistic processes over the intuitive. The superficial supremacy of emotionality over spirituality cripples the prayer of the so-called religious.

The Spirit helps our infirmity. This help is not a mechanical process memorized prayer. The Holy Spirit touches the most imperceptible aspects of our human spirit, tracing its many motions and seeking to direct that impression to the Will of God. Through the Holy Spirit's influence on our

> *It is true that whatsoever we ask the Father in the name of Jesus, He gives it to us. This means that the problem is not that our prayers have not been answered but we have not yet spoken the language of that which has been given to us.*

soul, we commit to the Christological Kingdom process. The Holy Spirit uses prayer to transition us from inefficiency to effectiveness. In prayer, the Holy Spirit is the agent of Divine effect that can raise our immediate situation to eternal realities. Why is the help necessary? Why is praying in the spirit necessary? We often know how to pray, we know who to pray to, but the language of the alignment of our circumstance and true need with the Will of God escapes us. Here the Spirit, being God, speaks to God. The Holy Spirit can align our will with the Divine Will and give us the linguistic vehicle for what we need for God's manifested will.

The Spirit helps our infirmity by taking upon itself to make intercession for us. The Holy Spirit functions as the go-between for the believer and the Father, to plead on our behalf about things which are hidden in our unconscious that we cannot put into words. Here, the Holy Spirit bears the burdens of our lives and pours them directly into the heart of the Lord God. This is not about us interceding for others but the Holy Spirit operating in our lives and picking up and cleaning hidden things that may lead to self-deception. If we consider the struggle in which the believer is engaged with the enemy, the fact that God chooses to use His Holy Spirit to impact us directly and create an atmosphere favorable to the union of our will to God's Will should not surprise us.

We do not know why we sometimes get the sense of urgency to pray. The Holy Spirit strikes the chord of our spirit, propelling us to produce sound in the supernatural sphere. This sound or voice (קול, - kol) allows an entrance of light that swallows darkness and opens the channel for us to tap into eternity. We enter the place where time, as we know it in the world, is no more. Through this helping of our infirmities, we hear the tone of the Heavens as our soul passes through various dimensions and is impressed upon by the Will and Thought of God. Our being becomes a wing for the flight of the harmony of worldwide wholeness.

The helping of our infirmity by the Holy Spirit changes how we conceive Divine process and how we calculate and understand time. Guided by the Holy Spirit in prayer, our being enters into the mind of God and hence beyond time. Since we are there by the very Spirit of God, we can become agents of changing time by seeing it from eternity. When time is seen from eternity, it ceases to be! Literally, we become the seat of Divine light piercing the dark background of night. Through this helping of the Holy Spirit, we develop spiritual lucidity which transforms all subsequent (and I dare say even past) actions!

> *Why is the help necessary? Why is praying in the spirit necessary? We often know how to pray, we know who to pray to but the language of the alignment of our circumstance and true need with the Will of God escapes us. Here the Spirit being God speaks to God.*

The Spirit Knows The Heart of God

In helping our infirmity, the focus is not to fit God into our ego or to force God to conform to our prescribed patterns. The Spirit allows intentional, genuine communion of God with God. It is an inner divine conversation to which we are privileged to eavesdrop. Only that which God does truly communicate with God at a God level and can truly affect a Divine outcome. When God ceases to act with God and leaves us to ourselves (or one another), it becomes demonic and subject to Divine judgment. For prayer to not be demonic, it must be directed by the Spirit of God who is God and summarized in the love of Christ.

In helping our infirmities, the Spirit helps us to remember Divine thoughts, ideas, and images, erased by the trauma of incessant attack of demonic powers against us. We certainly cannot find fault with the memory of the Holy Spirit. For as God is all-seeing and all-knowing, so is the Holy Spirit. One specific thing that the Holy Spirit does in helping infirmities is to bring up Scriptures in our mind and then give us the unction to speak the Word to accomplish a particular purpose. The Lord Jesus said, *"But the Helper, the Holy Spirit, whom the Father will send in My name, He will teach you all things, and bring to your remembrance all things that I said to you."* (John 14:26). In my estimation, "all things that I said to you" is not merely from the three years of His earthly life but also the eternal Logos and Rhema proceeding from God to humanity - all that God has spoken from the creation of man to the end of time. Logos is eternal speech from eternity and has the very nature of God. The Holy Spirit brings into our mind that which has been eternally in the mind of God. This is essential in intercession because what is at stake (and held up by the weakness of man) are the eternal purposes of God seeking to work itself out in the life of humanity.

This intercession flowing from the unutterable groaning refers to kind of a divine code decipherable only by God. How do I know it is code? In verse 27 we read, "Now He who searches the hearts knows what the mind of the Spirit is.". This is similar to the code book of Revelation which no one in Heaven or on Earth or beneath the Earth could open except the Lamb of God. In speaking of praying in the spirit, Paul affirms the idea of the spirit code: *"For he who speaks in a tongue does not speak to men but to God, for no one understands him; however, in the spirit he speaks mysteries."* (1 Corinthians 14:2).

Praying in the spirit puts our thoughts far away from any creature and communicates a prayer directly to God. One of our infirmities is the tendency toward repetition that Jesus warns against in Matthew 6:7. But the spirit bypasses this by providing us with language and capacity far exceeding the vocabulary of our ordinary learning. Another mode then of our infirmity is the fact that our natural communication is understandable even to the enemy of our faith. The devil can read our strategies and fears in our prayers. Our language of prayer carries with it our inner fears that the enemy cannot know. The heart of man is a closed book to everyone, even man himself, except God. The Holy Spirit, on the other hand, is God and communicates with the Godhead in language that God has reserved as intimate conservation between Him and His children. Thus Paul says it is a mystery, yes, even to the one in and through whom the Holy Spirit operates. How do I know that it is a code decipherable by God alone through His Holy Spirit? Paul says, "No one understands him for he speaks mysteries."

Furthermore, our infirmities consist in not always being certain of the Will of God. We tend to pray in cross-purpose to the Will of God, especially in situations where we have very heavily vested our emotions. The constant themes, ideas, needs, and images that strive to influence our lives may cause us to choose lines of action merely to maintain our comfort. The results become detrimental to our well-being. The Spirit is not affected the same way by these pressures that combine to assault our loyalty to the Divine Will!

The Spirit is not prevented either by emotion, rational limitation or lapse of memory from absorbing completely into the Will of God - since He is God! He understands our circumstances, but they are unable to sway Him away from the Divine will and purpose. The Holy Spirit does not fall prey to forces that separate us from God, for again, He is God.

> *When time is seen from eternity it ceases to be! Literally we become the seat of Divine light piercing the dark background of night. Through this helping of the Holy Spirit we develop spiritual lucidity which transforms all subsequent (and I dare say even past) actions!*

The Holy Spirit in helping our prayer is perpetually conversing to the Godhead the pressure under which we live. Through the Holy Spirit, the Godhead comes to move upon the waters in the dark places of our soul, bringing the God nature to bear and transforming our habits and motions. The Holy Spirit, as intercessor, holds the solution to our linguistic, rational and temporal disorientation that subject us to vanity and limiting our communication with God and one another. Praying in the Holy Spirit can also help us communicate effectively with other human beings whose human reasoning (or other factors) prevent them from grasping what our heart is trying to communicate. By praying in the Holy Spirit, our spirit can communicate with divine clarity to them.

The Holy Spirit, by praying through us and for us, creates for us a supernatural system. Divine energy flows from the eternal realm into the structure of our spiritual communication system. But it must be remembered that this work of the Spirit. This ability of the Spirit to indwell humanity and flow between people and God is only made possible by the "hypostatic union" of humanity and God in Jesus Christ. The Holy Spirit talks to God from inside humans because God first became human in Jesus Christ. Now, God does not only see our infirmity but, through Jesus Christ, the Godhead can be touched deeply by our weakness and seeks to help us. The Spirit, by interceding through us, can now use human nature to reveal hidden mysteries lying deep in the recesses of people back to Heaven!

In helping our infirmity, the Holy Spirit performs the task of intercession in us now here on Earth, which the ascended Christ performs in the presence of the Father and the angels. Some of the tasks of the Holy Spirit are:

- to open the door so that we can continually tap into the vast powers made available to us by God, by praying directly into the heart of God;
- to enlarge our revelational knowledge that comes through times of intimacy with God;
- to bring about the expansion of feelings of absolute dependence upon God that causes us to cry out to God for our total salvation.

The Holy Spirit has the Divine Technology that can cause our emotions to conform to the nature of Christ. This is called the Mind of Christ. The interweaving of our emotions and the Holy Spirit allows us to pray effectively and in harmony with the Will of God.

CHAPTER FOUR

VARIETIES OF PRAYER

> *With all (types of) prayer and petition pray at all times in the Spirit, and with this in view, be on the alert with all perseverance and petition for all the saints*
> (Ephesians 6:18)

Prayer flows in various ways and is carried by various currents and maybe affected by the individuals ministry or spiritual gifts. Anyone may pray in a particular flow, but a person who is powerful or passionate in a particular stream of gifting may cause higher vibratory resonance (by the greater deposit of the charismata in them in that area). All prayer calls for spiritual vigilance and perseverance, its main purpose to edify and build up the body, as Paul says, "for all saints." Let us look at 5 different types of prayer found in the scriptures.

1) PROPHETIC PRAYER

Prophetic prayer is both a re-appropriation and a transformation of the insights of divine man. This kind of prayer is based on need and love. It is not mere incantation or meditation, but a spontaneous outburst of intuitive insight. Indeed, heartfelt supplication is the essence of true prayer. Prophetic prayer does not involve begging and complaining! Prophetic prayer is not the same as what scholars call 'prophetic religion.' It is a verbalization of a divine intuitive grasp which literally prophesies to the circumstance based on what it has seen in the supernatural realm. One of the reasons for the giving of the Holy Spirit is the Lord's desire to move prayer from mere petition to prophetic output. When we fall down at His feet to worship and adore his Lordship as His servants we are open for the saturation of the Spirit of Christ and the release of prophetic prayer. We read in Revelation 19:10 (emphasis added);

> *Then I fell at his feet to worship him. But he said to me, "Do not*

> do that; I am a fellow servant of yours and your brethren who hold the testimony of Jesus; worship God. **For the testimony of Jesus is the spirit of prophecy."**

Hear Ye The Word of The Lord!

As followers of the Son of Man, our prayer is a prophetic annunciation of the Kingdom of God and a prophetic denunciation against the kingdom of darkness. In prophetic prayer we call on the universe to obey our God as we proclaim His majestic name. Prayer, when it flows from the testimony of Jesus which is the "spirit of prophesy," says to the world, "Hear ye the word of the LORD." By this prayerful prophetic statement, "Thus says the Lord GOD," we call for the world to cease its foolishness and following its own spirit and begin to see God's purpose. This is the essence of the infilling of the Holy Spirit which we read in Acts 2:17-21 (emphasis added);

> *And it shall come to pass in the last days, saith God, I will pour out of my Spirit upon all flesh:* **and your sons and your daughters shall prophesy,** *and your young men shall see visions, and your old men shall dream dreams: And on my servants and on my handmaidens I will pour out in those days of my Spirit;* **and they shall prophesy:** *And I will shew wonders in heaven above, and signs in the earth beneath; blood, and fire, and vapour of smoke: The sun shall be turned into darkness, and the moon into blood, before that great and notable day of the Lord come:* **And it shall come to pass, that whosoever shall call on the name of the Lord shall be saved.** *(KJV)*

The reasons for the outpouring of the Spirit is the empowerment for prophesy, vision, dreams, prayer, and the capacity to call upon the name of the Lord for signs and wonders. All these are geared to the salvation of the individual person and the whole world. The blood, fire, and smoke are reminiscent of sacrifices offered under the Mosaic Covenant. The final goal of all the sacrifices is the salvation of they who call upon the name of the Lord. Prayer has become for many a process of nagging at God and the very sense of prophetic prayer has been put on the back burner. Those who look for the great and terrific Day of the Lord must turn to prophetic prayer.

Prophetic prayer removes the shroud of darkness which grows from negative confessions. It illuminates our stammering language by the outreach of the Spirit, bringing it into pure articulation of Kingdom outcomes. The Holy Spirit moves prophetically to help us release creative life processes into the body of Christ. It is by this inflowing of prophetic prayer that there is empowerment to construct the channel through which divine energies of life flow - until the knowledge of the glory of the Lord covers the world as the waters cover the sea. That this prophetic mode of prayer is essential for the spiritual health and growth of the people of God is seen in the early church where prophetic announcement was seen in prayer.

There is no solution for the present loss of spiritual force, poverty of soul and body and the feebleness of visionary input of the church - except the people of God awaken to the fact that merely having gatherings is not going to cut it! There must be an applied prophetic mode of prayer at various levels of the universe which reinserts Divine value into the realities of the world. Prophetic prayer flows from a deep embrace of fellowship, drinking from the deep well of God's throne. We must become inebriated from this spring of Divine mystery, imbibing from the pure love of its creative force and letting it flow as a pure living spring from our innermost being. Prophetic "prayer is born out of the intense earnestness and out of the consciousness that only God, through us as feeble organ of his will, can accomplish what we seek and what we need" for the true transformation of the world. By prophetic prayer brings clarity of vision for the people that results in profound changes. When we enter the realm of prophetic prayer, light breaks through and we are often immersed with the river of God's energy from the throne. Such unbounded power comes when our prayer moves from mere utilitarian petition to prophetic outflow - a release from the Holy Spirit which has been freely given to us by the Lord.

> *Prophetic prayer is not the same as what scholars call prophetic religion. It is a verbalization of a divine intuitive grasp which literally prophesies to the circumstance based on what it has seen in the supernatural realm.*

Grace Warfare

Prophetic prayer is warfare prayer - conquering obstacles, refreshing the soul and settling the vast storm of restlessness. Prophetic prayer works in a mighty way throughout the world and upon the lives of God's people. It is an operation of grace given to those who search for God with the same fervency as the early church. When prophetic prayer comes, the people of God will influence the course of the cosmos, causing the secret channels of the universe to give up their treasures for the benefit of the Kingdom of God. In the words of Rufus Jones, "(Prophetic) prayer will lift us to new levels of experiences, put us in touch with an intensely transforming fire that brings transfigurative energy and make our impossible possible."

Prophetic prayer flows throughout the Book of Psalms. Often we see David move from petition to prophetic affirmations. Sometimes prophetic prayers may come as the result of a specific revelation from the Father:

> *Simon Peter answered, "You are the Christ, the Son of the living*

God." And Jesus said to him, "Blessed are you, Simon Barjona, **because flesh and blood did not reveal this to you, but My Father who is in heaven.** I also say to you that you are Peter, and upon this rock I will build My church; and the gates of Hades will not overpower it. **I will give you the keys of the kingdom of heaven; and whatever you bind on earth shall have been bound in heaven, and whatever you loose on earth shall have been loosed in heaven.**
(Matthew 1:16-19, emphasis added)

We see this also in Matthew 18:18-20:

Truly I say to you, whatever you bind on earth shall have been bound in heaven; and whatever you loose on earth shall have been loosed in heaven. "Again I say to you, that if two of you agree on earth about anything that they may ask, it shall be done for them by My Father who is in heaven. For where two or three have gathered together in My name, I am there in their midst.

Though they do not deal directly with prayer, these two passages show there are revelational, edificative, authoritative, and communal aspects to prophetic prayer. There is unique and greater flow of revelation in prophetic prayer.

The Hebrew word "***halipet** tefilah*" is the act in which the divine in man corresponds with the ultimate, which is at the heart of the prophetic. The very act of entering into intimate conversation with God unleashes the prophetic. It calls forth the source of plenty in times of need, mercy in times of judgment, peace in times of war, love to transcend hate, light to overcome darkness, and God to abide with people in the frailty of our humanity. Prophetic prayer can call forth joy in times of sorrow. At the depth of prophetic prayer in its true authenticity is God breaking into human consciousness by a creative word. By this prophetic inherency, prayer speaks forth Heaven's blessing and well-being. Prophetic pronouncement in prayer can help the one for whom it is being offered and hold the demonic storm surges at bay. By its revelational declaration prophetic prayer, what is called in the Hebrew *kavanah* aligns the word, mind, thought, and imagination with the spirit and open the pathway for the inflow of the glory of the Lord - the **Shekinah** - into the earthly realm. Prophesy flows from the **Shekinah**, hence when prayer taps into the Shekinah it stops being mere petition and becomes prophetic utterances. Prophetic prayer will often manifest when the praying one has touched that sphere of the glory with the divine arrow, causing its cloud to

> One of the reasons for the giving the Holy Spirit is the Lord's desire to move prayer from mere petition to prophetic output.

shower the soul and earthly realm with manifestation. Prophetic prayer does not imply that only official prophets can pray, prophetically. Prophetic prayer transcends whatever systems the religious systems of the world and its false consciousness have concocted as the final expression of God apart from the Word of God. If this is the case then the expression of prayer now possessed by a majority of the church must change in favor of the dynamic of the Holy Spirit, which Christ has given to the church.

Manifesting The Kingdom

Prophetic prayer is not the description of the circumstances we face; prophetic prayer is a speaking to God of the inner truth of our situation using the Word of God to transform it and dethrone it of whatever false power that has raised itself against God's Will and Kingdom. It is consistent with the Word of God and calls forth deliverance. By this prophetic prayer we identify with the Word of God and not with the statistics of human rules and principles. It announces what God wills and allows, because its revelational insight puts it in touch with the current of Divine energy, which it then helps to flow through the people of God. Furthermore, this is not just one individual praying for the people while they listen in awe to their prophetic skill; it is in itself a release of the Kingdom impulse within the people of God. This kind of prayer allows the people of God to corporately affect the manifestation of life upon the plane of human existence. Here the body vividly envisions the Kingdom and calls it into manifestation from its hidden realms. Prophetic prayer because of its revelatory insight taps into heart of the Father for those in the shadow of death and touches His desire to move them into the dayspring of life. The poor and oppressed are released and the windows of heaven are opened over the thirsty plains of human souls.

Because the body of Christ is a prophetic body, it is important that we should attempt to understand the place of prophetic prayer in the world in light of our definition of the Kingdom of God in which we now live. Prophetic prayer illustrates the difference between transformative prayers flowing in power from the timid pleas without insight and reveals the true meaning of our new humanity in Christ. The understanding of any prophetic prayer depends on the conviction that the praying believer has a unique place in God's heart and God's Kingdom and the salvation of the human race for which God has so graciously granted the Son.

Prophetic prayer is deeply rooted in the fact that human thought and action, life and suffering, are the subject of God's redemptive purpose. Of course, prophetic prayer does not ignore the realities of the person's community but plumbs the inexhaustible depth of Divinity and causes us to understand and depict the destinies of humankind with conviction flowing from an appreciative comprehension of the living sympathy of Christ. The Holy Spirit flows through our prophetic prayer posture, gives unction and draws the believer into cosmic order, binds the spirit of man to the spiritual sphere and fills the whole life with the pervading consciousness of the interconnection of worlds. It is here that the mighty phenomena which bring refreshment and receptivity into the wasteland of human hopelessness and despair can move people to steadily receive the mighty wind, propelling them to escape life's fragmentation and bringing them into wholeness— *shalom* in Christ.

When the church engages in prophetic prayer in earnest it organizes its spiritual energies to deal with the injurious effect forced upon people's lives in the form of thoughts, imaginations and concepts that raise themselves against the knowledge of Christ (see 2 Corinthians 10:3-60). The power of people who engage in prophetic prayer is not their perfection but finds its strength in the organization and practice of the Word of God as written in Scripture and apprehended in the innermost sanctum of the Spirit as the throne of God. Thus by prophetic prayer one seeks to reach in that moment the Holy of Holies behind the veil, calling forth the abundant life made possible by the death of Jesus Christ upon the cross. New vistas of power open from above, releasing below an overflow so that the praying person becomes an embodiment of heaven on Earth - possessing joy, truth and peace, providential immediacy and protective ability as it is in heaven.

Prophetic prayer should be saturated with praise, adoration and worship. Prophetic prayer is prayer centered wholly on God and His eternal characteristics and announces this as such to the world for its transformation. In prophetic prayer God's majesty, glory, and power; His beauty; His eternal love; His mercy and grace should be grounding point. Prophetic prayer must always begin here.

CLEANSING PRAYER

As we approach God in prayer we come through many formative issues that have affected our clarity of motivation. In the inner levels of our souls we have learned some lessons; many of them are valuable but many of them are hindrances to our honest and transparent approach to God. Some of our actions, attitudes and mentalities are nothing but rubbish and must be brought to the fiery altar and the purging waters of God before we can proceed any further in prayer. In fact, if we are honest many of them are as tares, which have grown with the divine wheat of God's love. We need to find them by prayer, detach them by the process that David sets forth in his psalm of confession, and burn them. They must come under the purifying fire of God's Holy Spirit. This facing of the worst aspects of our lives as we seek to become more intimate in prayer is demanded by the nature of God. A cleansing prayer does not bring us salvation, but it prepares us to intercede and be an effective witness to others. David said, "Then I will teach transgressors Your ways, And sinners will be converted to You." (Psalm 51:13).

We do not do this mainly because we are afraid of punishment from God but for the purification of our inner motives so that we are not living our lives or praying for others from a false center, thereby hindering our power and effectiveness. Pain may result if we do not let go of the ungodly aspects of our habit, mood and behavior and the pain is not caused by God but by exposure of uncleanness to the perfect Son of a holy God. Our inner world with all the things we still carry does not stop God from loving us; it stops us from being completely available to God in particular ways. Unless these undesirable elements of our lives are dealt with we may not make full proof of our gifts, power and ministry. So if we must be truly effective in our prayer lives and become healers in the world we need to continually come to the place of purification and cleansing - at the foot of the Cross, the place where sacrifice is made and the blood of the Lamb is poured out. We do not come out of fear because there is no more wrath; we come out of love without condemnation to pour out our "reasonable service." We want to present our bodies as living sacrifices, holy and acceptable to God" (Romans 12:1). This cleansing prayer needs to be at the foundation of all prayer to make us burn with affection and zeal for God and for others as opposed to burning with the fullness of our ego and lust for things.

> *Prophetic prayer removes the shroud of darkness which grows from negative confessions. It illuminates our stammering language by the outreach of the Spirit, bringing it into pure articulation of Kingdom outcomes.*

Transparency & Transformation

Naturally then, one important step in personal prayer is asking for forgiveness of sins if one is to be effective in the walk with God. Psalm 51 is our best known prayer of penitence in the Bible. Cleansing prayer places us on the altar of God's fire so that the flame may pierce our innermost being. Effective relations with God means that our lives must be transparent (not perfect in activities, but in love) before Him at all times. We are transparent before God. It is not the transparency that we have before God by virtue of His omniscience that is really the issue in our prayer; our own transparency toward Him removes our spiritual blockades. God's ability to see all our sins does not remove them but our ability to lay them bare, in a sense, permits God to remove them. Until God's transparency becomes my transparency, my sins remain because I am still attempting to hide my sins in the face of divine transparency.

Cleansing prayer is more than confession. It is the deep penetration of the inner core of our being to see the root cause of our sentiments, moods and behavior. This is what David does in Psalm 51. Sometimes a confession can just be the flippant "I was wrong." It should not be so when dealing with God. However, when seen from a deeper perspective we can see that cleansing prayer is reaching to the marrow of the act, sentiment, mood or behavior. It is laying everything bare in all its ugliness and shame before the Lord, being assured of grace because we come through the doorway sprinkled by the blood of God's Son. When we come to cleansing prayer, we ought to move away from the confused attempt to generalize our sins and the tendency to explain them away. In cleansing prayer we move away from the partiality inherent in our understanding of our own act. Above all we must seek a cure from the hopeless tendency to externalize our faults and project them to a source outside ourselves. In cleansing prayer we place before God every single occurrence - every habit, every mood, every behavior, every spiritual incompetence as a matter of spiritual urgency whose removal is indispensable to our spiritual survival.

The end (or at least the lessening) of every evil habit is the removal of the defenses of self-justification and self-righteousness. Unless deep cleansing prayer is undertaken, many of our prayers remain in the lower realm and do not pierce through the Second Heaven into the Third Heaven because often they are still founded on a dung heap of unresolved spiritual incompetence (sins). No progress is going to be made spiritually unless this aspect of prayer is restored to the church. Every movement which ignores cleansing prayer merely deals with the superficial externalities and does not have the power to transform its generation in their core being. Spiritual warfare is not a substitute for cleansing prayer. In fact, many become casualties of the war because they engage in spiritual warfare without dealing with the hold which the other side has on their soul. Any attempt to replace this cleansing orientation of prayer with warfare may result in the enemy being able to turn the weapon of the presumed warrior against him or her. Where cleansing prayer is not real, people may change how they dress, dance and speak but their inner core remains far away from God's heart and His Kingdom. All that happens in such cases is that the people become more and more self-focused, seeking new spiritual thrills and spectacular stories about the spiritual dimensions but having no real effect on the community. When we engage in cleansing prayer we open up ourselves to the tide of the cleansing flood of God's Son who then unleashes in us the creative force of the Father for the changing of our world.

> When prophetic prayer comes, the people of God will influence the course of the cosmos, causing the secret channels of the universe to give up their treasures for the benefit of the Kingdom of God.

The Merciful King & I

To show how deep cleansing prayer works in us, notice that in Psalm 51, David approaches the Lord Elohim based on the inner structure of the nature of God and not on his own merit. God's multifaceted mercy is reached: David said "*Have mercy on me, O God, according to thy lovingkindness; **according unto the multitude of thy tender mercies....***" (51:1 KJV, emphasis added)). Mercy is like a river's waterfall which, in its multicolored crashes, washes upon the contrite. The first thing that cleansing prayer is conscious of is the inundating flow of the mercies of God. The heart of Heaven, and the compassion that flows from it, are the only reason for the opportunity to approach God. The second thing that cleansing prayer must be conscious of is the deep and intensive nature of filth that fills the one who approaches the holy throne of the Lord. David uses several phrases to describe what must be done to the stain carried by the person who comes to cleansing prayer: (1) blot out, (2) wash thoroughly, (3) cleanse, and (4) purge. To grasp the issue here, look at the words which David uses to describe the act, habit or behavior: (1) transgression, (2) iniquity, (3) sin, and (4) evil (which is four-dimensional, affronting every quarter of the Divine name!). It did not just affect David, it affected every aspect of the kingdom, yes, even to the sixth dimension—the height, the depth, East, West, North, and South. How is the sin to be dealt with? I must put "I" at the center as the perpetrator of the act. It is "I" who transgressed.

The cause, the originator is I. The ego cannot be absolved of its place in the activities that stain and separate me from the ideal image and likeness in and for whom I was created. Secondly, the act was generated by me, not as a surrogate for someone else and cannot be casually banished from my presence. Because it is mine, I cannot remove my gaze and focus from it without lying to myself and (trying to lie) to God (1 John 1:8-10). The cleansing prayer demands that "I" be placed as the center of the act. As a possessive personality, "I" must acknowledge that whatever sins "I" have committed belong to me. It is this that moves one in the cleansing prayer to justify God and not the self. David put it this way: "Against You, You only, I have sinned and done what is evil in Your sight, so that You are justified when You speak and blameless when You judge," (Psalm 51:4). While this is something I do and possess, and while I am the originator of this act in the now, I am not the origin of its species. I believe this is what Paul meant when he said, "*But if I am doing the very thing I do not want, I am no longer the one doing it, but sin which dwells in me*" (Romans 7:20). The existence and power of transgression go beyond my formation as "I". Its flow is in my being as the result of a spiritual-genetic inflow, which has been part of my race. I must then resort to someone greater than me, more ancient and more adept than myself to deal with this act.

Knowing this, David resorts to God and asks God to do seven things:

1. Hide his face from the act,
2. Create in him a clean heart,
3. Renew the right spirit within him,
4. Restore unto him the joy of the salvation,
5. Uphold in him God's right spirit,
6. Deliver him from the guilt of misleading others to lose their soul,
7. Open his lips and he shall praise Thee.

The target of cleansing prayer is to let God into the innermost sanctum of the person, where truth resides in the inward parts, and to know wisdom in the hidden parts. What happens to the praying person when the cleansing prayer has done its work and God has been released to do His work in the person?

- Purity - "I shall be whiter than snow."
- Knowledge of Divine wisdom is gained.
- Knowledge of divine joy emerges.
- Spiritual alignment - broken bones shall rejoice.
- Continuous consciousness of God's presence is developed.
- Instructive - "I shall teach transgressors thy way."
- Doxological lifestyle - "**Then my tongue will joyfully sing of Your righteousness.**" (Psalm 51:14)

A cleansing prayer touches the core of our being and causes us to face our personal, communal and genetic line sins. This type of prayer brings us face to face with what God wants from us. God is not looking for material sacrifice. He is looking for a living sacrifice which was given in His Son Jesus Christ. When we sin as Christians we must go deep into our innermost being and allow God to deal with what we have done and who we are.

SUPPLICATIVE PRAYER

"Supplication" can mean either to ask simply for something, to pray or entreat someone's favor, or even to call for something. In some rare instances supplication can mean to demand for something. I am using it here in terms of a reverent asking for or calling for someone's help in time of need (Luke 11:9-13; James 5:17-18; 1 Kings 8:37-40, 54-55). The prayer of supplication involves a clear focus on the area of need in which we desire God to make an impact in our life. If we take up the prayer of supplication we acknowledge our limitation in resolving an immediate or anticipated issue or need. To supplicate means to petition or entreat someone - in this case God - for something.

Supplicative prayer must be undergirded by deep passion and fiery zeal for relationship; otherwise, it veers into idolatry. It is not unusual for supplication to be fueled by a deep spiritual burden. In supplication we come to God as Father and King who has the fullness of all the resources that are more than enough to meet our need. God is rich enough, strong enough, powerful enough. Prayers of supplication flow from that point of need. All children of God are aware of this kind of prayer.

Your Will Be Done

Our hunger to seek God's face often leads to this prayer; "Ask and it shall be given to you…" (Matthew 7:7). This asking for something that adds value to our lives here on Earth comes under the prayer of supplication. It is not the same as seeking or knocking, for Jesus Himself makes a distinction among them. Petition means to ask for something. Because we are wholly dependent upon God for life, He loves to have us ask for things. Perhaps this is the most used and misused prayer of all time. We all want material prosperity and popularity, but whenever we ask for material things we should remember to add, "Your will be done." Although God cares about anything that concerns us and He wants us to ask Him for what we need, it pleases Him most when we ask for the Holy Spirit and the characteristics of Jesus.

> *In supplication we come to God as Father and King who has the fullness of all the resources that are more than enough to meet our need. God is rich enough, strong enough, powerful enough.*

This asking dimension of prayer is underscored in the teachings of Jesus in Matthew 7:7. This asking dimension of prayer is also seen Psalm 2:8 where, just for the asking, God is willing to turn the nations over, "Ask of Me, and I will surely give the nations as Your inheritance, And the very ends of the earth as Your possession." In Isaiah 7:11-12, God says to one of the kings of Judah whose heart was filled with fear through his prophet:

> *Ask a sign for yourself from the Lord your God; make it deep as Sheol or high as heaven." But Ahaz said, "I will not ask, nor will I test the Lord!*

But asking the Lord for anything is not a temptation. The purpose and use of the gift carries within it a blessing or curse for the supplicant. To show how powerful this prayer of supplication can be in the believer's life, hear what Isaiah said in 45:11: *"Thus says the Lord, the Holy One of Israel, and his Maker:"Ask Me about the things to come concerning My sons, And you shall commit to Me the work of My hands."* In Zechariah 10:1 the supplication is directed to the weather and the atmosphere: *"Ask rain from the Lord at the time of the spring rain - The Lord who makes the storm clouds; And He will give them showers of rain, vegetation in the field to each man."* The supplicant receives, whether they ask alone or in agreement with others of like mind or like needs. *"Again I say to you, that if two of you agree on earth about anything that they may ask, it shall be done for them by My Father who is in heaven."* (Matthew 18:19).

It is interesting to note that in most places where Jesus tells us to *ask*, there is a context of the idea of God as Father. This is a type of prayer that affirms our Divine linage and our place as children of God. There is nothing out of limits in the prayer of supplication. We read in Matthew 21:22, *"And **all things** you ask in prayer, believing, you will receive."* (emphasis added). But this cannot be taken in isolation of other scriptural texts. We also read in John 14:13-14, *"**Whatever you ask** in My name, that will I do, so that the Father may be glorified in the Son. If you ask Me anything in My name, I will do it."* (emphasis added). In most of the contexts where Jesus tells us to ask there are foundational assumptions. First, that God is our Father. Relationship with God is assumed. At one point Jesus says, *"**Your Heavenly Father** knows what you need before you ask him"* (Matthew 6:32, emphasis added). It is this relationship that puts us in the right to pray. Prayer of relational affirmation should undergird prayers of supplication.

> It is interesting to note that in most places where Jesus tells us to ask, there is a context of the idea of God as Father. This is a type of prayer that affirms our Divine linage and our place as children of God.

Second, out of this relationship grows the other foundational assumption or condition, to "believe." Children believe that their parents can afford what they ask for until they are told otherwise. That relationship births a confidence that can move the hardest of hearts. This trust is indispensable to asking God the Father for anything.

Thirdly, there must be an abiding, unwavering and continuous dwelling in the presence of the Master, as opposed to the constant materialization of petitions. In John 15:7-8 Jesus says;

If you abide in Me, and My words abide in you, ask whatever you wish, and it will be done for you. My Father is glorified by this, that you bear much fruit, and so prove to be My disciples.

In The Name

The asking must be done in the name of the one who has these three following conditions summarized in Him. First, Jesus is the Son, showing a relationship with the Father that is inseparable. Secondly, He has unshakable trust in His Father and only does what He sees the Father do. Thirdly, He always abides in the Father and the Father is always abiding in Him. In fact, this abiding is so strong that He says, "*I and the Father are one*" (John 10:30), and at another place He says, "*he that has seen me has seen the father*" (John 14:9). Thus, the use of His Name to ask is a confirmation of our relationship, trust and rootedness in the Father.

> *"In that day you will not question Me about anything. Truly, truly, I say to you, if you ask the Father for **anything** in My name, He will give it to you. Until now you have asked for nothing in My name; ask and you will receive, so that your joy may be made full. These things I have spoken to you in figurative language; an hour is coming when I will no longer speak to you in figurative language, but will tell you plainly of the Father. In that day you will ask in My name, and I do not say to you that I will request of the Father on your behalf."*
> (John 16:23-26, emphasis added)

For His Glory

There is another condition for asking which is revealed in the life of our Lord and revealed for us in James. The purpose of our asking must be in tune with the glory and praise of the Father. We must not ask merely out of lust or for the purpose of hurting others. These are the only hindrances to obtaining our desire from the Father. Our asking must not be for war and strife. All these things are contrary to the nature of our Father and the one in whose name we pray. These are internal conditions of the heart that may hinder us from receiving what we ask. There is a strange connection between asking out of strife and internal restlessness, which is really unbelief. Faith is peaceable and restful because it is confident in its relationship with the one from whom it is asking. James also tells us another reason for our not receiving. We simply do not ask. We just wish. **We complain therefore we do not have. We must ask**! James says, "*You do not have because you do not ask.*" (James 4:2).

For what purpose are we asking? If the purpose for the asking is consistent with the nature and intention of God then we cannot be said to be asking amiss. Note the language of James: "You ask and do not receive, because you ask with wrong motives, so that you may spend *it* on your pleasures." (4:3). This is an issue of intention and motivation.

PRAYER OF THANKSGIVING

> *"In everything give thanks; for this is God's will for you in Christ Jesus"* (1Thessalonians 5:18).
>
> *Gratitude unlocks the fullness of life. It turns what we have into enough, and more. It turns denial into acceptance, chaos to order, confusion to clarity. It can turn a meal into a feast, a house into a home, a stranger into a friend. Gratitude makes sense of our past, brings peace for today, and creates a vision for tomorrow.*
>
> Melody Beattie
>
> *The transmitter of Divine gifts to man is the heart, continually moved to gratitude, and the transmitter of temptations to the soul is discontented thought for ever moving in the heart. Again, lips forever giving thanks receive God's blessings, and a heart filled with gratitude unexpectedly receives grace.*
>
> (The Philokalia: Direction to the Hesychasts)

Gratitude Restores Wonder

The way we use the phrase "*be* thankful" suggests that gratitude is not merely an act but "who one is." So when we read over 35 times in the *Authorized Version* "give thanks," there is an implicit assumption that these words verbalize who we are and frame our attitude in the world. If we look at the Book of Hebrews (and combine all the words that convey the idea of gratitude to God and even to human beings) we notice that it is used more than a thousand times. This tells us that if we would pray effectively we must cultivate a kind of **ontology (nature of being) of gratitude** which creates a **cosmology of praise**. Gratitude is in itself a spiritual practice that can transform our world. It is not a state of mind - but of *being*. It is intrinsically a grammar of being, and spirituality that communicates authenticity. For the believer, it is the environment within which their spiritual life has its ebb and flow. The way each of us goes about showing gratitude may differ but, for the believer who has an effective prayer life, this mode of being in the world is indispensable. The believer's relationship with God and the created world, which he/she believes is the gift of a gracious God to humankind, calls forth this flow of gratitude in the believer.

The practice of gratitude in prayer can increase our ability to deal with the circumstances that befall us. A prayer of gratitude is a way of looking beyond the causality of life and, instead of adapting a 'ho-hum' attitude, to return to joy by being surprised by the wonder in the so-called mundane.

Ingratitude Creates Idols

Prayers of gratitude put us in a place where, instead of feeling cheated by God and by life and looking incessantly for things to get better, we see ourselves as being intrinsically better than the situations, no matter what they are. Comparing, competing and cross-referencing our achievement and inadequacies burdens us with care. It can have devastating consequences for our spiritual lives, grown out of ingratitude. When this happens, we are led to live in perpetual dissatisfaction. This creates artificiality and exaggerates our lack, thereby causing us to set up idols other than God who we believe can meet our ever-gnawing need. But these idols never meet our need. The problem with absence of gratitude is that the things we want are never really for the glory of God or the benefit of others, but for relieving our greed - which remains ever present, eating up the soul's energy - until we develop this life of gratefulness.

Open Your Heart to the Universe.

Gratitude is a devotional, because it grows out of our love and hunger to see the Will of God done. When we are grateful and committed to the will of God, our hearts receive good medication, helping us to realize our commitment - though the process may be painful. Paul's injunction "in every thing give thanks" (1 Thessalonians 5:18) challenges us to take a posture of expressive gratitude for

> *There is a strange connection between asking out of strife and internal restlessness, which is really unbelief. Faith is peaceable and restful because it is confident in its relationship with the one from whom it is asking.*

everything and everyone based on how we see God, rather than on how we see the situation or what may appear to be the immediate failure.

There is an adage that describes people in terms of seeing a glass half-full or half-empty. I encourage you to use gratitude as your inner eye to look at the inherent goodness of life in all its ebb and flow. For gratitude is an affirmation of the goodness of God and the prodigious outpouring of mercy upon us.

Prayers of gratitude turn our eyes away from gaps or lack to providence and plentitude. Gratitude is not about how we see things; rather, it is about how we know God. The problem many prayers offered even among believers is that, rather than exude a life-state of gratitude, it tends to focus on lack and how difficult life has been. So many prayers are spent reminding God of how we can barely make it and how little good can be found in life itself. It is any wonder that God does not roar thunderously from the Heavens? This is not a denial of the difficulty we often go though as we pass this way, but rather a call to set ourselves above circumstances and embrace the joy of the Lord as a way of healing our innermost disappointments. A prayer of gratitude is focused on God, not on the often tedious process by which we take hold of our daily purpose or destiny. Gratitude says, "I will focus on the goodness and plentitude of God."

When our lives are charged with gratitude, we will give thanks for anything or anyone who has benefited us, and even for our enemies! Prayers of gratitude spring from a deep sea within the innermost sanctum and bubble up to the mouth of the righteous effortlessly. "Sing for joy in the Lord, O you righteous ones; Praise is becoming to the upright" (Psalms 33:1). For those of us who love God and whose life overflows with His love, gratitude is like a free-flowing tap pouring forth pure satisfying water - both for the us and those with whom we come into contact. Establish a habit of gratitude, sign it upon your heart and you will be made whole in more ways than one. A heart flowing with prayers of gratitude will chase away anger, pride, resentment, and selfishness. Prayers of gratitude open our hearts to the universe. Practice the prayer of gratitude by making giving thanks and praise and blessing a major part of your everyday life - and see how many miracles the universe releases to you. There is a Hebrew tradition that calls us to express gratitude at least a hundred times a day; thus, saturating the day and total environment with gratitude.

> The way we use the phrase "be thankful" suggests that gratitude is not merely an act but "who one is."

Howduw!

The word often translated in the KJV as "thanks" is the Hebrew הוֹדוּ(howduw). For example in Psalm 136:1, "Give thanks to the Lord, for He is good, For His lovingkindness is everlasting." In Psalm 136:1, we see another instance הוֹדוּ לַיהוָה כִּי־טוֹב כִּי לְעוֹלָם חַסְדּוֹ ("Howduw la-Yahweh kiyTowb Kiy la `olaam chacdow."). This word is more connected to the raising of the hand in acknowledgment of God, not just as the source of good but as good itself. Nonetheless, it carries with it the idea of gratitude, as duty embeds in grace. The wordsתודה (toda) translated "thanks"; ברכה(bracha) translated "blessing"; and הלל(halal) translated "to shine" or "to shine a steady light upon someone or

4 - Varieties of Prayer

something" is usually translated "praise" in scripture. It can also mean to raise high. These are all the words of gratitude and power. These words convey a sense of the universal obligation of gratitude which humankind, especially believers, owe God for His beneficence. Even a casual look at one's life demands gratitude for all the benefits of Divine Providence. There are general and personal gifts of divine inflow that, in all our wildest dreams, we could not conjure up, so we bow in the prayer of gratitude.

A Powerful Safeguard

The gifts which God gives each day are indescribable, so we join Paul and say "Thanks be to God for His indescribable gift!" (2 Corinthians 9:15, NKJV), Learning **to be thankful** is one of the best ways to combat a sense of victimization and self-pity, despair, hopelessness, and perpetual fatigue. Thanksgiving should be a part of every conversation, not just prayer. One of the major sins of many people today is that of ingratitude. According to Romans Chapter 1, lack of gratitude is the seed of most evil acts that go against the will and purpose of God. The members of the perverted generation of Romans Chapter 1 are not grateful to God for being God; they want him to be something else, so they make a substitute. They idolize. The women are not grateful for being women, they seek to act as men. The men are not grateful for being men or for the creation of women - they must substitute themselves and even animals for women. Children are not grateful for the parents they have. Their parents can never do enough for them; they are not grateful for the little their parents are able to afford for them. Parents are not grateful for their children; they compare, complain, castigate and complicate. This lack of gratitude ends in the removal of the Spirit of God from their heart and they become darkness instead of light.

An understanding of gratitude is of great significance to the flow of God's power in our lives. Gratitude is one of the key ways to avoid many of the error against which the Scripture cautions. Prayers of gratitude keep us in the place of truth and check the sinful impulse to believe that we are the source of our successes. The prayer of gratitude opens our eyes to see, so that we do not arrogantly presume that our developments and progress are based on our own resources. A prayer of gratitude can be an antidote to the type of thinking which marginalizes God and misjudges others. Our objective in the spiritual life should be to integrate gratitude into every aspect of our prayer life. It is the oxygen that causes prayer to move. When gratitude becomes the environment in which prayer is exercised, we would receive more extraordinary answers to prayer. Often our immediate situations (and the pain they cause) move us to justify our accusations, complaints and even curse our lot in life. Gratitude is the cure.

Answered Prayer and Presence

This is why every prayer must be girded and saturated with praise, adoration and worship of God. We come to God in praise and glory, requesting that our prayers be answered and then return, glorifying and praising God for all. When our prayers have been answered, it is God incarnating Himself in the name of His Son into our lives again. In praise, adoration and worship, we are not being sentimental about our feelings for God. We focus on God's nature and this focus leads us into a reverential awe - out of which flows worship. We worship in spirit and in truth as gratitude helps us to focus on God who is Spirit and Truth. A grateful heart knows there is a God who based on the goodness of His nature answers prayers. Prayers of gratitude embody praise and thanksgiving as exemplified in Psalm 100; Acts 16:16–34; Psalm 149:4–9; and 1 Thessalonians 5:15–19. We find that as gratitude saturates and atmosphere, the glory of the Lord flows freely into the atmosphere, as we see in the dedication of Solomon's temple:

> *When the priests came forth from the holy place (for all the priests who were present had sanctified themselves, without regard to divisions), and all the Levitical singers, Asaph, Heman, Jeduthun, and their sons and kinsmen, clothed in fine linen, with cymbals, harps and lyres, standing east of the altar, and with them one hundred and twenty priests blowing trumpets in unison when the trumpeters and the singers were to make themselves heard with one voice to praise and to glorify the Lord, and when they lifted up their voice accompanied by trumpets and cymbals and instruments of music, and when they praised the Lord saying, "He indeed is good for His lovingkindness is everlasting,"* **then the house, the house of the Lord, was filled with a cloud, so that the priests could not stand to minister because of the cloud, for the glory of the Lord filled the house of God.**
> (2 Chronicles 5;11–14, emphasis added)

Gratitude will bring down the cloud of glory even easier than fasting! A prayer of gratitude is a revelation of delight and reaches the throne quicker than most prayers. It is written, **"Delight yourself in the Lord; And He will give you the desires of your heart."** (Psalm 37:4, emphasis added). To delight is to move delicately and with finesse, to express joy with a kingly flair yet with softness and fluidity. At least that is my understanding of the Hebrew word עָנַג (*awnawg*). It is to be in constant motion as one who is dancing with a beloved partner and enjoying the movement. As we see here, it is the harmonization of the atmosphere with God's nature and purpose. When that is done, it makes way for the release of the glory of the Lord. One of keys to this is gratitude.

The effect of the prayer of gratitude on negative conditions is well attested in Scripture. The best known example of the power of prayer of gratitude in the midst of a negative situation making a big difference is the prayer of Jehoshaphat in 2 Chronicles 20:21–23:

> *When he had consulted with the people, he appointed those who sang to the Lord and those who praised Him in holy attire, as they went out before the army and said, "Give thanks to the Lord, for His lovingkindness is everlasting." When they began singing and praising, the Lord set ambushes against the sons of Ammon, Moab and Mount Seir, who had come against Judah; so they were routed. For the sons of Ammon and Moab rose up against the inhabitants of Mount Seir destroying them completely; and when they had finished with the inhabitants of Seir, they helped to destroy one another.*

With the watering of a prayer of gratitude, we dispose ourselves to quickly answered prayers. Sometimes it is not that our prayers are flawed in and of themselves that keep them from being answered but that these prayers are bathed in the waters of ingratitude and discontent. What

> *Gratitude is in itself a spiritual practice that can transform our world. It is not a state of mind - but of being.*

hinders us from praising God will hinder us from effective prayer if we let it. It can also hinder us from loving others. A heart of gratitude beings us into the inner chamber of God. When we give thanks, with all the facets of what that means even in seemingly negative situations, we are affirming our faith in God. This brings joy to God, because it lets Heaven know that we are not confused about what is ultimate and who is truly in charge. Gratitude is one of the most powerful weapons available to would-be intercessors. Gratitude removes one of Satan's greatest weapons against our lives out of his hands. Here is where we silence his roar and his movements. Be thankful. Count your blessings. Delight yourself in the LORD.

PRAYER OF INTERCESSION

The word התפלל (ythpalal - to entreat) is what is translated "to intercede" in some versions of the Bible. This is really to entreat the favor of a great person of behalf of one who has wronged them, or needs their help. To intercede is to come between two parties and plead before one of them on behalf of the other. In the New Testament, it is the translation of the word ἐντυγχάνειν (entygchanein). The Latin word is *interpellare*, found in Hebrews 7:25. Some theologians suggest that we separate intercession from "mediation," - which means standing in the midst between two contending parties, for the purpose of bring them together.

"Mediate" is what Christ did for us. To intercede is travail in prayer for another to God. When we take it upon ourselves to pray earnestly for other people, we enter the realm of intercession. To enter into intercession, we must have a heart that really loves the Lord and cares about the things God cares about. In a sense, it is to pray for someone that they may receive a special dispensation of grace from God.

Protecting The Heart and Community

The great danger surrounding any people who have no intercessors is aptly stated by Ezekiel:

> *I searched for a man among them who would **build up the wall and stand in the gap before Me for the land**, so that I would not destroy it; but I found no one. Thus I have poured out My indignation on them; I have consumed them with the fire of My wrath; their way I have brought upon their heads," declares the Lord God.*
> (Ezekiel 22:30–31, emphasis added)

One who does not intercede is a breaker of the wall and, in fact, is in danger of letting their serpent nature express itself. Often one who is not interceding is complaining, gossiping, passing judgment, and condemning. Let not that one think the serpent will spare him, for he who breaks the wall ("hedge" in KJV) or even leaves it in disrepair will feel the bite of the serpent. Where intercession is not constant, there is indignation, fire, wrath and overpowering Divine vengeance. So God actively seeks someone who can in fact make up the hedge by standing in the gap. Prayers of intercession mean that the believer has taken upon himself to stand between two people who have a quarrel and plead for peace. The following Scriptures bear this point out. Moses the man of God says:

> *And the LORD was angry enough with Aaron to destroy him, but at that time I prayed for Aaron too.*
> (Deuteronomy 9:20, NIV)

Righteous Hezekiah interceded for the people:

> *Although most of the many people who came from Ephraim, Manasseh, Issachar and Zebulun had not purified themselves, yet they ate the Passover, contrary to what was written. **But Hezekiah prayed for them**, saying, "May the LORD, who is good, pardon everyone."*
> (2 Chronicles 30:18, NIV, emphasis added)

Job's healing and goods were restored when he interceded for his self-righteous friends:

> ***After Job had prayed for his friends***, *the LORD restored his fortunes and gave him twice as much as he had before.*
> (Job 42:10, NIV, emphasis added)

Jesus Christ our Lord interceded for Peter even though He knew that Peter would deny Him:

> *"But **I have prayed for you**, Simon, that your faith may not fail. And when you have turned back, strengthen your brothers."*
> (Luke 22:32, NIV, emphasis added)

A group intercessory prayer was compellingly responsive:

> *When they arrived,* **they prayed for the new believers there that they might receive the Holy Spirit.**
> (Acts 8:15, NIV, emphasis added)

Like Christ

Jesus' major work for us in Heaven, before the throne of the Father, is entreating God's favor on our behalf. "*Therefore he is able to save completely those who come to God through him, because he always lives to intercede for them*" (Hebrews 7:25). When we intercede for others, we come closest to God's heart. We are more like Jesus. Jesus, in Heaven, is our High Priest and His ministry is to intercede with the Father for His disciples (us) and for all humankind. When we join Him in praying for others, we are most like Him.

The natural outflow of being like Christ is to pray for others, especially as relates to salvation and deliverance from the evil one. Jesus tells us as disciples to pray for others who are being called to the vineyard. In Matthew 9:37–38 (NIV) we read, "*Then he said to his disciples, 'The harvest is plentiful but the workers are few. Ask the Lord of the harvest, therefore, to send out workers into his harvest field.'*" In praying for workers in the vineyard of the Master, we are interceding for the salvation of the world. The key to the harvest of souls is that God sends effective harvesters into the field of human souls where love has given birth to true intercession. It is true that we are to pray for the unsaved, but the direct intercession is for believers and for workers that God is calling from the body of His Son. The New Testament does explicitly teach intercession for the believer and the unbeliever in the command to pray for all men. We may go from the fact that Jesus died for the world to the idea that He was given for the world to intercede for them. But the general orientation of the New Testament points believers to intercede for one another. Our effective witness to the non-believer is powered by our willingness to intercede for them.

Powerful Intercession Through Scripture

The first occurrence of intercession is the picture painted of our father Abraham as he stood face to face with the Lord and pleaded for the mercy over Sodom and Gomorrah. The word also occurs where others are pleading on behalf of Abraham as he seeks land to bury his late wife. Abraham said to the elders of the city *"If you are willing to let me bury my dead,* **then listen to me and intercede** *with Ephron son of Zohar on my behalf"* (Genesis 23:8, NIV, emphasis added). "Intercession" is also used in 1 Samuel 2:25 where Eli asks, *"If a man sins against the LORD, who will intercede for him?"* But Eli did not intercede for his sons, so they died from the judgment of the Lord. The man of God, Samuel, exemplifies intercession. *"Then Samuel said, 'Assemble all Israel at Mizpah and* **I will intercede with the Lord for you**'*"* (1 Samuel 7:5, emphasis added). In 1 Kings 13:6 (NIV), we see how a stubborn king got himself in trouble with God and, through intercession, was restored to wholeness.

> *The king said to the man of God, "Please entreat the Lord your God, and pray for me, that my hand may be restored to me." So the man of God entreated the Lord, and the king's hand was restored to him, and it became as it was before.*

Another great example, which in my mind is the greatest in the Old Testament, is the intercession of Moses for the people of Israel when God wanted to wipe them out. Moses put his own welfare on the line to shield the people from the wrath of God. We read in Numbers 21:7 (NIV), *"The people came to Moses and said, 'We sinned when we spoke against the LORD and against you. Pray that the LORD will take the snakes away from us.' So Moses prayed for the people."*

There are several things we must understand about intercession. First, it is directed to the Lord God and *never* to the devil or demons or human beings. We are not told to intercede for a demon oppressed, possessed, or depressed person. Rather, we are told to cast the spirit out. Second, good intercessors may place themselves in the line of God's fire and must be willing to lay themselves down for the people for whom they intercede. There is always a sacrifice that the intercessor must make. It may mean that they need to spend hours in prayer and fasting for the person who is in need. We may intercede for someone to be saved from the legitimate consequences of their action. Third, we may intercede for healing of sickness. Fourth, we may intercede for direction in life's journey. Fifth, we intercede for salvation of our unbelieving friends, family and fellow citizens. Sixth, we can intercede for the weather to change in favor of the work of God. Seventh, we can intercede for the government of the land. We can intercede for people in any geographic location. Eighth, we may also intercede for believers who are in trouble because of their work in spreading the Gospel. This is exemplified in Acts 12:5, "*So Peter was kept in prison, but the church was earnestly praying to God for him.*" This prayer of intercession was answered when God sent an angel to set him free!

A Word of Caution

Intercession is not just for the super-spiritual, as has sometimes been conveyed. Any believer can get involved in a prayer of intercession. A command in the Book of James is directed to the general body of Christ. Specializing in intercession is problematic, because it seem to excuse many from interceding. It creates a self-styled elite class of Christians who disdain and disregard their brethren.

> *Prayers of gratitude turn our eyes away from gaps or lack to providence and plentitude. Gratitude is not about how we see things; rather, it is about how we know God.*

> *Confess your trespasses to one another,* **and pray for one another***, that you may be healed. The effective, fervent prayer of a righteous man avails much. Elijah was a man with a nature like ours, and he prayed earnestly that it would not rain; and it did not rain on the land for three years and six months. And he prayed again, and the heaven gave rain, and the earth produced its fruit.*
> (James 5:16–18, NKJV, emphasis added)

The prayer of intercession which we see here is directed for the benefit of the body of Christ. Elijah is only used here to illustrate the power of prayer, not as an example of intercession.

We must not confuse judgment prayer with intercession. It has become common for people to pray down judgment on people and call it intercession. Intercession is directed toward healing and deliverance. A prayer of judgment runs along a different stream from intercession and must be distinguished if the believer is not to veer off into witchcraft and self-seeking vengeance, which may in fact poison his/her spiritual stream. It is not intercession when judgment is called for (Luke 9:54-55). A prayer of intercession promotes healing and seeks achievement of reconciliation.

CHAPTER FIVE

METHODS OF PRAYER

"With all prayer and petition, pray at all times in the Spirit"
Ephesians 6:18

VOCAL METHODS

In the vocal method, prayer is said out loud alone or in groups. We make statements such as "say your prayers," "speak a word to the Lord" or "cry to the Lord." In the *King James Version* of the Bible the psalmist uses the word "call" 22 times to refer to his prayer to the Lord. This shows how common the vocal type of prayer is. In fact, this method of prayer is so common that many church people consider other types of prayer irrelevant or unchristian. In the simplest terms prayer is talking to God, speaking to the Creator in a conversational manner. The problem is that many of us speak to God but we do not wait to hear Him talk back to us.

Vocal prayer features three main benefits. First, the power of vocal prayer articulates our hidden desires. Second, it makes our unconscious conscious so that we are clear about what we are saying to God. Third, vocal prayer creates a certain level of confidence in that we hear our voice as it resounds in the environment, giving us the feeling of not being alone and not merely talking to ourselves. Everyone from Adam to Moses to David to Jesus and all the way to the present day talks to God in some form or another. But the real issue is who does God speak back to? True vocal prayer is manifested when it moves from merely being our talking to a conversation between us and God. One of the ways to make vocal prayers effective is simply to put our thoughts into the form of questions to the Father as a child would. In this way, rather than telling God what to do, you elicit a conversation with Him. Vocal prayers should be interspersed with moments of quiet waiting for responses from the Father. **Let God talk too.**

CONTEMPLATIVE METHOD

Contemplative prayer has been given a bad name among many brethren who view it as merely an eastern religious invasion into Christianity. This is a misunderstanding of the impact and meaning of spiritual methods. There are phrases that convey the idea of contemplation in the Scripture. The dictionary defines contemplation as thoughtful, meditative, deep in thought or to be lost in thought, pensive, reflective or introspective. Contemplative prayer involves being "lost" in the beauty and wonder of God and His creation, acknowledging His greatness in all things. It begins in silence. "Silence is the mastery of the future life," said an ancient Christian father of the Hesychast movement.

> One of the ways to make vocal prayers effective is simply to put our thoughts into the form of questions to the Father as a child would. In this way, rather than telling God what to do, you elicit a conversation with Him.

In contemplation we lay aside all thoughts that do not have direct bearing on the work of salvation. It is in this silence and stillness that we come to know God in a unique way. "Be still and know that I am God" (Psalm 46:10 KJV). We can only practice this method successfully if we remove all distractions from our inner self man and our external surroundings. The second way then to be effective is to find solitude. It can be done with Scriptures, the lives of recognized men and women of God or even by revelative reflection on the creative genius of God our Father. At issue is the place of the intuitive imagination in prayer, not the mind. Psalm 119:148 can be translated "Within my imagination I picture your precepts." Scripture supports the harnessing of the intuition and imagination as instruments of prayer. The Hebrew words translated "meditation" can also be translated "contemplate," as in Joshua 1:8. The word translated meditate is the Hebrew word הָגִיתָ ("wagiyhaalah," - thou shall mediate). The idea here can mean to imagine, mourn or mutter and study a matter. It can also imply to contemplate in isolation. Another word used is the Hebrew term שׂוּחַ "suwach" (in Genesis 24:63), which speaks of communing or complaining in a mournful way or musing, talking and simply praying. In this case it is nurturing of a thing in the mind until it comes to fruition or manifestation. This method of praying focuses on the creative imagination and can be harnessed to focus prayers' power on its target. By the use of the mind we can reproduce the patterns of the upper realm in the mundane realm. Here the believer uses his spiritual capacity and gifting to reproduce in the material realm the things which the eyes of the spirit have seen.

The Spiritual Mind and Imagination

The imagination of the believer, when focused absolutely on God or any aspect of

God's being, can bring success and fulfillment because the mind joined to Christ synthesizes the future and the present. When we use this method of prayer we structure our spiritual experience for greater reception of divine inflow. Focusing the mind in prayer is not necessarily achieved by the use of the natural mind, for the natural mind is enmity with God. It is the spiritual mind which is called for here. There must be a release of the self from the carnality of the natural mind. This intentional release of the natural mind and moving into the spiritual mind (or the mind of Christ) facilitates our cooperation with the mind of God. In this method of prayer we are moved to clear the field of all mundane and worldly anxiety, honing into and focusing on the beauty of the Lord, or some aspect of His being that moves us at that moment. In contemplation we quiet our inner tumults and phase out all worldly sounds by centering our spiritual imagination on what is ultimate and lofty.

In this we rest in God. This is our inner being enjoying God's Sabbath. Getting into this kind of prayer demands a positive posture that causes the soul of the praying person to come to grips with the fact that all it knows about God is nothing compared to that which can be known of Him. In that place the praying person then enters into willing release or a self-emptying of what is known in order to plunge headlong into the mystery called God. The power and effect of the mind, when turned over into the mystery of God, causes us to transcend our present tendency to list, describe and analyze our situation for God. Rather we move into a faithful resting because our mind is saturated by Him and not our needs. Actual intimacy with God culminates in points of knowledge, love, ecstasy or other empathic experience of the heart of God. Praying thus, our soul gazes in loving awe on the glory of God.

MYSTICAL METHOD

> *For one who speaks in a tongue does not speak to men but to God; for no one understands, but in his spirit he speaks mysteries.*
> (1 Corinthians 14:2)

The word "mystery" is used so many times in Scripture by Paul that it seems strange to me that there are some Christians who avoid it. Prayer is meant to penetrate the mystery of the universe. It is communing with divine mystery in our inner man, calling it to reveal itself. According to Heiler, the two highest types of prayer are the mystical and the prophetic. Mysticism, in its Christian context, is not a synthesis of sound, light and feelings, it is the silencing of all in the presence of the indescribable and incomprehensible nature of God. It silences human thought and language.

In mysticism the depth of our intellect, our will, our hearts and soul communicate beyond normal language. Words which we know are much too weak to convey the height, extent and depth to which we have been brought. That is why only those who speak in tongues really approach this. But even they can come to the place where only groaning will do. It is also a universal religious phenomenon in which one allows his spirit to plunge into the unknown by faith in order to access the celestial sphere. Here the aim is union with God, who is generally portrayed in supra-personal terms, unknowable by reason, beyond description, overpowering light or depth to which man can only answer with silence. In mystical prayer the idea of silence - not just of sound but of the thought - is very important. Sometimes this prayer begins by picturing God in terms of the substances that are used to describe Him in Scripture but the prayer pushes the mind or the imagination to the point where it loses its denotative and descriptive ability. One is left only with silence. Ideas about God are not transformed into pictures on which the human soul or spirit soars beyond the terrestrial but becomes silenced as one plunges into God.

The Spirit Gives Life

Mystics see God as transcending personality, best described as the Absolute, the infinite abyss, or the infinite ground and depth of all being. Mystics see prayer as the elevation of the soul and spirit to God. Though the mystic does not deny the intervention of God in history as we find in the Bible, he or she sees revelation as effective mainly in terms of an interior illumination rather than the literal letter of Scripture. A mystic understands what Paul meant when he said, *"for the letter kills, but the Spirit gives life"* (2 Corinthians 3:6). To a mystic, the Master's statement *"the words that I have spoken to you are spirit and are life"* rings true (John 6:63). Mystics often speak of a ladder of prayer or stages of prayer, and petition is always considered the lowest stage. The highest goal in prayer is to culminate in divine ecstasy. They may use singing, chanting, moaning and groaning, joy, music, hymns alone or in groups - but these are seen mainly as a means to reach that silence in which one plunges into the depth that cannot be described. They crave a silence in which the material universe is "dead" and closed out. The world's distraction and noise hushed, the door of the heart opened to the Lord and the will disappearing into the Will of the Godhead. The mystic may use a "working prayer" which is dedicating the day's work joyfully and honestly to the Lord. They may also turn daily vernacular into prayer, bringing God's name back into everyday language—saying "Thank God" or "Thanks be to God" during conversation. The mystic prays from the Heavenly place. Mystics are supernatural travelers who can locate themselves spiritually in any place and pray across dimensions.

MEDITATIVE METHOD

By "meditation" we are referring to the active use of the mind, which may include the feelings. Meditation is conscious awareness of God, self and the world by taking into oneself the Word, acts, or a precept of God and allowing these to saturate one's being. Christian meditation requires, as its testing instrument, the Word of God. There are proven methods of meditation in the Bible and in the experiences of Christian saints which have shown results to which believers may resort, depending on their maturity.

Meditation is the road many Christians travel to becoming truly spiritual in their walk. Unlike some of the other methods of prayer, meditation is not simply an intuitive art veiled in mystery. Usually it is applied to a passage of Scripture, or our own situation in life, or to any active way in which we try to understand God or ourselves. It is **thought-focused** on God or God's Word. Meditation has great richness. Meditation is easier to do than contemplation because the tools are ready for it - such as language and other symbolic expression. We may think about the meaning of joy or a wonder or sign performed by God. It is more akin to the thought grasping an idea. Moving the mind from hostility to genuine love and reverence takes work and cooperation with the Holy Spirit.

Words, Thoughts, Meditation and Memory

This conformity of our mind with the mind of the Holy Spirit demands that we develop a way of concentrating deeply and considering the Word of God. The meditative capacity of the mind is affirmed by several New Testament passages such as: Romans 8:6; Romans 12:1; and 1 Corinthians 2:16. The Greek word used usually is $\mu\varepsilon\lambda\acute{\varepsilon}\tau\alpha$ (*meletao*), which means to revolve an idea in the mind and use the imagination. Most of the time in Scripture when the word occurs, it is in the context of meditating on the Word of God. In Psalm 1:2 this is clear, "*But his delight is in the law of the Lord, And in His law he **meditates** day and night*". Thus in meditation we create a kind of respite in the outside world so that we can lift up our mind's eye and behold the beauty of the Lord out of the world. In Joshua 1:8 we read:

> *Contemplative prayer involves being "lost" in the beauty and wonder of God and His creation, acknowledging His greatness in all things. It begins in silence.*

> *This book of the law shall **not depart from your mouth**, but you shall **meditate on it day and night**, so that you may be careful to do according to all that is*

written in it; for then you will make your way prosperous, and then you will have success.
(emphasis added).

Three key points about meditation are mentioned in this passage. First, the mouth is important for meditation. Taking phrases from the Word of God and repeating is a vital part of meditation. This is not vain repetition. For no repetition of the Word of God or the true name of God is ever vain. The second aspect involves **thinking** on the words and concepts and using the reasoning as way to grasp the concepts in the Word of God. Third, part of meditation is to active adhere to the ideas and concepts contained. Doing something for God can also be seen as meditation, a way of getting into the meaning of what one is meditating on. The idea espoused here is also supported by Psalm 77:12, "*I will meditate on all Your work and muse on Your deeds.*"

The memory is also important in meditation. Hence the principle of remembrance as David says in Psalm 63:6, "*When I remember You on my bed, I meditate on You in the night watches,*" (emphasis added). We can meditate by deliberately recalling our experiences with God or other works of God. When Jesus said, "Remember Me" it was a call to meditation. When God says to Israel, "Remember the Sabbath to keep it holy" He calls us to meditate on the creative work of God and His power. The Sabbath is meant to be a day of meditation. It is a day of creative focus on the nature and work of God. Furthermore, in Psalm 119:15, David insists that meditation is a way of developing reverence for the ways of God: "*I will meditate on Your precepts and regard Your ways.*" According to Psalm 119:23, meditation is one way to handle verbal attack by others. "*Even though princes sit and talk against me, Your servant meditates on Your statutes.*" When we lift up our minds unto the celestial and express our love, our memory of the mighty acts of God is activated and recreated in our mind.

> *In contemplation prayer we are moved to clear the field of all mundane and worldly anxiety, honing into and focusing on the beauty of the Lord, or some aspect of His being that moves us at that moment.*

Self Transformation

Meditation on God and His might shames our base pride and deals with perversity within us. "*From Your precepts I get understanding; Therefore I hate every false way.*" (Psalm 119:104); "*Mine eyes prevent the night watches that I might meditate in thy word,*" (Psalm 119:148); "*I remember the days of old; I meditate on all Your doings; I muse on the work of Your hands*" (Psalm 143:5); and "*Settle it therefore in your hearts, not to meditate before what ye shall answer,"* (Luke 21:14, KJV). Paul tells us, *"Meditate upon these things; give thyself wholly to them; that thy profiting may appear to all."* (1 Timothy 4:15, KJV).

Meditation on the person of Jesus Christ can produce in the believer a sense of the full joy of which our Lord spoke. It is a way of forming the image of the Master in our inner being. As we practice meditative prayer we enter into God and God enters us. We open to the source of tranquility available to us as human beings in our Father. By this kind of prayer Christ is formed in us and we are able to deal with some of the personal conflict and chaos that threaten to invade our lives. Deep meditation on the things of God and on the Word and work of God allows wholeness and Divine love - the beauty of God streams into our daily experiences. When we meditate on the things of God we open up ourselves to the eternal nature of God which then takes form within us and flows into the world.

Meditation is a great tool for self-discovery, self-examination and honesty to God and the universe in which we live. As we meditate we can get to know ourselves and our purposes in life as the Holy Spirit lights our inner self and names our soul for the Kingdom. Meditation allows us to look deeper beyond the temporary, helps to rouse us up from our deep bondage to the unconscious and prepares us for better visions of ourselves and the world. It is a great way to arouse the prophetic spirit and unleash dreams of great things within oneself.

Part of meditative prayer is also the principle of self-questioning. Ask yourself who you are in God. Who were you yesterday? Who are you today in the now? Who will you be in light of what you know or think you know about God? Meditation is a way to live life in wakefulness, moment by moment. Meditation increases awareness of yourself, your world and the spiritual world in which you move that is actually going on behind your own eyes. Meditation has intrinsic value or else God would not have recommended it to Joshua, nor would the psalmist have spoken so eloquently of the indescribable joy and comfort it brought to him.

ACTION OF GRACE AS METHOD OF PRAYER

This is a prayer not accompanied by word or deep contemplation but a simple thought of doing something for someone which carries the grace of God into one's life. Offering an act to God as a prayer is one of the easiest prayers, yet it's often neglected by us in our daily life. It is the intention and focus of the act that makes it a prayer. In giving alms or offering help I offer it up to the Lord as prayer for the person to whom it is given. Doing a particular act in this way can help others experience the grace, power and glory of God.

CHAPTER SIX
ATMOSPHERES OF EFFECTIVE PRAYER

EFFECTIVE BODY PRAYER MUST BE PRAYED IN THE SPIRIT OF AGREEMENT

The principle of unity and agreement is seen even in the building of the tabernacle of worship in the wilderness. God says to Moses in Exodus 26:11, "**You shall make fifty clasps of bronze, and you shall put the clasps into the loops and join the tent together so that it will be a unit.**" (emphasis added)

Psalm 133:1-3 states unequivocally the benefits of the principle of unity for the flow of Divine blessings:

> **Behold, how good and how pleasant it is for brothers to dwell together in unity!** It is like the precious oil upon the head, coming down upon the beard, even Aaron's beard, coming down upon the edge of his robes. It is like the dew of Hermon coming down upon the mountains of Zion; **for there the Lord commanded the blessing - life forever.** (emphasis added)

The exclamation of David in this passage, שֶׁבֶת אַחִים גַּם־יָחַד *(shebet 'achiym gam- yaachad -* "For brethren to dwell together in unity!") points to the unity of the people as a symbolic expression of God's nature. This God is also One, His Name is ONE. The Hebrew word translated "dwell," (שֶׁבֶת- shebeth) is derived from the root word "yashab" (יָשַׁב) which means to sit down in proper order - as judges will sit on the bench with the intent toward justice. They are not gathered as spiritual vigilantes, nor are they gathered to destroy one another. They have gathered in the Rest of the Lord as an expression of the inner covenant of the Lord. It is also a word which may also have reference to matrimonial harmony. The use of the form "shebeth" (שֶׁבֶת) in my view could be seen as a reference to the Sabbath, where the brethren gathered and all the tribes came together in unity to worship and to praise the name of the Holy One. Also of note is the phrase "together in unity" (גַּם־יָחַד *gam-yachad*). It is the idea of the unity which grows from the unified nature of Divinity. This unity is very important for creating an atmosphere of effective prayer. The LORD is one, therefore we are one.

The Lord Loves Unity

The Lord affirms this and clearly makes a big deal on this issue of unity for effectiveness in prayer. He says in Matthew 18:19 (NIV), "*Jesus said, 'Again I tell you that if two of you on earth agree (are united as one) on anything you ask for, it will be done for you by my Father in Heaven. For, where two or three come together in my name, there am I with them.*" God the Father and His Son Jesus Christ will join you in any prayer where there is agreement or unity that is prayed in the Name of Jesus. You say, "How do I create this unity?" You can do it simply by focusing on His Name. Jesus Himself said that He would be with you in that moment of that prayer.

> *If there is agreement, He not only prays with us but through us, thus making our prayers more effective. If He joins us, then all creation under the authority of God joins us also!*

The Lord Jesus Christ is attracted to the environment of unity and agreement in prayer. Our agreement with Jesus needs to work out into our agreement with one another, especially when we pray. If there is agreement, He not only prays with us but through us, thus making our prayers more effective. If He joins us, then all creation under the authority of God joins us also! It means that our prayer has the capacity to bypass every created obstacle, for the Lord of creation is in agreement with us. This plural, "you" conveys the idea that God delights in agreement and unity among His people. The Lord Jesus Christ in His intercessory prayer for the church makes mention of this unity of the believers four times and bases these mentions on the agreement between Him and the Father:

> *I am no longer in the world; and yet they themselves are in the world, and I come to You. Holy Father, keep them in Your name, the name which You have given Me, **that they may be one even as We are.***
> (John 17:11, emphasis added)

> ***That they may all be one;** even as You, Father, are in Me and I in You, **that they also may be in Us,** so that the world may [a]believe that You sent Me. The glory which You have given Me I have given to them, **that they may be one, just as We are one;***
> (John 17:21-22, emphasis added)

Free Will

We must be in agreement with one another. Agreement is the turning over of the will to the fulfillment of the things being prayed for. God gave us free will, He does not delight in violating it. Our agreement then affirms the purpose of God in creating us as free will agents. Prayer of agreement is one of the highest expressions of our divine nature and is an expression of freedom in the spirit. To see the power of agreement read the following passages: Genesis 11:1-9; Matthew 18:19-20; Exodus 17:8-13; Psalm 133:1-3; Acts 4:23; Hebrews 10:24-25. The prayer of agreement is not a forced conformity of thought but a willing desire to see God's goodness manifested in someone's life. It is so powerful because here we become less self-focused and seek the good of the other, as God seeks our good. We throw our will into the pot, so to say, for the good of the other. Its power comes from the fact that it gives purpose. Biblically the prayer of agreement is when two or more people come together and agree with one another and with the Word of God that something specific will be done. People who do not worship God, or indeed worship Satan, can also stand in agreement and see power released (Genesis 11:1-9). God has given power and authority to the Church. When we stand together in unity we can see more of God's power released (Matthew 28:16-20).

Unity is standing together with one purpose, sharing a joint vision and trusting God's Word to be fulfilled. We need to value the power of unity if we are to see God's power released through our prayers.

ATMOSPHERE OF FAITH BIRTHS EFFECTIVE PRAYER

Prayer demands an atmosphere of faith. There is such a thing as the 'prayer of faith' as used in the Book of James. This environment is one that invites God and goes over what God has stopped doing or is unwilling to do. Faith rises above the circumstance and changes the atmosphere with radiating optimistic expectation, placing godlike demand on God's power and ability. This belief in the desire of God to move on behalf of His children is so burnt into the spirit and the atmosphere that those who pray can taste and see what it is they are asking God for before they receive it. While Jesus often berated His disciples for lack of faith, it was not so much that they could not muster enough faith within themselves. Rather, they were in an environment charged with faith by the presence of Jesus but were oblivious to it and chose to create a contradictory atmosphere. The verbal request, gratitude, and the songs and praise are all meant to create an atmosphere of faith, which makes it possible for our request to become manifested.

That faith which is ignited in the soul of the soul of the believer

by the light of grace; art which through the evidence of the mind, fortifies the heart in sureness of hope removed from all self opinion, which shows itself not in inclining the ear of hearing but in contemplating with spiritual eyes the mysteries hidden in the soul, those graces, concealed from the eyes of the sons of the flesh, and revealed by the Spirit to those who feed at the feast of Christ.
(Philokalia: Directions to the Hesychasts)

A Place to Receive

In an atmosphere charged with faith it is easy for even the most spiritually weak to receive. This is why great outdoor evangelistic campaigns see more miracles than churches. The evangelistic campaign's atmosphere is charged with faith—intense expectation and anticipation. When Jesus says in Mark 11:24, "'**When you pray, believe that you receive ... and you shall have...**'" He is speaking about forming an environment for the manifestation of the request, creating a space on Earth in which heaven can be manifested. Not to believe God is to create an environment in which God is not "comfortable" but absent. Because it is God who will give you your request, the atmosphere must be one in which God can come to stay.

One of the atmospheres conducive for the presence of God is that of faith. "**And without faith it is impossible to please Him, for he who comes to God must believe that He is and that He is a rewarder of those who seek Him.**" (Hebrews 11:6). Therefore, a refusal to believe that God has given it to you makes your environment non-conducive for answered prayers. Faith is a spiritual thing seeking a place, so in praying we need to be in the spirit. We must have faith. "**Now faith is the assurance of things hoped for, the conviction of things not seen**." (Hebrews 11:1). The place of prayer, our lives or our church must first be saturated with faith for God's gift to be substantiated or evidenced in those contexts. Faith is activated when we stand and speak in an atmosphere immersed in the Word of God. Faith comes by hearing and hearing by the Word of God. Our desires can be incarnated from the spiritual into the natural when we allow the Word to birth faith. Walking in the environment and speaking the Word of God will change the vibration of the area so that we can decree what is needed within that context - and it will come to pass! (see Mark 11:12-14, 20-25; Luke 7:1-10; James 5:13-18; Matthew 9:18–26).

Creating an environment of faith happens when we develop an inner unshakable **confidence** in God's willingness and ability to answer prayer. We have a triangular unshakable relationship between us, Jesus and the written Word of God. This becomes a square of faith as we take over the environment where we are to pray.

Because the prayer of faith is a call for the Word to be made flesh in our immediate circumstance, we must have a clear picture of the incarnate Christ. True prayers of faith call into effect John 1:14. It is calling for the physical tangible manifestation of the spiritual realities into the material realm. The environment of faith is created through our confidence in God's Word. The woman with the issue of blood (Matthew 9:20-22) created an environment in herself so that in the midst of the crowd she could touch Jesus, receiving her health. Her inner resolve and focus on Jesus released for her the environment of her healing despite the press of the crowd. You can create an environment of faith by offering positive confessions until the atmosphere is saturated with faith.

> God has given power and authority to the Church. When we stand together in unity we can see more of God's power released

AN ENVIRONMENT THAT BIRTHS EFFECTIVE PRAYER MUST BE ONE OF LOVE

God is found in love. Love is the whole law. Anything not done in love is not of God. With God, love taps into the highest level of Divine energy and joins forces with God to affect self and others. This world can only be changed and God's will done if we are filled with the love of God. It is because the love of God in Christ Jesus has been shed abroad in our hearts that the Spirit is freed to energize our weakness. In this loving flow of energy, God gives knowledge and insight into the supernatural that is then expressed for the deliverance of our brothers and sisters. He searches our hearts and knows the mind of the Spirit, because the Spirit intercedes for the saints in accordance with God's will.

Effective Prayer

From this love comes our real power. This holy love knows the heart and mind of Christ because this is who He is. By this love our spirit knows what is happening to other saints and moves toward them with compassion. When we are praying in love, the power of our prayer is multiplied many times by the very nature of God. The thing about love is that, like air, it does not choose who can or cannot breathe it. Love carries Christians' prayers into those parts of the world that need God to intervene for them. The believer filled with the love of God and love for human beings affects life at a much deeper level. Love interrupts the negative flows and infuses the life of God into our situations.

If we are filled with the love of God our prayers will be different and more effective. Right now, those of us who believe that we are to pray, must tap into love. So much intercession has been informed by hurt and anger that it is little wonder why our prayers are often hindered. But holy love does bring us to the fullness of life in the body of Christ. Love has great authority to empower our prayers in a manner that our heart has not yet received. When prayer is bathed in the environment of holy love, we are enabled to do God's work effectively on Earth. Part of creating an atmosphere of love is to be a covering for those who have transgressed - to seek to minister the love of God instead of repeating the issues until the body is divided and the unity that is so necessary for prayer is sundered. According to Proverbs 10:12, "*Hatred stirs up strife, but love covers all transgressions.*" Wherever there is strife there is hatred at its root no matter how it is painted - prophesy, righteous indignation, speaking one's mind, standing up for right. Hatred is what stirs up strife and hinders prayers, especially those that are geared toward the healing and deliverance of people.

An atmosphere of love is not one where we shout out our love for God, but one in which genuine divine love flows from us to others, even our enemies. I am at a loss to understand how we can stand to say prayers of hatred couched in so-called warfare and still expect our prayers for our personal healing to be answered. The atmosphere in which we pray must be charged with love, both for God and for our neighbors:

> *And thou shalt love the Lord thy God with all thy heart, and with all thy soul, and with all thy mind, and with all thy strength: this is the first commandment. And the second is like, namely this, Thou shalt love thy neighbour as thyself. There is none other commandment greater than these.*
> (Mark 12:30-31, KJV)

> *A new commandment I give to you, **that you love one another**, even as I have loved you, that you also love one another. By this all men will know that you are My disciples, if you have love for one another.*
> (John 13:34-35, emphasis added).

The measure of this love is not our feelings, ideologies, shame, guilt - but the love which Jesus Christ Himself has always had for us - "*as I have loved you.*" Why is it that whenever Jesus opened His mouth miracles happened? The love of the Father was manifested in and through Him. He is love incarnate. Why are millions flocking to Him even now? It is a response to the story of His love. In fact, Jesus says that as His disciples whatever we ask the Father in His name the Father will answer. Yet here He says that we are His disciples "*if you have love for one another.*" We are not candidates for answered prayers if we do not love one another. You want to look for reasons why so many prayers are not answered, here it is - the absence of an environment of love.

In John 15:17 Jesus says, "*These things I command you, that you love one another.*" He also says, "*If you love me, keep my commandments*" (John 14:15). The new commandment is LOVE. If we can cleave to love, if we can love without pretense, cleaving to what is good, how much godly energy and power will flow in our prayer meetings! Paul puts it this way: "*Be devoted to one another in brotherly love; give preference to one another in honor;*" In Romans 13:10 he says, "*Love does no wrong to a neighbor; therefore love is the fulfillment of the law.*"

If we are to pray as Jesus prayed, and be saturated by an atmosphere of answered prayers, we need to walk in love - as Christ loved us. It must be a love which will lead us to give ourselves up as He did "*and walk in love, just as Christ also loved you and gave Himself up for us, an offering and a sacrifice to God as a fragrant aroma,*" (Ephesians 5:2). Love is God saturating the atmosphere of prayer.

Let's look at some passages of Scripture and see how important love is for creating an atmosphere of effective prayer.

Love infuses prayer with life:

> "*We know that **we have passed out of death into life, because we love the** brethren. He who does not love abides in death.*"
> (1 John 3:14, emphasis added)

Love creates a habitation in which we dwell in God:

> *This is His commandment, that we believe in the name of His Son Jesus Christ, and love one another, just as He commanded us. The one who keeps His commandments abides in Him, and He in him. We know by this that He abides in us, by the Spirit whom He has given us.*
> (1 John 3:23-24)

Love is the key to Divine knowledge:

> *Beloved, let us love one another, for love is from God; **and everyone who loves is born of God and knows God.** The one who does not love does not know God, for God is love. By this the love of God was manifested in us, that God has sent His only begotten Son into the world so that we might live through Him. In this is*

> *love, not that we loved God, but that He loved us and sent His Son to be the propitiation for our sins.* **Beloved, if God so loved us, we also ought to love one another. No one has seen God at any time; if we love one another, God abides in us, and His love is perfected in us.**
> (1 John 4:7-12, emphasis added)

Love is the principle of perfection creating boldness even in the face of judgment:

> *We have come to know and have believed the love which God has for us. God is love, and the one who abides in love abides in God, and God abides in him. By this, love is perfected with us, so that we may have confidence in the day of judgment; because as He is, so also are we in this world. There is no fear in love; but perfect love casts out fear, because fear involves punishment, and the one who fears is not perfected in love. We love, because He first loved us. If someone says, "I love God," and hates his brother, he is a liar; for the one who does not love his brother whom he has seen, cannot love God whom he has not seen. And this commandment we have from Him, that the one who loves God should love his brother also*
> (1 John 4:16-21)

These are the several things that make love an ingredient which creates an atmosphere for effective prayer. You too can have a powerful and effective prayer life if you can create these atmospheric conditions.

I truly believe that your prayer life, intimacy, likeness and knowledge of God will be greatly increased as the Holy Spirit helps you understand and implement the principles as expressed in Part 1 of this book. They have benefited me, as they have Christians and Jews through history, and are part of your inheritance.

Now let us turn out attention to the deep mysteries and wisdom of the prayer given to us by the Lord Jesus Himself …

Part 2

The Golden Cord – The Alchemy of the Lord's Prayer

Chapter Seven
Key #1: Relationship

Pray, then, in this way: 'Our Father...'
(Matthew 6:9)

Relationality (our relational nature) is the primal axis on which all destinies in the universe turn. "Our Father" (our relationship with God) activates that destiny and turns the axis of the universe to its fulfillment. Jesus refers to God many times as "Father." This was to activate His destiny and direct the universe toward its release and fulfillment. The word "Father," as referring to God, occurs 126 times in the Gospel of John alone. To show its importance for prayer, Jesus uses it six times in His intercessory prayer recorded in Matthew 6. Jesus taught this prayer to us this way because His primary relationship with God was that of Son to the Father. Jesus does not call God "Father" to suggest that God created Him and then adopted Him. Rather, He does this by insisting that He is generated by God as God's internal and eternal seed.

Jesus is Our Example

When Jesus says "Father," He sees God as the complete embodiment of glory and the giver of glory. He sees God as the keeper of those who believe. Jesus implies that "our Father" is the source of Unity. His prayer implies the problem of the world is that they do not know God as Father and righteous keeper of those who believe in Him. The world does not know the Father because they do not have knowledge of the Spirit of the Father. At the onset of this prayer, the Master teaches His disciples to tap into that primal reality. That which is not in relationship ceases to exist. Relationship is the DNA of existence itself. To exist is to be in relationship.

In the Fatherhood of God we connect to the source of this blessing which is rained down upon the children of God. As the Heavens send down rain upon the Earth, so the Father rains down His goodness upon those who call out, "Our Father." This relationship is in every implied and explicit place in the Scriptures.

The Plan From the Beginning

According to Genesis 1, when God created Adam, God formed man from the dust, making him a result of God's active craftsmanship. The purpose for Adam's creation, as stated by God Himself in Genesis 1:26, was intrinsically Divine. These purposes could only be carried out by one who was more than a simple material creation of Divinity. In Genesis 1:26–28, we find the intent of relationality and communion leading to the idea that God wanted one who carried within them the essential nature of God. One with the capacity to soar to the Heavens and descend to Hell, and the ability to make decisions and carry out activities that could affect the relation of the Earth to both. We read:

> Then God said, "Let Us make man in **Our image**, according to **Our likeness**; and let them **rule over** the fish of the sea and over the birds of the sky and over the cattle and over all the earth, and over every creeping thing that creeps on the earth." God created man in His own image, **in the image of God He created him; male and female** He created them. God blessed them; and God said to them, "**Be fruitful and multiply**, and **fill the earth**, and **subdue it**; and **rule ove**r the fish of the sea and over the birds of the sky and over every living thing that moves on the earth." (emphasis added)

In Genesis 2:6–7, we are then shown that Adam is more than just fabricated, mechanical pottery fashioned by God: "*And the LORD God formed man of the dust of the ground, and breathed into his nostrils the breath of life;* **and man became a living soul.**" (KJV). To make sure that the man was more than a mechanical entity (and could go on to live as a dynamic spiritual being who shares intimately the nature of God), God placed a living soul into man, making it possible for man to be the one upon the Earth capable of manifesting the very life of God! This idea so fascinated Luke that he ends his genealogy of the Lord Jesus with the phrase "*and Adam the son of God."* God was longing for a father/son relationship when he created Adam. That intention of God is reactivated in Christ who now calls it forth from within us by telling us to say, "Our Father." The entire objective of what God does comes from the lips of God, turns on relational communion and calls for intimacy with God. We read in Deuteronomy 14:1–2:

> **You are the sons of the LORD your God**; you shall not cut yourselves nor shave your forehead for the sake of the dead. "For you are a holy people to the LORD your God, and the LORD has chosen you to be a people for His own possession out of all the peoples who are on the face of the earth. (emphasis added)

> *All of God's demands and dialogue presume that human beings can be children of God, dedicated to Him and inhabited by Him. In Psalm 82:6 we read, "I said, "You are gods, And all of you are sons of the Most High." We read in 1 John 3:2, "Beloved, now we are children of God, and it has not appeared as yet what we will be. We know that when He appears, we will be like Him, because we will see Him just as He is."*

Just Like Your Dad

Fatherhood and Heaven typify the relationship of seed to the seed bearer, and the location of the seed bearer. Fatherhood is a primary relation in which the child, son or daughter realizes that there is a fundamental, non-severable inner connection between the child and the source of their being. God, as the bearer of the seed called Adam, transfers the divine DNA, if you may, to the seed.

> *For in Him we live and move and exist, as even some of your own poets have said, '**For we also are His children.**' Being then the children of God, we ought not to think that the Divine Nature is like gold or silver or stone, an image formed by the art and thought of man.*
> (Acts 17:28–29, emphasis added)

By virtue of being in the father's nature, the child carried the possibility of the nature of the father in seed form - and thus has potentially of the father's character embedded in them! This line of prayer puts the believer above principalities and powers. Yes, though we are created, yet by virtue of this father-child relationship, we moved beyond the

> *Jesus refers to God many times as "Father." This was to activate His destiny and direct the universe toward its release and fulfillment.*

realm of mere creation to intimate sharing of the nature of God. There is a difference between fabrication and being begotten. We are begotten of God. This affirmation of God as Father serves notice to all of creation, angels, demons, principalities, things above, things below, things to come, and things past, that we are not like them. We are intimately linked with God and have God's heart open to us. His power is available to us without reserve. God is our Father.

This relationality is the basis for the release of power and presupposes that God is intent on intimate relations with those who call Him "Father." It is the release of freedom into the beloved, which provides a place from which they, like Archimedes, can move the Earth around on its spiritual axis. It is the true inner signification of our souls' highest moments in substance of Divinity. Rather than being a declaration of want, it is declaration of fundamental relationality, serving as launching pad for us to take our place in the royal activities spoken by the mouth of God at the creation of Adam. Dominion, rulership, authority, fruitfulness, multiplication capacity - all presumes this fundamental relation to God, not just as the Creator, but also as our Father.

Human Experience Versus Heavenly Reality

We have a tendency to understand this relationship as negative, wherein God bullies us into doing what He wants us to do with threats. But Jesus made this Father-Son relationship primary in His life's teaching, activities, death, and resurrection. In Jesus' prayer in John 17, He uses the word "Father" at least four times to refer to God. When this relationality is foundational, we no longer live under compulsion but in true freedom, which allows us to come into the fullness of what Adam was created for by God. The point is that it is impossible for us to be independent of God. Even our negative choices are made in reference to God and, therefore, must face the nature of the God in whom they are made. This relationality then means that every prayer is an affirmation of communion with the ultimate substance of the universe. Those who do not pray, or do not believe in its effectiveness, are usually those who refuse this relational communion with the Eternal for one reason or another. Some declare their independence from this relational communion because of upbringing, some because of what they consider failure on the part of God as Father, and others because of the failure of an earthly father. But this does not take away from the need for this relational communion, which serves as the fulcrum for the turning of our human bodies, souls and our spirits' cry to the Heavenly sphere.

> *By virtue of being in the father's nature, the child carried the possibility of the nature of the father in seed form - and thus has potentially of the father's character embedded in them! This line of prayer puts the believer above principalities and powers.*

True prayer is only possible here, in this place of relational communion with the Creator, in His Fatherly outreach toward our inner man. This cannot be discarded, it cannot be marginalized, nor can it be ignored. It is the ground of what James calls *"effectual fervent prayer of the righteous"* (5:16 KJV). Without it, prayer becomes a program that is void of any power. It is by means of this relational communion that good success in prayer is guaranteed. What a marvelous manifestation of glory, when one begins to grasp the awesome and powerful potential of our prayer, growing out this intimacy with God our Father! Those who do not have knowledge of this intimacy cannot really pray.

In this relationship, the Face of God by the brooding Holy Spirit, flashes forth into the face of the dark, deep waters of our needy souls, calling us out and causing light, generativity and fruitfulness. This flash of God into our soul, enabled by intimacy, which we have found with God through Jesus Christ, moves us to join in the battle for the world's souls. In His flashing intimacy, we see through eyes enlightened with God, feel His heartbeat, and desire what God our Father desires for this world. This relational communion encompasses and makes available to us the full panoply and possibility of Heaven's solutions into the temporal circumstance of our lives.

We live in a time when those who have had pathological and negative experiences with their earthly fathers, and thus see relational communion as being fundamentally problematic, want us to forgo the pleasant experiences we find Jesus having with the Father. They desire we join them in decrying the Fatherhood and the intimacy which this brings to us in prayer. If we are to pray effectively, we cannot use people's pathological experience as the basis for judging our relationship with God as Father. This relational communion is primordial, primeval and fundamental. This present tendency to exalt bad experiences over good, and to make them the springboard for spiritual understanding, must cease for prayer to become effective. For the power of prayer to be manifest, God's desire to be in relational communion must be seen as a substantial and pragmatic good. The psalmist said *"To declare that the LORD is upright; He is my rock, and there is no unrighteousness in Him,"* (Psalm 92:15).

True Relationship

Now this relationality is not some idle sentimentality subject merely to our whimsical view of what is good in human feelings. This intimacy accepts all that happens within God into whom we have entered. This intimacy causes us to know that God relates to the whole universe in a loving fashion, even in our failings and misery, and seeks to have a relationship with everyone. Thus, out of the inner heart of God's love to which the believer is related, flows prayer that seeks to manifest the heart of God into the world. In this Divine intimacy, we receive the compass of eternity for navigating times and seasons in which we find ourselves. With this intimacy, we avoid crashing into the black hole of existential despair.

Relational communion is not a program. If we make it into a program, we miss the mark and, in fact, make our prayers ineffectual. The truth is, that for too long, we have programmed God out of prayer. Rather than being a dance of freedom, it has become a bondage to patterns and plans. It becomes an unwilling cross that we carry - and no unwilling cross ever led to salvation. It is out of this relational communion that life-giving prayer dialogue arise. Here our thought, speech and action carry God into various human contexts of needs. Not only is our progeny Divine, as we are related to God as Father in a fundamental way, our location or position is with Him. When we move from being the image of the man of dust - Adam - we are changed into the image of the Son of God and, thus, we bear the image of the Heavenly man. When we pray "Our Father," we call on this relational aspect of God.

A Compassionate Father

We activate the compassion of God for us when we suffer, as it is written, *"As a father pities **his children**, So the Lord pities those who fear Him"* (Psalm 103:13, NKJV). God shows compassion to His sons as we find in Exodus 4, where we find the reason why God felt such pain at the suffering of Israel. God says:

> *Then you shall say to Pharaoh, 'Thus says the Lord, **"Israel is My son, My firstborn**. So I said to you, 'Let **My son** go that he may serve Me'; but you have refused to let him go. Behold, I will kill your son, your firstborn.*
> (Exodus 4:22–23)

It is this relationship that led God (YHVH) to be gracious unto them, and to have compassion on them. His regard and respect for Israel cannot be separated from this claim which God makes of them as His sons (2 Kings 13:23). It is this fatherhood of God that activates His compassion. "Our Father" is an inner cry to experience God's compassion and pity. Just as children are often helpless, so we find ourselves often helpless in life's situations. The cry "Abba, Abba" activates God's deep compassion. The Hebrew word used here is רַחֲמִם (*rahamim*).

Compassion is stronger than sympathy or empathy. As we find in Exodus, this fatherly compassion on the part of God is what gave rise to God's active involvement in the deliverance of Israel from bondage in Egypt. If, as Thomas Merton said, *"The whole idea of compassion is based on a keen awareness of the interdependence of all these living beings, which are all part of one another, and all involved in one another,"* then God as Father is the ultimate expression of compassion - for in Him we all live, move and have our being. He is the fundamental source of universal interconnection. This Fatherly compassion is what gives rise to the care that God gave Israel in the wilderness.

In another passage of Scripture, this Father/son relationship between Israel and God is reiterated.

> *The Lord your God who goes before you will Himself fight on your behalf, just as He did for you in Egypt before your eyes, and in the wilderness where you saw how **the Lord your God carried you, just as a man carries his son**, in all the way which you have walked until you came to this place.*

(Deuteronomy 1:30–31, emphasis added)

As a father, He will fight for them and carry them along when the way is long and rough in the wilderness. When Moses wanted to see God in His essence after proclaiming His Lordship, God opens up the description of this character with word "compassionate," - translated from the Hebrew רַחוּם (*rahum*), or in the Septuagint is **οἰκτίρμων** (*oiktirmon*).

> **καὶ παρῆλθε Κύριος πρὸ προσώπου αὐτοῦ καὶ ἐκάλεσε· Κύριος ὁ Θεὸς οἰκτίρμων καὶ ἐλεήμων, μακρόθυμος καὶ πολυέλεος καὶ ἀληθινός,**
>
> וַיַּעֲבֹר יְהוָה ׀ עַל־פָּנָיו וַיִּקְרָא יְהוָה ׀ יְהוָה אֵל רַחוּם וְחַנּוּן אֶרֶךְ אַפַּיִם וְרַב־חֶסֶד וֶאֱמֶת
>
> *Then the Lord passed by in front of him and proclaimed, "The LORD, the LORD God, **compassionate** and gracious, slow to anger, and abounding in lovingkindness and truth"*
> (Exodus 34:6).

In many of the English translations, the flow of the passage is short-circuited. רַחוּם (*Rahum*) and **οἰκτίρμων** (*oiktirmon*) are translated as 'merciful' rather than 'compassionate'. But as we look at the original, the flow makes perfect sense. Compassion serves as the springboard from which we see **ἐλεήμων** (*ele ee moon* - sympathy), **μακρόθυμος** (*macrothumia* - longsuffering), **πολυέλεος** (*polueleos* - the expansion of mercy or plurality of mercies) and **ἀληθινός** (*alethinos* - true dependability). All these grow from the father-child relationship, which this prayer evokes in the simple phrase "our Father." So the text should read: "*And the YHVH passed by before him, and proclaimed, Yod, Yod, Yod, Elohim, compassionate, sympathetic (gracious), long-suffering, ever expanding in mercy and full of true dependability.*" When we speak of God as Father, these are the characteristics that should come to mind.

When we pray "Our Father," we activate the grace of God. As children, we have no deserving work or act which should endear us to Him except that He calls us His children. Grace is what allows us to get mercy which we do not deserve, as God based our relation to Him as Father, holds back from us the judgment we

> *Yes, though we are created, yet by virtue of this father-child relationship, we moved beyond the realm of mere creation to intimate sharing of the nature of God. There is a difference between fabrication and being begotten. We are begotten of God.*

deserve. In mercy, the Father forbears and does not inflict harm because of our willful provocation. Though God has power to inflict harsh punishment, because of His mercy, He withholds it. Though we often offend, and set ourselves as adversary against His will, He expands His mercy toward us.

His Nature, not Our Ability, Brings an Inheritance

As Father, God has a covenant with the children. This covenant is based on His person, and not on the ability of our faithfulness to Him. As Father, He makes promises and keeps them. As Father, He searches for and finds His lost children. Even when they have sold themselves to enemy, He pays for their redemption. He is the Father who redeems the children as the fathers in Israel were told to redeem their firstborn children from the curse of death in Egypt. As Father, God provides a place of refuge in Himself for those whom He calls His children. His overflowing mercy is ever present to forgive erring children who return. His goodness and mercy are tied together forever. As Father, God will defend and require justice at the hands of those who mistreat the children. Yes, God is Father.

The fatherhood is nowhere made clearer than in the person of Jesus Christ, His Son. When we say "Father," we enter into the same relationship that Jesus had with God the Father.

> *It is by means of relational communion that good success in prayer is guaranteed. What a marvelous manifestation of glory, when one begins to grasp the awesome and powerful potential of our prayer, growing out this intimacy with God our Father!*

"Our Father" activates our total inheritance. For it is written, "*In Him also we have obtained an inheritance, having been predestined according to His purpose who works all things after the counsel of His will,*" (Ephesians 1:10b–11). This inheritance is sealed until we take possession of it. Only when we, as children, understand how to offer praise and glory to the Father, does our inheritance emerge from its hidden place. We cry out "Father" so that we might see with eyes of the Father and feel with the heart of the Father. It is only by this crying out that we come to know the hope of our calling.

The riches of the glory of God's inheritance for the saints is couched in this simple formula of "our Father". As father, not just as Creator, that God made us partakers of the inheritance of His Light. God is the Father of Lights, and we cannot inherit this light until we are birthed by, in and through this light. Only those of us who have been called His children will receive the promise of the eternal inheritance. We are told in 1 Peter 1:4 that our inheritance which the Father gives us is "*an inheritance which is imperishable and undefiled and will not fade away, reserved in heaven for you.*" Since God is our Father and we do indeed cry out "Father," we "*no longer a slave, but a son; and if a son, then an heir through God.*" (Galatians 4:7). If we say "Our Father," then all that belongs to God now is open to us - even the most valuable of all His possessions, His Son.

One Family

"Our Father" also underscores for us the fact that we have a fundamental connection one with another. We are part of God's family. In God as Father, we are interrelated through Jesus Christ who serves to bring us together with Him and His Father. Not only are we related to one another, we affect each other by our being. This relationality means that we cannot act as if we are isolated and alone. This relationship with others calls forth care. This care grows out of love and compassion. Thus, the nature of our Father is the compass by which we locate ourselves relationally in the world. When our interconnection with one another is understood in the context of "our Father," it becomes the key to the transformation of the world. The authenticity of our existence is measured by the way we relate to each other in the context of "our Father". There is no way of getting around the fact of our interrelatedness which flows from this opening line of prayer. Our destiny waits impatiently for us to come to the awareness of our interrelatedness. It is only in relationship that we reach our fulfillment. Romans 8:19 tells us that all creation awaits the revelation of relationship as the children of God. This sonship with God is also the interrelation of human to human.

When you and I pray "Our Father," we invoke the relational principle which is called the fruit of the Spirit. We read:

> *But the fruit of the Spirit is love, joy, peace, patience, kindness, goodness, faithfulness, gentleness, self-control; against such things there is no law. Now those who belong to Christ Jesus have crucified the flesh with its passions and desires. If we live by the Spirit, let us also walk by the Spirit. Let us not become boastful, challenging one another, envying one another.*
> (Galatians 5:22–26)

The spirit-filled life is a life of relationship. Love is about relations with God, self and others. Joy is the response of our whole being to the interrelated web of human experience filled with exuberance and optimism which encourages others. Peace is the ability to be at one with the self and to connect with other human beings without violence to self, God, or the other. All of this fruit is activated when we pray to God who is Spirit as Father.

"Our Father" contains two portals which open us to relationship with the Godhead and with one another. The greatest example of this is the incarnation of Christ. We find in Him relationship with God and with man. Relationship is the key to the universe and to individual destiny. Its most effective key is to call out "our Father."

Chapter Eight
Key #2: Heavens

"Which is in heaven,"
(Matthew 6:9)

"Πάτερ ἡμῶν ὁ ἐν τοῖς οὐρανοῖς"

In the Torah, the word for "Heaven" is the fourth word of the text. So, in the beginning, God created the Heavens. The Hebrew word for "Heaven" is always in the plural הַשָּׁמַיִם (Hashamayim) in the TNK (Tanach or the Old Testament). The use of the plural suggests that the idea was to include the vast expanse of space as the realm of God's activities, including all possible galaxies and star systems.

How Many Heavens?

There are scriptural suggestions of at least three Heavens, for we read that Paul knew someone who was caught up to the Third Heaven (2 Corinthians 12:2). In some of the Jewish canonical books, such as the apocrypha of Levi and Baruch, we see five Heavens spoken about. We also find in the Ethiopian book of Enoch the idea of a Seventh Heaven. This is more likely to have been derived from the idea that Earth was created according to the patterns of the Heavens in six days, and the seventh day is the day of the Lord. In later times, some have even suggested that there are 12 Heavens, since the Children of Israel are to be used as the measure of what God does with the universe. No matter how many numbers we assign to it, the truth is that the Heaven of the Heavens are not enough to contain the infinite God! That notwithstanding, I subscribe to the idea that God fills the vast expanse of the universe and God is the principle of their very expansion. There may also be mysterious imagery with which the Bible defines as Heavens. *(For an in-depth understanding, please see my "Hashamayim" book series).*

The Scripture, especially in the New Testament, subscribes to the idea also of single Heaven. That single Heaven Jesus refers to as a *place*. This is where the Throne Room of God is located and from where God judges the world. It is written in Romans 1:18, "*For the wrath of God is revealed from heaven against all ungodliness...*" There is also Heaven as paradise. But this is believed to be the paradise that was on Earth, but has been transported away to another part of the universe until man is redeemed and comes to maturity. But it seems that paradise is just a part of the Heavens, not all of the Heavens. Furthermore, Jesus speak of "my Father's house" in John 14:2. Later on in the epistles, Paul speak of a city, and in Revelation, there is hardly any reference to the plural concept of the Heaven.

Heavens, translated **οὐρανοῖς** (*ouranois*) in their plural, conveys ideas that are important for their complexity and the simplicity of their function. **οὐρανοῖς** (Ouranois) conveys the idea of the Father continually seeding the dark edges of His creation with new possibilities and inhabiting it. In that sense, it carries with it the very nature of the One whose location it is claimed to be! The one who inhabits these Heavens is infinite. It is not so much a place as it is an organism, whose complexity and simplicity befits the one whom this prayer is offered: "*Our Father who is in the heavens...*". No simple description can give an adequate idea of it. When the Heavens open, even in the most limited way, their visual effects cannot be neglected for they "declare your glory". Heaven is the building up of all the external and inner hope to which all human action points. It is the intervening idea that impacts our choices and allows us as believers to adapt to the various circumstances with joy. It is the finality that brings together all human plans with a view to a Divine end. So then, Heaven is regarded as the reward to all the labor of the pilgrim workman. This reality of Heaven leads us to outward forms of behavior which reflect the one with whom we identify when we say, "our Father." Heaven is shown with increasing clarity to us as our allegiance to it is carried by strong faith.

Our Father is Greater than the Heavens

According to this prayer, and many other passages of Scripture, the Heavens belong to God. The vast expanse of infinite space is where Divine creativity is at play. Clearly the vastness of these Heavens is far too difficult for creatures to handle. The Heavens are regarded as the abode of God and the emerging dimension of God's work. There is no particular point from within the Heavens to point at God, for He is at once everywhere present. He affects the Heavens as a king seated on his throne affecting the entirely of his kingdom. When we consider that Solomon said Heaven is considered the habitation of this one who we call Father, we must also take into consideration that He is larger than the Heavens. Though there are myriads of Heavens, this ONE God YHVH whom we call Father, rules over all of it. Thus, no matter where we find ourselves in space or time, we find ourselves in the presence of our Father. His voice is heard in the Heavens, pushing creatively at the edge of nothing. If it be true that *"the heaven of the heavens cannot contain"* our Father, then it appears that we, as His sons and daughters, make our abode beyond the stars as we enter into the heart of God, whom we so lovingly call Father. God's power is loftier than we can grasp. By saying "Heaven," we acknowledge that we are connected

When the Heavens open, even in the most limited way, their visual effects cannot be neglected for they "declare your glory".

to all of creation (Genesis 24:7). In this, we declare that we are not bound even now by the materiality of our existence, but that our spirit can soar to dimensions and realms unknown by human scientific research.

Heaven is the prototype, the archetype of all the ideas seen and unseen, all the joys, happiness, pleasures, and fulfillment to which human beings ever aspire. Man on Earth is measured by the unseen forms, according to the worlds not made with hands. It is as the prayer says: the habitation is the Father's essence and, therefore, the full embodiment of all the benefits which the Father is willing to bestow on the one who is a son or daughter. When this relationship is recognized, we are raised up and conducted from Earth to Heaven. I speak not merely of the Heaven of the afterlife, but the Heaven that is apprehended and appreciated in the daily flow of our earthly life.

God draws us up from this world to Himself. God shows Himself to us and we are able to behold God's glory. In the eyes of those not born from above, this is impossible, but for those who have been born from above we read, *"They shall see the kingdom of heaven"* (John 3). Heaven is accessible to them because they have the spirit of the Father which can carry them upward - not by mere intellect, but by the kindling of the fire of the Holy Spirit which is in them. Heaven, as it is established in the microcosm of the Earth, is revealed and their spirit ascends as John ascended on the Lord's Day (Revelation 4:1).

Heaven is to be construed in this way: it is the place of truth. It is the place of the birth of spirits. It is the place from which we are clothed with power - for it is written, *"You shall receive power from heaven when the Holy Spirit is come upon you."* Heaven is the habitation of power, authority, rulership, dominion, and thrones. It is a place of ever-flowing love, for God is love and necessarily so, for in Him all people are loved without partiality. Heaven is a place of diligent devotion and worshipful attention. Heaven is the place where the fragmented relationship of humankind with God and the world is reversed and submitted to the one eternal will and agency of the Holy Spirit. No more false imagination and bad will of a mind possessed with a false grasp of supreme authority over all.

Aspects of Heaven

In Heaven, where the Father makes His abode, the imperfect give way in to the perfect. Those who are here reflect the true likeness of the Deity they call Father. There is in Heaven an unbroken flow of virtues from the same Being.[7] For clarity, let me list the ideas of Heaven which we find in Scripture:

> The Heavens are regarded as the abode of God and the emerging dimension of God's work. There is no particular point from within the Heavens to point at God, for He is at once everywhere present.

1. The vast expanse of the universe, which according to modern science, has many systems coming to life and some even dying. This has innumerable galaxies; some undiscovered. Man has not left this galaxy and can only peer into them through a telescope. All of those systems are included in the plural reference in the Bible to the Heavens. In this Heaven (*ouranois*), we have what we call nested Heavens interwoven with one another in a web of interconnection (see Hashamayim book series). This interconnection and nested web is due to the fact that all the Heavens are created by One Being, God. The Heavens are the expanding created order of space, referred to in the plural. However, when speaking of the new Heaven and the new Earth, the Targum (the Aramaic text of the Hebrew TNK) uses the singular "Heaven," translated *shamaya* (שְׁמַיָּא).

אֲרֵי הָאֲנָא בָרֵי שְׁמַיָּא חֲדַתִּין וְאַרְעָא חֲדָתָא וְלָא יִדְכְרָן קַדְמָיָתָא וְלָא יִתַסְקָן עַל לֵב:

The same usage is found in the Greek New Testament in Revelation 21:1,

> *Καὶ εἶδον οὐρανὸν καινὸν καὶ γῆν καινήν· ὁ γὰρ πρῶτος οὐρανὸς καὶ ἡ πρώτη γῆ ἀπῆλθαν, καὶ ἡ θάλασσα οὐκ ἔστιν ἔτι.*

> And I saw "a new **heaven** and a new earth," for the first heaven and the first earth had passed away, and there was no longer any sea. (NIV)

In the above Greek text, the first use *οὐρανὸν* (*ouranon*) is the 'accusative masculine singular' and the second use *οὐρανὸς* (*ouranos*) is the 'normative masculine singular'. My intention in pointing this out is to show that the first usage of word "Heaven" in the Lord's Prayer has to do with all that is beyond the realm of the Earth. The second usage is a reference to a particular place. I am suggesting that it is not all of Heavens that will be discarded but only the Heaven that has to do with the Earth. This is probably referring to our solar system.

2. We also know that the word "Heaven" can refer to the sky, which we see which serves as the covering of the Earth. This Heaven is nothing but the clouds and the atmosphere, which includes the ozone layer, for example. So when we say "who art in the Heavens," we are not referring to some kind of sky god. Neither are we speaking about archons and angels who traverse the sky or even in the sun or the constellations. We are referring to God in whom all "lives move and have their being."

3. Heaven can also refer to the realm of paradise or the Garden of Eden which was taken up to a different region of the universe after the fall of man. We know that God met Adam in the Garden which the Lord planted on Earth. In that garden, Adam was expected to do the will of God as it is done in the specific Heaven that God built. When man fell, God caused the garden to disappear. There are many Jewish legends that say God took the Garden to another dimension of the Heavens. This Heaven was specifically prepared for man in fellowship with the Father. We shall deal with this Heaven when we deal with the key of 'the will' in prayer.

4. Heaven can also have specific reference to the city which is part of the Eden and is also referred to as Heaven. The Bible calls it the New Jerusalem and insists that it comes down out of Heaven from God.

> *He who overcomes, I will make him a pillar in the temple of My God, and he will not go out from it anymore; and I will write on him the name of My God,* **and the name of the city of My God, the new Jerusalem, which comes down out of heaven from My God, and My new name.**
> (Revelation 3:12, emphasis added)

Here there is a "new Jerusalem" coming out of Heaven from God. Heaven coming out of Heaven which comes from God. What a wonder! So then we see the New Jerusalem is in Heaven - which is in God. At least in this case we find two things nested in God. I do believe that there are more things in the Heavens nested in God that we can imagine!

Heaven and Heavens

The two Heavens mentioned in the Lord's Prayer indicate two realities. The first mention of Heaven (οὐρανοῖς) in the Lord's Prayer in the plural. This is directly in contrast to the second mention, "thy will be done on earth as it is in Heaven (οὐρανῷ)." I submit that the difference is this:

- the plural (*"who art in* **Heaven***"*) refers to the whole of Heaven as God's creative domain. It is where God continuously displays His creative energy and infinite imageries of His beauty. We may even say that there are all kinds of interrelated beings. *"Of whom the whole family in Heaven and earth is named"* (Ephesians 3:15).

- the singular (*"as it is in **Heaven**"*) is used when speaking of Heaven as the home and place of rest for those who have acknowledged and accepted the Fatherhood of God

When we say *"who are/is in the Heavens,"* (plural) we speak of the all-inclusive presence of our Father and all the beings who may inhabit other spheres. There is not a place in the universe or, as some scientists are suggesting, the "multi-verse" that is not ruled and controlled by our Father. There is not a race of beings who do not come under the authority of our Father. Here is the reason for the plural Heavens. It puts in one swoop the whole universe in its present form and its becoming. As Paul expressed clearly:

> *For I am convinced that neither death, nor life, nor angels, nor principalities, nor things present, nor things to come, nor powers, nor height, nor depth, nor any other created thing, will be able to separate us from the love of God, which is in Christ Jesus our Lord.*
> (Romans 8:38–39)

References

7 Philo of Alexandria QG 3:42 (taken from Bible Works version 7).

> I speak not merely of the Heaven of the afterlife, but the Heaven that is apprehended and appreciated in the daily flow of our earthly life.

Chapter Nine
Key #3: Hallow the Name

"Hallowed be Your name"
(Matthew 6:9)

One of the first things Moses asked God was, "Who shall I tell them sent me?" God gave him three forms of His name as way to deal with Israel and with Pharaoh. When YHVH appears to Moses, God says, "*I am the God of your father, the God of Abraham, the God of Isaac, and the God of Jacob." Then Moses hid his face, for he was afraid to look at God*" (Exodus 3:6). God calls this name a memorial. That is a name which sets up a territorial claim. In further conversation, YHVH (LORD) tells Moses what this name entails divine care and divine concern for the human condition and liberation and providence for the oppressed. Then Moses presses God for more details!

> Then Moses said to God, "Behold, I am going to the sons of Israel, and I will say to them, 'The God of your fathers has sent me to you.' Now they may say to me, '**What is His name?**' What shall I say to them?" God said to Moses, "I AM WHO I AM"; and He said, "Thus you shall say to the sons of Israel, 'I AM has sent me to you.'" God, furthermore, said to Moses, "Thus you shall say to the sons of Israel, **'The LORD (YHVH), the God of your fathers, the God of Abraham, the God of Isaac, and the God of Jacob, has sent me to you.' This is My name forever, and this is My memorial-name to all generations.**
> (Exodus 3:13–15, emphasis added)

Power of The Name

God gives His names and title as an instrument of transaction for Israel in the midst of Egypt. "I AM that is the Becoming ONE" is given as a name that produces a response within the individual and the community. A response of anger in the case of Pharaoh or of hope and possibility in the case of the Israelites. It is a key for unlocking the awareness of those who say or hear it. I AM evoked in Moses a rekindling of hope for liberation. The name is capable of evoking a variety of responses, but there is one response that will unlock its potential for those who call themselves sons and daughters of God - faith!

As a key for unlocking awareness, I AM raises the consciousness of the one who enters into it on a Heavenly level. When this name is grasped, suddenly activities, events and symbols take on deeper and larger significance. It did for Moses and the Israelites. God's Name made all the difference for Israel and still makes the difference for us who believe. When Jesus teaches prayer, He places the phrase *"hallowed be thy name"* in the first poetic triangle.

So, what is this name supposed to do for us? *"Hallowed be thy name"* does three things.

1. It is a request that our contexts bow to the name of the one we call Father.
2. It is an affirmation of God as intrinsically holy. We declare the holiness of God's name and command the sphere in which we live to be brought into alignment with the holiness, power and glory of the name.
3. It is a declaration of right, as those born of God. To say "hallowed be thy name" is to require that all existence come under the dominion of man and compliment the Creator. It is true that the location for hallowing God's Name is not specified. However, everyone and everything in the universe must come under His authority. As those assigned by God to be His representatives, we must pay God this compliment that He is the Lord God and that His name is the instrument for manifesting effective good in the universe. David understood this and used this reverential intimacy with God to insist that all creation "hallow the name of God" by continual praise of the Name. *"Let everything that has breath praise the Name of the LORD."*

The Name is Sacred

The Name of God carries the identity of God and displays His power. By hallowing the name of God, we keep the identity and power of God as the Lord God intact in our minds and our hearts. One of the commandments given to Moses by the Lord reads, *"Thou shall not take the name of the LORD thy God in vain."* Taking the name of the Lord in vain is the cousin of materialist idolatry in which we make creation, or things created by us, to become objects of our worship. Simply, this name is not to be attributed to anything or anyone other than God, the Creator of the world. Hallowing the name of God then means that verbal idolatry must be avoided. In its place, we must put a continual affirmation and protection of the reputation of God. To hallow then is to make God's reputation great at all times and in all places no matter where, or with whom, we may be. In this line of prayer, we command that the identity and reputation of our God and Father be revered and remain sacred in the world.

This respect of the name of God comes from the fact that we know that this name of God is the house in which God's power for us dwells. If the name is made unholy, then we cannot expect a clear flow of the power we seek for the transformation of our circumstances. There is loftiness to the name of God which causes one who is in that name to rejoice and to bring joy to the world. To 'hallow the name' is to take responsibility for the sanctity of that name in the realm of life which

> When this name is grasped, suddenly activities, events and symbols take on deeper and larger significance. It did for Moses and the Israelites. God's Name made all the difference for Israel and still makes the difference for us who believe.

has been entrusted to us. The name of YHVH services life and regulates the power and structure of cosmic relationality. When the name of our God is used, either in its spiritual sense or especially in the manifestation of God as Man in Jesus, there is no withholding of God. There is no withholding of intimacy to those who know the name. The writer of Proverbs says, "*The name of the LORD is a strong tower, the righteous run into it and is safe*" (18:10). That name in its holiness is the weapon for penetrating all spheres. By this hallowed name, we prevail against all the wiles of the enemy. In this Name is the principle that helps keep relationships and lives from disintegration. If we want to experience the power and holiness of this name, our being must be saturated in the name. We can do this by praying the names of God prophetically. When we do this, we evoke all the powers of God!

Call Upon The Name

The name of the Lord cannot truly be hallowed where the name of the Lord is not called. That is why it was important that, after the birth of Enoch, according to Genesis 4:26, "***men began to call upon the name of the LORD***" (emphasis added). In a sense, it can be read that men began praying the name of YHVH. Calling the name of the Lord is vital because it distinguishes the righteous from the unrighteous. The Hebrew *wayiqra* וַיִּקְרָא , from the root *qara'* (kaw-raw'), is rooted in the idea of engaging a relative or the king by name or using a horn to call them out. It is to properly address them by name and by title. This call is not just the yelling out of a name but carries with it the mood of deference. Many times the Bible uses the phrase "call on the name of the LORD" as a euphemism for the prayer.

> The Name of God carries the identity of God and displays His power. By hallowing the name of God, we keep the identity and power of God as the Lord God intact in our minds and our hearts.

There had been six generations of fear for the name. Having been kicked out of the garden, Adam could not call the name without fear and shame. By the seventh generation, men began again to pray and seek God's presence. So indeed we can say that men began to pray the name of the Lord. In some cases, it may mean to cry out the name of the individual or even preach the name. In many African cultures, which would have been similar to that of Israel in this regard, an individual wanting the audience of a famous man will begin by declaring their name with words that describe the fame of such a person. In fact, a host may lavish such called-out names upon his invited guest, mentioning his/her accomplishments and giving him/her new names in his proclamation! These pronouncements made their renown public to those who may not know. In this case, anyone challenging the proclamation will force the receiver to defend his honor!

We also read that when Abraham moved "*to the mountain east of Bethel, and pitched his tent, with Bethel on the west and Ai on the east; and there he built an altar to the LORD and called on the name of the LORD*" (Genesis 12:8). He was not only calling the name but declaring the holiness of the LORD. Thus he was also sanctifying the land for the Lord God by placing the name of the Lord upon it. Through that calling on the name of the Lord, the land and atmosphere carried the renown of the God of Abraham and echoed it back when the children of Abraham came back. In another place, Abraham came back "*to the place of the altar, which he had make there at the first. And there, Abram **called on the name of the LORD**"* (Genesis 13:4, emphasis added). In many cases, calling of the name of the Lord is done where altars were present or being built and thus making it an anchor of prayer. The principle of holiness is in the name of the Lord. When we call on the name of the Lord, holiness is released. We call upon the name of the Lord in truth and so hallow the name of the Lord. This call implies a dependence on the Lord. Because this calling of the name of the Lord is tied to the holiness of the same name the law was given in Exodus 20:7 (NIV), "*You shall not take the name of the LORD your God in vain, for the LORD will not hold anyone guiltless who takes his name in vain.*" The calling of the name of the YHVH implies what Schleiermacher calls "*absolute dependence which forms an ultimate concern.*"

Effect On Earth

In kingdom prayer, the phrase "hallowed be thy name" is an imperative to the universe to keep the name hallowed and also an implicit commitment on the part of members of the Kingdom not to misuse the name of the Lord. The misuse of the name will constitute a breach between Heaven and Earth. Conversely the correct use of the name constitutes a connecting of Heaven and Earth. The name of God carries the identity of God, its misuse will not only defame God, but will rob creation of its sustaining power. If God's name is not hallowed or deliberately misused, either as a curse upon others or the oppression of others, there is a tragic interruption of the commerce of the supernatural in that sphere. The misuse of God's name usually ends in some form of exploitation of the weak and marginalized, because the broken reverence for the Name is the result of broken fellowship with the owner of the Name. Since God works effectively in an atmosphere of trust, this becomes the breaking of trust between God and the person, place or sphere in which the name of LORD is not hallowed. Praying the name of YHVH is a way to build trust and faith.

The effectiveness of the ministry is based on this hallowing of the name of the Lord. Speaking of the Levites, Moses says in Deuteronomy 18:5, "'*For the LORD your God has chosen him and his sons from all your tribes, to stand and serve in the name of the LORD forever.'*" (See also Deuteronomy 28:10.) This means that effective ministry is carried out only in the context of the hallowedness of the name of the Lord. Only when one serves in the name of the LORD God can a person stand before the LORD. Both prophet and priest must carry out their task in the name of the Lord for their work to be effective. When a prophet speaks, he must do so in the name of the LORD, not in the prophet's own name or other entity. The name of the Lord carries the seed of prophesy to its fruition. Here is why the prophet must not speak falsely in the name of the Lord, because the prophet's false speech dishonors and defiles the name in which they speak. What sets the believer apart from the unbeliever is that we are called by the name of the LORD. This name into which we have been baptized exudes the majesty and glory of the Lord and causes those who see us to experience nature of God. They may become afraid of us because of the name or be drawn to us because of the inherent majesty and holiness of that name. For this reason, Moses says "*For I proclaim the name of the LORD; Ascribe greatness to our God!*" (Deuteronomy 32:3)

This line of the Lord's Prayer is so important, because the name of the Lord is a battle sword by which we overcome. "*Then David said to the Philistine, "You come to me with a sword, a spear, and a javelin, but I come to you in **the name of the LORD of hosts**, the God of the armies of Israel, whom you have taunted."*" (1 Samuel 17:45, emphasis added). The name of the Lord God our Father brings divine offering into our lives and enhances peace. Out of the name flows blessing for the people of the

LORD of hosts. The name is the source that births the stones that build the altar of lives. It is this hallowing of the name that holds the seed of our victory. Nowhere in the Bible is this victory in the name more pronounced than in Psalm 118:10–12, 26:

> *All nations surrounded me;* **In the name of the LORD** *I will surely cut them off. They surrounded me, yes, they surrounded me;* **In the name of the LORD** *I will surely cut them off. They surrounded me like bees; They were extinguished as a fire of thorns;* **In the name of the LORD** *I will surely cut them off ... Blessed is the one who comes in the name of the LORD; We have blessed you from the house of the LORD.* (emphasis added)

Singing and Sozo

One of the ways in which we hallow the name of the LORD is to sing as David sang in Psalm 7:17, *"I will give thanks to the LORD according to His righteousness And will sing praise to the name of the LORD Most High."* The name deserves trust, remembrance, reverence, kingly glory, and declarative praise by the children of Zion. It is the majestic embodiment of splendor. So, *"Praise His name O servants to the LORD, Praise the name of the LORD."* Hallowing the name is speaking well and saying with David, *"Blessed be the name of the LORD from this time forth and forever more"* (Psalm 113:2, NASB).

Salvation (***sōzō***) finds its ground and process in hallowing. When we take up the name of the Lord, we take up the cup of salvation. It is by taking up the holiness of that name that we go up to the LORD Himself and perfect our testimony in Israel. The holiness of the name engenders thanks to the LORD. To show that the name of the Lord is not distinguishable from the Lord Himself, the psalmist in 124:8 says, *"Our help is in the name of the LORD, Who made heaven and earth."* Joel 2:32 says, *"And it will come about that whoever calls on the name of the LORD will be delivered; for on Mount Zion and in Jerusalem there will be those who escape, as the LORD has said, even among the survivors whom the LORD calls."* This is not just a one-time shouting out of the name but a continuous calling of the name; in a sense, it is to have the name of the LORD as our song. Yes, indeed, when we are in danger or dire need, we call out the Name and we are delivered. I have had so many experiences in my Christian walk where just the call of the name of the Lord has wrought great deliverance.

> *When I was a young pastor in Jalingo in the northern part of Nigeria, only 19 years of age, I saw the name of the Lord work great power. No one told me that miracles did not happen anymore! On several occasions, I had encounters with people who practiced witchcraft and deep devilish*

> incantation. In one particular occasion, after witnessing to a man and his family, the wife and some of the children gave their lives to Christ. The man with candor told me, "Tonight we shall see if what you preach is real." I thought the meant he was coming to church that night to witness the power of the Lord. He did not come to church that evening! In the middle of the night with all my doors and windows closed, the man appeared in my room. He said to me, "Today you die and let's see if your God can deliver you." Immediately I began to sense the life going out of me. From the deep recesses of my being, I began chanting the name of the Lord Jesus Christ. He placed his hands on my mouth to keep me from making a sound. The name of Lord whirled in my innermost being until, like a flash of light, it came bursting forth out of my mouth: "Jesus, Jesus, Jesus Christ, Son of God, Savior!" It was like a beautiful Gregorian chant welling up in my soul and coming out with a powerful sound, piercing the whole room. The man left the room as darkness disappears in the presence of light. The next morning, he was moaning and crying on how he lost his power by attacking me in the night.

There are many incidents in which the Name of the Lord has been invoked and has brought great deliverance in my life.

> Once I had a strong urge in my spirit to sing the name of God. For over two hours I ululated His name. I was caught up in the Heavens and saw visions of wondrous things. When I left the house that evening, armed robbers were waiting for me. With calm and ease, I stood there and looked at the two men. I could sense no fear but the presence of the Lord God - into whose name I had been immersed for hours - was so real. These two men with their weapons looked steadily upon me and their faces became pale and they took off running as fast as they could.

Whatever we need, whatever the situation, we can change these by immersing ourselves in the Name(s) of the Lord. We are saved not just because we say the name of God once. We are saved because we continually pray the name of the Lord and are hidden in that name. We have been baptized into the use of the Name. It is our birthright as sons and daughters of God to call on the Name(s) of the Lord. It is not my way to tell personal stories, but I will tell one more (and that will be it for this book so as not to take away from the Lord and the message of the book).

> In 2007, while preaching in Lagos, Nigeria, I had to spend about five hours in prayer using various methods, such as contemplation, meditative, mystery (praying in tongues), and just chanting the Names of God and all the titles of the Lord Jesus Christ. That evening at the

services, I had the church chant and sing the name of Jesus as we showered Him with titles befitting His Kingship. In the midst of the ululation, my eyes were open and I saw companies of angels beautiful, radiant and some fearful. I remember saying to the church, "What are these angels doing here?" I was so caught in the glorious manifestation of Heaven I must have seemed 'out of it' - as I was not in Africa! After the service, still inebriated by the powerful presence of the Lord, we went into the car with a pastor, George, his wife and another young man, Humphrey. They were all from Christian Pentecostal Mission headquarters in Ajao Estate, Lagos. They were to take me to hotel near the church. I was still chanting the name of the Lord. I found myself chanting quietly, "Yod Heh Vav Heh" and then "Yeshua moshieny." At one moment, I told the driver I did not like the road he was taking but he said it was okay. In 15 minutes or so, we ran into armed bandits with all sorts of weapons. They stopped the car and shot their guns into the air.

Then they commanded everyone to get out the car, but I sat there calmly as I was caught up in the beauty of the name of the Lord. Suddenly, one of the bandits got angry and began to shout, "I am going to blow your head off." He placed the gun into the window upon my head and, in a flash, I saw the same angels I had seen at the church. He opened fire, but to the glory of God, he fell about 15 feet away from the car. Everybody thought I was dead. The pastor's wife shouted, "They have killed Bishop!" I responded, "I am all right." The bandits panicked and began shooting into the air. I remember muttering, "Lord Jesus, release them before they hurt anyone," and they took off in a Jeep, taking all my documents and all my money. That whole night, I praised the name of the Lord. The next morning, my documents were found intact.

The name of the LORD is a strong tower. When we pray "hallowed be thy name", we should proceed to hallow the name and saturate our being and atmosphere with the name of the Lord. Be like David: when you take up the cup of salvation, call upon the name of the LORD and hallow it. When you offer the sacrifice of thanksgiving, call upon the name of the LORD and hallow it. In proclaiming God's names, you build a fortress around yourself and your family. When we sing, speak or even mutter the name of the Lord from our heart, we attribute value to the Name. In so doing, we release its inherent power. It is by calling the name of the Lord that we are saved from our enemies (Psalm 55:16; 86:7). In the day of your trouble, call on the name of the Lord for He will answer you.

Here is a summary of the Names of God in One. It is above all names in Heaven, on Earth and underneath the Earth:

HEBREW	ENGLISH	MEANING AND USE
אֵל	EL	The strong one. Should be used sparing alone because of its tendency to attract the gods of the nations because the term is common for all that may be called God in all the world.
אלהים	Elohim	God in all His Trinitarian majesty. Used to invoke the plenitude of divine powers. Powerful as Name of agreement especially when used as YHVH ELHM.
God in all His Trinitarian majesty powerful as Name of agreement.		
אֲדֹנָי	ADNY	Lord, Master, a term for the rulership and mastery of God over all circumstances and being. Used more than 300 times in the Bible. When used in combination with ADNY YHVH, it can really mean LORD of Lords. But also power to create unity from where there is division among God's people.
אֵל שַׁדַּי	EL SHADAI	God all-sufficient, used to strengthen Abraham (Genesis 17:2); Lord of the plenitude of all life.
יהוה	YHVH	The ineffable name of God. The root combination of all life proceeding from God. The Self-Existent source of life.
אֶהְיֶה אֲשֶׁר אֶהְיֶה	AHIH ASHR AHIH	I AM that I AM, the name of divine deliverance from bondage revealed to Moses.
יְהוָה יִרְאֶה	VHYH YRH	The Lord of provisional insight who shows His people how to find provision in tough times. (Genesis 22:14)
יְהוָה נִסִּי	YHVH NYSY	The Lord who is the flag of victory in battle. The flag that remains forever standing—this is a battle name of the LORD dealing with particular battles not general war.
יְהוָה, רֹפְאֶךָ	YHVH ROPHE	The LORD as the remover of diseases. To remove disease plagues and sickness.
יְהוָה קַדְּשְׁכֶם	YHVH MQDSH	The LORD of who sets apart in purity—the Lord is the purifier, the sanctifier able to make even the most unclean clean. While denoting holiness of God, it denotes God's ability and power to make holy.
יְהוָה שָׁלוֹם	YHVH SHLVM	The LORD our fulfillment and wholeness. This is God as the source of the welfare and safety of His people.
יְהוָה רֹעִי	YHVH ROEH	The LORD who is Shepherd, nurturer and guide, protector in a land of my vulnerability. (Psalm 23)
יְהוָה צִדְקֵנוּ	YHVH TZDKNV	The LORD our righteous balance in the scales of justice and mercy. (Jeremiah 23:5)
יְהוָה שָׁמָּה	YHVH SHMMH	The LORD who is ever present. Wherever you go HE is there. (Ezekiel 38:45)
יְהוָה צְבָאוֹת	YHVH TZBTH	The LORD of Hosts is the LORD of the innumerable armies. This is the name of the LORD as it relates to war not just one battle.

> Hawfy YSHVH JESUS
> *Given by God as source of human salvation*
> Matthew 1:21; Luke 1:31
>
> *This is the Name of Supreme Salvation given humankind*
> Acts 4:12
>
> *Wherefore God also hath highly exalted him, and given him a name which is above every name: ¹⁰ That at the name of Jesus every knee should bow, of things in Heaven, and things in earth, and things under the earth; 11 And that every tongue should confess that Jesus Christ is Lord, to the glory of God the Father.*
> (Philippians 2:9–11)

In our prayer life, the best way to hallow the name of the Father is to honor the name of the Son - in whom the Father has implanted all of His Names and the functions of the Divinity in humanity. Throughout history the church used to chant the name of Jesus all day and reported tremendous experiences of grace through Jesus' name in prayer.

CHAPTER TEN
KEY #4: CALL FORTH THE KINGDOM

"Your kingdom come"
(Matthew 6:10)

The word "come" is translated in the Greek as ἐλθέτω (*elthetow*), which is an 'aorist active imperative third person' denoting a *command*. It should read as an apostolic supernatural command to manifest the Kingdom of God in the context within which we find ourselves. (This does not remove the call for the eschatological manifestation of the Kingdom of God). The Greek speaks imperatively and we can read it something like this, "*Come, the kingdom of you.*" We must then command the coming of kingdom by our faith. If indeed what we bind on Earth is bound in Heaven, then we owe it to what we believe to speak imperatively that the kingdom of Him whom we serve be manifested in every sphere to which our king sends us. This must be our primary aim as it relates upon the Earth. The primacy of the Kingdom of God cannot be overstated. In all that the Lord Jesus did, the Kingdom of God was primary. According to Mark 1:14–15:

> *Now after John had been taken into custody, Jesus came into Galilee, preaching the gospel of God, and saying, "The time is fulfilled, and the kingdom of God is at hand; repent and believe in the gospel."*

Manifest Kingdom and the Omega Point

Not only must we pray this imperative, we must make this an imperative lifestyle (and not just speech). We are told by the Lord Jesus Christ in Matthew 6:33, "*But seek first His kingdom and His righteousness, and all these things will be added to you.*" The kingdom lifestyle is God-oriented, Christ-centered, Holy Spirit propelled and saints propagated. The kingdom is life liberated from the false consciousness of cosmic materialism. It is a supernatural and immortal life, infused into the earthly realm. It has its foundation in God, whose desire is for us to participate in it. The

Kingdom of God is not the domain of one particular group of people, but the diffusion of the name and nature of God into the world through those who believe in Jesus. When the Kingdom of God comes in any form, the old ways of people vanish. As Paul says, *"Behold, all things are become new"* (2 Corinthians 5:17). The Kingdom is not a mere marginal insertion into the problems of those who find it or are born into it. It is the very constituent of their being in the world.

The Kingdom that must come is the structure by which the entire intentions and purposes of God flow into manifestation. Kingdom is a barrier overcoming process! The coming of the Kingdom causes a face-to-face engagement with the structures and processes of the cosmos in light of the purpose of God. As we command the emergence of the Kingdom and respond honestly to its manifestation, we move toward the purpose for which God created the world, which is that the kingdom of this world would become the Kingdom of our God and of His Messiah! But to see the Kingdom, there has to be a transformation of affection from mere *eros* love to *agape love*. Part of how the Kingdom is manifested in our consciousness is by our praying it into our own being.

"Kingdom come" is the purification, illumination and beatification of the universe by the full presence of God. In the Kingdom, our beings are infused with glory through the encounter with Christ. We preach up the Kingdom until the incarnational principle enters our being and we allow it to become manifest through us to the watching world. The Kingdom is not achieved by us but comes by direct apostolic-prophetic appeal to the Will of God in Christ. It comes from God and is revealed within the web of human relationship, undergirded by God's love. The purpose then of the Kingdom is the restoration of dominion, subduing power over the Earth, ruling authority, Divine fruitfulness and multiplicative principle, and the replenishing capacity of humanity as the image of God upon the Earth. The vitality of the coming Kingdom for which we pray can raise up new life which expresses itself in appropriate Divine forms. It is also by prayerful participation in its dynamic structure that we open its citizenry continuously to move toward it God desired and designed end - what Teihard de Chardin once called, "the Omega point."

Not of This World

The Kingdom for which the apostolic-prophetic voice calls refuses to be held captive by human institutional traditionalisms. Neither can the Kingdom be overtaken completely by meat, drink and belly-oriented emotional sentimentality. Rather, the Kingdom bends toward righteousness, peace and joy in the Holy Spirit who is its propelling force.

This Kingdom ought not to be confused with the church in its current institutionalism.

The church as an institution sometimes seeks to circumvent the Spirit that birthed it and to obliterate its dynamic mission for the maintenance of the status quo. Systems are created that deny the promptings of the foundational spirit. But the call for the Kingdom to come is a challenge to such fossilized systems! The Kingdom is the spiritual force of the supernatural, invading and transforming materialistic and naturalistic tendencies which have arisen in the course of time by those who have lost its first dynamic nature. Being spiritual and dynamic, the Kingdom does not allow for total self-isolation but demands a multifaceted responsiveness to God as He continues to be revealed in the Word and the world.

There is within us the Kingdom flow, the need to break out of the old, to de-fossilize and unthaw congealed forms that have taken over the church. This Kingdom, for which we call apostolically and prophetically, is constantly discarding old wine skins and old wine taste for new wine skins and fresh wine flowing from the innermost chamber of the Holy Spirit. It is in search for a form ready for

> *If indeed what we bind on Earth is bound in Heaven, then we owe it to what we believe to speak imperatively that the kingdom of Him whom we serve be manifested in every sphere to which our king sends us. This must be our primary aim as it relates upon the Earth.*

its manifestation and use. We read in the KJV, "*Thou has prepared a body for me*" (Hebrews 10:5). I believe it should be read, "*You continually prepare a body for me.*" The Kingdom suffered violence and the violent took it by force until the time of Christ. From the death of Christ, it does not arbitrarily impose itself upon the will of others, but rather, it signals divine intentionality to the space, place and people who are called to embrace and respond to it in love and freedom. It is not propagated by fear and violence, but by righteousness, peace and love. So if we are to pray "come this kingdom of yours," we must overcome our fear of the surging waves of new becoming, and respond without reserve to the dynamic urge and agency of the Spirit of that Kingdom.

Every new flow claiming to be a manifestation of the line of prayer, "*Thy Kingdom come*" must be tested following John's injunction, "*try the spirits*" to see if they are true (1 John 4:1). The Kingdom is not of the world. Therefore, we should not try to conform it to the worldly system, nor use the world's system as the primary means to assess it. What we call 'lack of order' and unconventional by the system of the world may be the Holy Spirit's kingdom dynamic refusing to be hemmed in by natural man into old wineskins. We may "*not know not know where it comes from and where it is going*" (John 3:8), as the Master said - yet, blow it must and flow it must! If we discern and follow its currents, we would experience its power. The Kingdom is always searching for appropriate forms of expression. We should be open to be formed into that which is appropriate for its manifestation at every given season.

Turn The World Upside-down

To call the Kingdom, *"come kingdom of you,"* we need to ask the hard questions of religious, political, social-cultural ideas, forms, and structures. If we watch the Master Jesus Christ, we notice how He called on these institutions to answer the tough questions concerning the mind and purpose of God. When religion, society or culture offered answers that had nothing to do with the Kingdom of God and the movement of the Spirit, He called them to account. He offered new ways for the world and people that were liberated from false religious consciousness. In His interaction, we see that the Kingdom is usually unconventional and on the margin of institutional conventions, religious systems and traditions which men have made for themselves. Such institutions and systems, even traditions, have made themselves enemies of spiritual renewal by unbiblical conservatism and ungodly liberalism. Both are sterile, ideological systems of materialistic convention that have no true openness to supernatural manifestations which Christ intended for the church. The Kingdom calls us to move beyond these systems into the heart and purpose of God for the world. We want the Kingdom to manifest in us and around us with power. Our prayers need to be seasoned with the consciousness of the Kingdom.

> *The kingdom lifestyle is God-oriented, Christ-centered, Holy Spirit propelled and saints propagated ... It is a supernatural and immortal life, infused into the earthly realm.*

When we call *"come, the kingdom of you"*, we are calling for a confrontation of powers and conversational engagement of wills within the sphere in which we seek to see the Kingdom come. It involves casting out the devils and structure to which they have attached themselves, be it in community, clan or person. We know then that our call for the manifestation of the Kingdom of God is heard when we are able, by the power of the King of our Kingdom, to cast the devils. We read in Matthew 12:28, *"But if I cast out demons by the Spirit of God, then the kingdom of God has come upon you."* The very personal aspect of this concept is also revealed in Mark 9:47, *"If your eye causes you to stumble, throw it out; it is better for you to enter the kingdom of God with one eye, than, having two eyes, to be cast into hell,"* It is only by praying the Kingdom that we cast out all that has sought to usurp the place of the King in our lives.

Calling on the Kingdom to come is to call for change in the fundamental mode by which we conduct relational business in the world. The world says make it easier for the rich and the famous to enter. "Bring them in, bring them in!" it cries - but keep the needy outside. The Kingdom turns that upside down and says in Matthew 19:24, *"It is easier for a camel to go through the eye of a needle, than for a rich man to enter into the kingdom of God."* This offense, to the present peddlers of greed, is in the name of the Gospel. The world's system insists that the self-righteous, the prosperous and the arrogant are going to inherit the world. The Kingdom says, "*tax collectors and prostitutes*" may actually go into the Kingdom of God before you (Matthew 21:31). The world's system says, "*Let the adults stand in the way of children, abort them, because they are mere inconveniences and make them second-class citizens in the kingdom of man and of God.*" The Kingdom of God says in Mark 10:14, "*But when Jesus saw this, He was indignant and said to them, "Permit the children to come to Me; do not hinder them; for the kingdom of God belongs to such as these.*" The world's system says, "Get yourself together and straighten up before you can come to our god and inner circle." The Kingdom says, "*Come to Me, all who are weary and heavy-laden, and I will give you rest.*" (Matthew 11:28). The King says, "I *will make your yoke easy and burden light.*" The world's system is full of disease, but the Kingdom of God, for which we call, comes to bring healing. The King of this Kingdom sends His emissaries with these words: "*And he sent them to preach the kingdom of God, and to heal the sick*" (Luke 9:2). "*And He sent them out to proclaim the kingdom of God and to perform healing.*" (Luke 9:11). "*But the crowds were aware of this and followed Him; and welcoming them, He began speaking to them about the kingdom of God and curing those who had need of healing.*" (Luke 10:9). Organized religion and its system says, "We will put obstacles on your path to the Kingdom." The Kingdom itself says clearly, "*You are not far from the kingdom of God*" (Mark 12:34).

The world is filled with hate, but the Kingdom for which we pray comes in love and brings love. The transformation of worldly consciousness to God consciousness marks the coming of the Kingdom of God. The Kingdom comes to us as a Divine mystery, spoken among the mature who speak with wisdom. God is our Father, God's name is for us, and this Kingdom is from God. We cast our Father's word-seed into the ground that the world might live through it. It is a kingdom of life, peace, grace, love and righteousness. All who stand within it shall not taste of death, because they have seen the Kingdom of God come with power and glory within their sphere of living.

Change Your Heart and Mind!

Because the Kingdom is an inner principle, it must begin with inner motion flowing from the depth of the heart of man. It must issue forth from the heart, the place of which the Scripture says, "*flow the issues of life.*" Thus, when it comes near, there is a revolution in the heart of those to whom it draws near. Lord came, saying "*Repent, for the kingdom of heaven is at hand,*" (Matthew 3:2). When we begin to pray "*come Kingdom of God,*" we in fact stir up repentance toward the Kingdom of Heaven and begin to be moved by its urgency. Repentance was preached based on the nearness of the Kingdom of Heaven. Human beings need to understand the bankruptcy and ineptitude of spirit in which they live.

The Kingdom calls us to become poor in spirit. This understanding of poverty is a Kingdom principle that reverse our bankruptcy and ineptitude into blessedness - and thrusts us into the possession of the Kingdom of Heaven. This poverty must be evidenced by the motion to repent that, in a sense, draws the Kingdom by divine magnetic impulse into the innermost being of man. This calling forth of the Kingdom is meant to fortify us for righteousness, so that we stand even when this repentance leading to righteousness causes us to be persecuted. When we imperatively call forth the Kingdom, we state that we will do so by more than words. By being fortified in suffering for righteousness, we not only possess the Kingdom of Heaven, but we call it forth into the lives of others even if they hate us and pour slander upon us. Our prayer for the Kingdom breaks through the command centers and strongholds of the enemy and teaches people to open up for the entrance of the Kingdom of Heaven. By our prayer, we command and teach the necessity of the Kingdom of Heaven for human greatness. Calling the Kingdom is of itself a stance of righteousness, since the least of the Kingdom of God is more than the greatest prophet of the law. This Kingdom consciousness causes the one who calls to exceed the scribes' and Pharisee's righteousness. It causes those who call to live, being saturated in their whole being with the Kingdom of Heaven.

We call forth the Kingdom because we desire that people enter into the Kingdom of Heaven and do the will of the Father. The will of the Father is to *"believe in the one whom He has sent."* When we say *"come, kingdom of God,"* our voice reaches to the east and west, north and south - and we shall sit down with Abraham, Isaac and Jacob in the Kingdom of Heaven. We proclaim the Kingdom of Heaven and command the world to respond to it. Our voice rings among men and women to raise a great host, baptized into the Spirit of Christ, making the least of them greater than the enemy of faith. This *"your kingdom come"* is God's answer through us. In our calling forth of the Kingdom through Jesus Christ, the mysteries of the Kingdom of Heaven are opened to those who seek it. Jesus Christ tells us, *"The kingdom of heaven may be compared to a man who sowed good seed in his field."* (Matthew 13:24). Our prayer in this vein is like seed poured forth into the ground of human hearts.

Calling forth the Kingdom, we put into practice Matthew 13:31. In this simple line *"your kingdom come,"* we carry the Kingdom of Heaven like a grain of mustard seed sowed into the atmosphere and into the field of people's hearts. By it, we leaven the whole world with Kingdom vibration and harmonize God and humanity and human beings to one another. The Kingdom of Heaven is full of treasures, hidden and prepared for the joy of the world. Our voice is needed. We must pray *"your kingdom come."* By this, we call forth merchants with the heart to seek its godly pearls at all cost. Cast your Kingdom prayer like a net into the sea and gather of every kind of fish. This is the command of the Lord.

A Transcendent Spiritual Reality

Humility is an inner vibration in those who pray this Kingdom. By this, we do not mean a beggarly attitude in prayer. Rather, it's a proportionate view of ourselves in light of grace.

> *At that time the disciples came to Jesus and said, "Who then is greatest in the kingdom of heaven?" ... "Truly I say to you, unless you are converted and become like children, you will not enter the kingdom of heaven. Whoever then humbles himself as this child, he is the greatest in the kingdom of heaven.*
> (Matthew 18:1, 3 - 4)

This inner vibration of humility is reiterated in Matthew 19:14, *"But Jesus said, "Let the children alone, and do not hinder them from coming to Me; for the kingdom of Heaven belongs to such as these."* When we pray accordingly, we call it forth for our King. We call into account all creation as His servants (Matthew 18:23). Call it forth, laborers, by this prayer (Matthew 20:1). In this prayer, we call forth His friends to the marriage feast of the King's beloved Son (Matthew 22:2).

Praying *"your Kingdom come,"* or *"come, Kingdom of you,"* means the alignment of subjective feelings, emotions and sensations to the ideal world of Heaven. It means walking in the spirit and inclining the hope of one's being toward Heaven. The Kingdom calls us to move our body, power of mind and all its potential, into becoming the arena of Divine activity. In the Kingdom, our common

> As we command the emergence of the Kingdom and respond honestly to its manifestation, we move toward the purpose for which God created the world, which is that the kingdom of this world would become the Kingdom of our God and of His Messiah!

duality is transcended. Praying this prayer with our whole being can cause us to experience going in and out of various dimensions of reality. In fact, the Kingdom shakes our rationalistic perspective for it calls us to transcend our mechanistic view of the world and enter into a spirituality that meshes with the boundary of the world. Jesus' statement, *"Except you become as a little child, you cannot enter the kingdom of God"* calls you to open up your inner imagination to infinite possibilities beyond anything you can even comprehend. This metaphorical transcendence is a reversal of our static universe and does not set well with our adult rationality. We see this in the response of Nicodemus. *"How can a man revert to his mother's womb and be born again?"* (John 3:4, KJV)

The Kingdom of God that we call to be manifested on the Earth as it is in Heaven at once shakes our view of reality. It turns upside down our criteria for acceptability and puts in its place an offensive idealism. This principle is carried farther when, as Paul said *"There is neither Jew nor Greek, there is neither slave nor free man, there is neither male nor female; for you are all one in Christ Jesus."* (Galatians 3:28). Now if the Kingdom removes the demarcation fixed by men upon themselves and upon others, it causes those who have come into its scope to move into a lifestyle of faith. It means to us that, in the Kingdom, things are not judged by our opinion or even experiences - things are judged by God's purpose and end goal.

Unity

When the Kingdom comes, the spirit-body problem is solved, the Heaven and Earth problem is solved, the male-female problem is solved, and the God-human problem is solved. This issue of exterior-interior is solved, because the Kingdom is the restoration of the harmony of the universe as God intended from the beginning. As for the external-internal problem, the Kingdom that is coming is already inside the believer. Jesus said, *"The kingdom of God is within you"* (Luke 17:21). The one who is prepared to pray this is someone who has received the Kingdom - in whom there has been reconciliation to Christ. In this person, the fullness of God dwells and Divine character and Kingship are carried out. Although this is hard for some to believe, the Kingdom is in a person as he or she receives it. It is quite obvious that the Kingdom of Heaven and of God will not come into our natural realm unless it first comes into human beings.

There is a profound difference between the life of someone who believes and accepts this Kingdom in its fullness now and one who sees the Kingdom merely as what appears at the end of life. To be engaged by the Kingdom of God as revealed in Christ, and now revealed in us, is to realign us with God's intention for creation. The Kingdom that comes to Earth as it is in Heaven is a kingdom of communion. This communion, as John states in 1 John, is between us, the Father, the Son, the Holy Spirit and each other. It is the removal of enmity, both Divine and human. If indeed in Jesus Christ the Kingdom has been revealed, and He is the living Word who structures this Kingdom, then our path must follow His example. In order to speak meaningfully of the Kingdom, we must ask, "How and when has it been seen?" And for all of us who believe, this how and when is answered in the

> *"Kingdom come" is the purification, illumination and beatification of the universe by the full presence of God. In the Kingdom, our beings are infused with glory through the encounter with Christ.*

"who" of Jesus the Christ, the Son of God.

Entering A New Dimension of Christ

If the Kingdom is embodied in the Person of Christ, then the purpose of the Kingdom is also manifested in what He can do and does do. The Kingdom comes to Earth as a way to deal with the dehumanization of sin and the entrapment of man by evil. If indeed the Kingdom is embodied in Christ, then our being in Christ puts us in the heart of the Kingdom. The Kingdom, as I have said, is a fellowship with its root in God's love. Its source is God from whom it springs. The very atmosphere in which it thrives is the love of God, His righteousness and His peace. When love reigns on Earth, movement to the Kingdom becomes irresistible and irreversible. Because love in the Kingdom is grounded in the love of God, there is sufficient power to conquer the innate selfishness of human hearts. In speaking of the Kingdom, Paul said, "*for the kingdom of God is not eating and drinking, but righteousness and peace and joy in the Holy Spirit.*" (Romans 14:17).

We can list several things which are part of the Kingdom into which we enter when we pray the Lord's Prayer:

1. Truths, so we open up and enter dimensions of truth;
2. Faith, so we enter dimensions of faith that bring release;
3. Grace, so we enter into dimensions of grace-filled walk;
4. Holiness, so we open up to ourselves the power to walk in holiness;
5. Wisdom and revelation; we enter into vistas of revelation previously unknown;
6. Righteousness, so we become the righteousness of God;
7. Peace, so we have peace;
8. Divine exuberance, so we live in joyful exuberance;
9. Dynamic power, so we receive power over all the powers of the enemy;
10. God's love, so we manifest love for one another and for the lost;
11. God's life, so we live life more abundantly;
12. God's glory, so we move from glory to glory; and most of all,
13. It is the kingdom of God our Father, and we are children of God.

So when we pray "*thy kingdom come*" or "*come, kingdom of yours*", we open up to an indwelling presence that aligns us to all of the above. The entire concept as articulated above is embodied in God's Son, Jesus Christ. These are wave patterns of the Kingdom of Heaven, as they are manifestation on the Earth and our lives among those who pray for the Kingdom to come.

The Kingdom comes through divine communication and is manifest wherever there is a communicative process of the Kingdom. The Kingdom that we ask in prayer to come to Earth is not some sort of ethereal occult communication. It is a communication from the Throne room of God which influences through and through the lives of those whose souls have been invaded and transformed by the idea of this Kingdom. Jesus puts it this way, *"But seek first His kingdom and His righteousness, and all these things will be added to you."* (Matthew 6:33).

The Kingdom of Our Lord and of His Christ

The Kingdom coming to Earth is to enhance God's influence and prestige by recounting all the marvelous works and qualities which God has manifested in the house of His creation.

There is also another side to this which, in our coming to the Kingdom, allows us to enhance our influence in both spheres. It enhances our personal attributes, revolutionizes our disposition, and imports at our disposal supernatural resources in terms of our enhanced health, emotional strengths and spiritual insights. Furthermore, it enhances the strength of our will in the expression of its moral and social strengths. It is not uncommon to see those who have been regarded as non-influential, gaining a level of influence after coming into the Kingdom that isn't due to the level of their education, pedigree or hard work. This Kingdom-flowing influence in many cases has enhanced property holdings and certain knowledge which has no other reference except the Kingdom to which they have been connected.

Because the Kingdom changes human disposition, it lends itself to the transformation of generational consciousness as well as tribal consciousness of those it has affected. It does so because, coming from Heaven and manifesting in the material world, it brings with it a new set of interactive systems not responsible to the earthly arena - but to a far more superior Kingdom. Its point of view is motivated by a deeper and higher dimension of thought and imagination grounded in God. By saying this, I do not mean that the Kingdom is for peddling mere influence and prestige, but rather that its power is so strong and so irresistible that those who embody it have an influence disproportionate to their social status and number. Though we pray for the Kingdom to come to Earth as in Heaven, the Kingdom cannot be an Earthly kingdom. It must be a Heavenly kingdom. The Kingdom of this world cannot remain the kingdom of this world. It must become, as we read in Revelation 11:15, *"The kingdom of our Lord and of his Christ."* Here we must take warning. We cannot reduce this Kingdom to mere human ideology. This is why the Kingdom is an object of prayer so that it remains in the realm of divine sovereignty, holiness and majesty.

Of course the Kingdom coming to Earth, and the kingdom of this world becoming the Kingdom of our God, entails the usage of every dimension of human existence as communicative instruments for the glory of God. Again, herein lies the danger that so easily besets people. The danger is that the Kingdom would become human economics, human education, human media mongering, human social uplift, human religious systems, human prejudice aimed at protecting human greed, arrogance and partisanship.

Our Origin and Destiny

Being conscious of the Kingdom through prayer helps us develop a new attitude of introspective spirituality which helps us discover ourselves as we are . I mean the real us. Not a received set of systems given to us by people who want us to avoid examining ourselves from the Divine perspective of the Kingdom as fully expressed in the Person of Jesus Christ! The Kingdom is humankind's origin and destiny. It is in the Kingdom of God that the true nature

> *The purpose then of the Kingdom is the restoration of dominion, subduing power over the Earth, ruling authority, Divine fruitfulness and multiplicative principle, and the replenishing capacity of humanity as the image of God upon the Earth.*

of human beings is revealed. We pray thusly because the Kingdom is the necessary and sufficient condition for discovery of who we are. We cannot be truly sincere about who we all are until the Kingdom comes into our lives. The very nature of the Kingdom generates a type of virtue contrary in its essence to the natural (actually unnatural!) ways of doing things to which we are so accustomed. Jesus Christ devoted His lifetime to outlining the Kingdom. Anyone who wants honestly to see the Kingdom on Earth will do well to recall that, without Christ in the affairs of humans, any Kingdom building is doomed to failure. Its manifestation will always escape humans' grasp as long as they hold to a false idea of God, self and the world.

Praying the Kingdom come is a way of facing the fact that: this Kingdom which is coming to birth on the Earth stems from being within God's mind in eternity and is manifested in and through us upon whom the fullness of time has come. This Kingdom is being made manifest as we welcome the disciplinary impression of the Holy Spirit upon our mind, soul, spirit, and body. As we open up to this move of the spirit over the waters of our chaos, the Kingdom of Light closes in upon our portable lights and the connecting causes and explosion of light in the universe. We then move from one state of being to another. Our words communicated in the sphere of the Kingdom of God pierce through all the dimensions. This does not just lead to introspection, which causes change in our person, but also changes everything we touch. "*Your kingdom come*" is not merely a gassing of ourselves - it is a focus on God and His glory which exhausts us of ourselves and causes us to lose all carnal capacity for false relationships with the world and with God. We are transported from a narrow, deformed, defensive stance against God to an enlargement of soul and openness to His inexhaustible depths.

The Infusion of Divine Word

When the Kingdom comes as we pray, it commands an entrusting faith that throws us completely into the unsearchable abyss of Divinity. This coming of the Kingdom into the Earth calls forth an expansion of time and space and, in actuality, an expansion of emotion and intellect, resulting in an expansion of care. That expansion of care develops in us a stance that justifies our confidence in the possible transformation and remaking of everything. From this perspective, our rambling life suddenly takes on illuminative excitement and the seeming contradictions become reconciled.

> *What we call 'lack of order' and unconventional by the system of the world may be the Holy Spirit's kingdom dynamic refusing to be hemmed in by natural man into old wineskins. We may "not know not know where it comes from and where it is going" (John 3:8), as the Master said - yet, blow it must and flow it must!*

The Kingdom remains a mystery. However, when it has come into our lives, we tie into the one who is an unfathomable mystery, whose spirit illuminates and clarifies it within us. The Spirit of God, who has delved into our innermost being, takes rule and dominion over us, opens our eyes to see His story as our story, and put the Kingdom in motion. To pray for the Kingdom to come on Earth as it is in Heaven is not a mere pursuit of a fantasy. It is a taking hold of the things which "*cannot be shaken*" (Hebrews 12:28). The Kingdom, in its coming, inscribes in us knowledge of the sameness of God and of His Christ and is not contradicted by the artificial ebb and flow of worldly illusions. The Kingdom which comes on Earth as in Heaven comes spontaneously and infuses spontaneity, so that the person of the spirit, like the wind, cannot be predicted. This is what makes the Kingdom and its movement so humbling and overwhelming to those who have found it or have been found by it. To those who have not found it, the Kingdom which comes on Earth as in Heaven presents a level of unnerving confusion which they cannot explain. Oh, but its discovery for the person who has called out truly "come, kingdom of you" and has tasted its beauty, it is sweeter than honey in the honeycomb! Just by praying this prayer, we are in the presence of a force so loving, so caring, so compassionate and so sweet, flowing into unending joy.

Living in authentic joy, peace and righteousness is not possible without the coming of this Kingdom. To say "*come Kingdom of you*" is to ask for the incarnation of the Word. It is a call for God to assume the form of this created world. To say this prayer is not just to believe in the present age as inhabiting God's possibility, but to see the possibility of its eternal transformation! Saying "*come, kingdom of God*" is to reject the structures of human ideology as the norm of things and to infuse the world and ourselves with Divine sound and thought - to activate the divine DNA, so that the present gives way to something completely new. The Kingdom is not about rules, moralities, legal systems, or rituals which turns us into automatons and self-righteous sleep walkers, deprived of Divinity. Rather, it is the intentional illumination of our darkness with its contrary light. It is only here, in the coming of the Kingdom that true creativity, love, evangelism, prophetic utterance, apostolic move, pastoral spirit, and teaching zeal flow into us and our world.

Get Real! Get Spiritual.

What is the Kingdom? Is it not the infusion of Divine Word from eternity into our present? Kingdom, as Paul tells us, is not just words but the acting out of God as love. Only in the Kingdom can we know God. "*Your kingdom come*" is the best place to begin for anyone who seeks to know God and obey Him. It is the linchpin of authentic prophetic imagination.

For those who are so bent on what they say is "real," we insist that the Kingdom is real in the sense of being rooted in the ultimate. Its realness, really, has nothing in common with worldly realism. It is not what we call real in our superficial materialism. In fact, our illusive reality directly contradicts the reality of the Kingdom. One of the first ways in which the Kingdom contradicts our idea of what we call real is that it is a Spiritual kingdom. Here again, the current church of Babel, with its materialistic pretensions, does not want to admit this. In fact, the modern church is bent on condemning the spirituality of the Kingdom as being "merely spiritual" (as if the "Spirit" can be called mere!). Our world's reality is meat and drink - but that is not the Kingdom's reality. We are told in no uncertain terms by the Apostle Paul that the Kingdom's reality involves "*righteousness, peace and joy.*" The reality of the world involves sin, war, sadness or pretentious joy. The vision of the Kingdom resides in the "Spirit," not the banal conversation of self-competing egos and material measurements that are not directed to the Person of the Son of God. It is not an escape from "reality," whatever that may be, but the insertion of Divine reality into the unreal world of human illusion. Remember, in this Kingdom into which we are called, "*walking by sight*" is contrasted to "*walking by faith.*"

Awake, Oh Sleeper!

This *"come, Kingdom of yours"* is a call to the transcendent level of life to reach out to us and awaken us from our sleepwalking nightmare. Once we say this prayer, we either consciously or inadvertently accept that our so-called reality is a nightmare from which we cannot wake ourselves and, thus, stand in desperate need of a transcendent wakeup call. We cannot undo the ravages of our greed, lusts and materialistic delusions. It will take a spiritual revolution to unclad our rags of certainly without faith. Faith is not worldly assertions but revelational affirmations which contradict the so-called rational course of things. Again, I must reiterate that the life of faith is expressed completely and perfectly in the contradictory life of Jesus Christ. Contradictory, not in character but in contrast to what the world considers important. Being God, He became man; being rich, He became poor; being eternal, He subjected Himself to time; being Lord, He became a servant; being Life everlasting, He died; being Holy, He became sin.

To call the Kingdom to come into our lives and into our world is to set us up for trouble with the world. In this sense, many of us are not in the Kingdom. It has not come to us. The world is too comfortable with us. Rules, regulations, moralities, and laws cannot bind the Kingdom. In fact, where we see in the life of Jesus, it messes with the so-called standard of righteousness which we have set up in the name of God. If this is not so, then must look to explain why He, and almost all who followed Him, died at the hands of the world because of their belief in God. All of this is summed up when with all our hearts we pray, "thy Kingdom come."

Chapter Eleven

Key #5: Aligning Will to Will

"Your will be done, On earth as it is in heaven."
(Matthew 6:10)

How do we unlock the floodgates of Heaven and allow the Kingdom to manifest on Earth in our earthen vessel here and now?

In this chapter, we focus on the *will* as a way to propel us into effective prayer. The human will [8] serves as the transitional key for moving the sound of Heaven to the Earth. In the lower sphere, it also serves as the key which allows (or disallows) the influence of others in our lives. It is through the act of the human will that, what is in Heaven, is translated into the earthly realm. What is God is transmuted into what is human. By the key of the human will, the blessings of Heaven are trans-located to Earth or held up in the ethereal realm. Will is key to the opening and release of the fullness of Heaven to humankind. Conversely, it can lock the gate and keep us, and our earthly realm, from experiencing Heaven's fullness. So we can see the importance of this line of the Lord's Prayer, "*Your will be done on earth as it is in heaven.*"

How Does The Kingdom Come?

Now, if Heaven is the place where God reigns as King, and is the model for the Kingship of God over the whole world, what is the key that can be used to speed up manifestation on Earth and in human life? The simplest answer is this: The Kingdom of God must first come into people as the model of God on Earth. The Will of God must first come into the sphere of humankind as beings capable of exercising free will in the acceptance of the Will of God. The Kingdom of Heaven must be accepted into our hearts so that as "*the LORD, is God in Heaven above, He may be so upon the earth beneath*" (Deuteronomy 4:39, KJV). There must be no room for anyone else to be the Lord and God. If the Heavens are the "holy habitation" from which

God blesses the people of Israel and the land God has given them, so man, who is taken from the Earth, must become the holy habitation of God. This cannot happen unless the structures and processes of Heaven are duplicated or birthed into the sphere of humanity, so that both the land and the life of humans flow with milk and honey. Ultimately man is the habitation of God, for man is made in the image of God and is intended to become like God. But for man to become truly like God, his will must be submitted to the Will of God.

As you read the Lord's Prayer, you will notice that *"Your Kingdom come"* occurs between "hallowed be your Name" and the prophetic call for the manifestation of the Will of God, *"on Earth as it is in Heaven."* What the world lacks is the structure for manifesting the Kingdom of God or the pipelines for the Will of God to be done on Earth. The problem is the misalignment of the human will to the Will of God, because people do not want to submit. The solution is in the submission and connection of human will to the Will of God so that the Kingdom can flow freely through it to this sphere.

The Will is fundamental to spirituality. The Will of God is important for the manifestation of the Kingdom of God. In people's willingness to do the Will of God, the way is paved for the manifestation of the Kingdom of God in our sphere here on Earth. This is one reason why Jesus our Master taught us to pray, *"Your will be done on earth as it is in heaven."* 1 Peter 4:2 tells us that our power and effectiveness lie in moving away from the desire of our flesh to doing the Will of God. Leviticus 19:25 says, *"If you are willing and obedient, you shall eat the fruit of the land."* The key to our fruitfulness and abundance is in the orientation of our will. The passage from Isaiah suggests that most of our problems in the area of prosperity lie in the area of our will. If we no longer want to live the rest of our time in the flesh, subject to the lusts of men, we must surrender our will to the Will of God.

The question then naturally arises, "What is will?" Specifically, "What is the Will of God?" Furthermore, "What is *will*, in a person? What is the relationship of the human will to the Will of God? How is the Will of God to be done on Earth?" Asking the Will of God to be done in our lives is the place to begin. *"Your will be done on earth as it is in Heaven,"* is one of the keys to unlock great things, as it was for the Lord in the Garden of Gethsemane. This line of prayer is sweeping and far reaching. Its power can reach into the depths and frontiers of our consciousness and self.

DEFINITION OF WILL

The definition of will in this book begins with the words and terms used in the Scriptures. In this definition, I hope to show that the will is not the same as the human soul, spirit, emotions, or the body. The will is the crown worn over the soul and the body, serving as the point of contact between the Spirit of God and a person's life.

The Crown of Being

The Hebrew word רָצוֹן (ratzon), meaning "will," is the spiritual principle serving as the valve that opens the flow from which comes from existence. It is the nerve center of all the activities of being. The human will is so powerful; nothing can stand in its way when it is full of forcefulness. The will is a pervasive power over the soul which determines purpose and destiny. In a sense, the will is the original of the head of the soul. It is the crown of being. The enemy of our soul focuses on poisoning the soul,. He understands that the soul is the formative, instrumental flow through which Divinity passes. It is in our will that we, as fallen man, are like God. In the goodness of the will lies our connection to God. In the evil of human will lies our separation from God. It is at the level of "originality," the human will gives no reason for its existence. This is the basis of the problem which modern scientific psychology has with the concept of will. There is no explanation of its existence, but it is there.

It is in the human will that Wisdom finds itself concealed, waiting to flow out in Understanding, Knowledge and action. In the Bible, the will of man is sometimes identified with the heart, but never with the soul. The will gives the soul the "right" of existence and rite of passage to manifest its purpose -

> It is through the act of the human will that, what is in Heaven, is translated into the earthly realm. What is God is transmuted into what is human.

ill or good. The Bible says, "*Guard your heart (will) with all diligence for out of it are the issues of life*" (Proverbs 4:23). Thus, the will is supra-rational and supra-emotive in its nature. It serves to control and direct from above in sovereignty over all of the soul's movements, stands majestically in its strength between the spirit and the soul, and can bypass the soul to act upon the body for its own purpose. It also allows or disallows what the 'thought' will think, or what 'desire' will desire. In folly, the human will may block God Himself from entrance into a person's life. The rational mind in its entire prowess may choose. However, the power to make choices, to pursue chosen objectives rationally and act on them, mentally and physically, are the prerogatives of the will.

As powerful as the Divine Will may be when dealing with non-rational creation, it finds itself thwarted by the sovereignty of the human will. This is seen in the fact that the Divine Will, when it comes to man, is expressed essentially in the commandments given to Israel in the Torah by Moses. God allows the possibility that man, by his will, may reject and refuse or, by the same will, may choose to accept and embrace. The way God phrases the commands *"thou shall not"* and *"if you"* shows that the human will is at the center of the Ten Commandments. The will of man sits in judgment over the possibility of obedience or disobedience. The commandments express the power of that will.

Yes and No

In the Greek New Testament, *"will"* is translated from two words. One is the word **βούλησῃ** (*boule*, pronounced "boo-lay"), meaning *volition*, has the sense of *advice*, and by extension may imply *purpose*. When Stephen says, *"David served his generation by the Will of God"* (Acts 13:36), he is speaking of the counsel of God or God's advice. Of course, God gives counsel based on His Will and purpose.

> Ultimately man is the habitation of God, for man is made in the image of God and is intended to become like God. But for man to become truly like God, his will must be submitted to the Will of God.

The other word which occurs in the New Testament is **θέλημα** (*thelema*, pronounced "thel'-ay-mah"), meaning determination of the fundamental property of a thing. It refers to that which gives a thing active movement. In human beings, it refers to the tendency toward choice. It is the determiner of purpose of an act. When you will something, you choose to incline to something or someone one way or another. The word **"θέλημα"** (*thelema*), which Paul uses in the "will of God" (**θέλημα τοῦ θεοῦ**, *thelema tou Theou*; Romans 12:2), finds its root in the **thel'-o** - which means to determine a subjective state that is disposed to something. *Thelema* speaks also to "intention" which drives certain action. It is, therefore, that which determines the compatibility of an act with one's nature. When one wills, one desires. In turn, the willing is meant to produce pleasure in the one who wills or pain in another who rebels. Both words point in the direction of the human will and its sovereignty in human thoughts and actions.

The will is sovereign in man, as the Divine Will is sovereign in God. As the sovereign decision making instrument in one's being, the will is the instrument of synthesis. The will synthesizes the "I" and the action. In it adheres coherence of the past, present and future. In its freedom, the possibility of being and non-being abide in their purity. It is the will that man exist as the image of God since the Fall. This is why deficiency in will results in evil action. Its nature, as the synthesizing element, makes the will the principle of human becoming. From its fountain the spring of righteousness bubbles up and is revealed in the life of a human being. From it may also flow the foul waters of evil that can overtake one's life. The will must be the focus of discipline, intense education, and spiritual inpouring for it to spring forth and the person to live righteously in the sight of God. Heaven and Earth, life and death, center on two words: *yes* and *no*. This is the declaration of the will in its fundamental freedom. In the will lies the kingly majesty of decision, direction, destiny and divinity. This is why the Lord Jesus Christ prayed, **"Father, if You are willing, remove this cup from Me; yet not My will, but Yours be done"** (Luke 22:42, emphasis added). The Lord could pray this prayer because He had spent His whole life disciplining His will and surrendering it in every act to the Will of the Father. Jesus gave us this line "*Your will be done*" as a vital prayer for this season.

Freedom, Choice and Surrender

Hidden in the inner sanctum of the will is the possibility of our sonship and Divinity. Inside our will, this Divinity lies dormant. Dammed up in this reservoir is the Kingdom of Heaven, waiting to flow powerfully into the world. Our thoughts, imaginations, dreams and visions must pass though the magisterium of the will. The will is not the product of emotional stimuli, or even the flow of ideas, though they may serve to strengthen or weaken it. The act flowing from the human will is the supreme expression of the personality. We meet an act of will only when an action is apprehended in distinct consciousness, deliberated upon and left to be determined by the free choice, not swayed by pressing emotions. The human will is intrinsically attached to freedom and intimately connected to it. Thus, when anyone asks for the Will of God to be done, the person intends to surrender to God's Sovereignty at the very basic level. In a sense, I stop pretending to be free and independent and allow myself to become dependent on God by freely submitting my will to God.

In this freedom to give over the will to God's sovereignty is displayed the true effectiveness of the will. Freedom is at the heart of the connection of the human will to the Divine Will. The uniqueness of will is that it can have no content other than that supplied by the involuntary flow of ideas from beyond itself. It is to touch this supra-rational source that we pray "*Your will be done on Earth as it is in Heaven.*" Our will, content with unrestricted freedom of choice, stands as gatekeeper over all other faculty of being, owning none yet controlling all by its majesty. Accordingly, we must flee to a greater will. In us, the will is the principle of resolution between ideas and intentions, standing between determination and variance. It is a good thing, but history is full of evidence that the human will can gradually accumulate and express itself in opposition to Divine Will. We have no guarantee that human will, left to itself in its fallen state, can always mingle together with God's Will so that they can act upon one another in harmony. No chance in a million years - except the will of man is given over to God as the perfect Will. God chooses to freely allow human will to come into conjunction with the Divine Will. By submission or submersion, willingly turning itself over to the sovereign Will of God, both can end up in the practical out-working of the Kingdom.

The Divine Will must direct and limit our will, even in our freedom. The limit of our misuse of the power of our will can only be brought about by dread and reverence from being submitted and submerged to the greater Will of God. The disturbance of the outer world is never the limit on human will. God, as God, puts a limit on human will. Thus, our will is only truly free in relation to the connection to God's nature.

Resting In Divine Will

The internal connection of Divine Will to our will, so to possesses unlimited freedom of resolution of the battle within and without, can only come by the united stability of our personal will resting on the broad security of the foundation of Divine goodwill. It is only in this link of Will to will that we find the perpetual Will of God combined with our will of effective Godly life. Only God's Will is sufficient cause. It has the capacity to combine the manifold waves of our being in relationship with the ultimate. God's Will is the clear pipeline of communicative holy actions. The Will of God, combined with the submitted will of man, makes possible an interaction with the world which leads to righteousness and transformation.

It is this will, submitted in prayer to the Will of God, that is the principle of resolution of our existential crisis. God's Will and our will in prayer affects our motivation. Accordingly, our will must come under critical examination. The truth is, that for the sake of emotional convenience, many of us do not regard our will with intense examination. Thus, we miss how the failure or weakening of the will may actually be a hindrance to our understanding of the motives that lay behind our actions or desires. We can become acquainted with our will by exercising keen observation of our choices and the inner processes by which they are made. We cannot allow ourselves to disregard the process of our will, because the influence of our will on our mind and body requires serious attention. The work we must do on our will must focus on how we allow our thoughts to flow through the various levels of our consciousness. All that comes in time and space and passes through the channel of the will is not necessarily good for us. So we must submit our will to God by praying *"Your will, not mine, be done."*

It is by the act of will that attention is given, sustained and applied to the thought life and the spiritual life. The permission of the will at the helm of human choice allows the sanctification of our acts. It is wrong to describe the will as a blind faculty. If left to itself, it will choose the easiest act and the quicker process without considering the impact on the whole person. It is the springboard, the root from which speculative thought finds its bearing. I admit with Dun Scotus that the will is an integral part of all that flows into human thought and its outcome. It is, therefore, rational at its very roots.

The Will of God

Now, let's ask the second question posed in the beginning of this chapter. What really is the Will of God? The question makes it seem that Will is a possession which God "has", as one may possess an object. That would be the wrong way to view God's Will. His Will is the most universal characteristic manifestation of who God is. It expresses the very essence of God as God. It is His Will that God seeks to express everywhere in all that He does - with terrestrial as well as celestial life, in Heaven and Earth. Will in God is indeed the creative universal element which gives purpose and fulfillment to all which exists. As there is one God, so there is one absolute WILL. The Will of God is the foundation of creation, as well as the process and destiny of that created world. God's Will, as the heart of nature and ideals, exists for the manifestation of the Kingdom of God. One can note the centrality of the Will in the phrase "*your kingdom come, **Your will be done**, on earth as it is in Heaven.*" The manifestation of the Kingdom of God is dependent on God's Will being done on Earth. It is the alignment and interweaving of His Will between the Heavens and the Earth - by the act of His created beings - that releases the Kingdom principle upon the Earth.

We know that "*in the beginning was the word*," - but before the beginning was Will and in the end shall be Will. Will is foundational and 'teleological' (focused on purpose). The word is the instrument for the expression of the Will of God. Words are spoken as afterthought. The process might be stated / visualized like this:

Being ⟶ Will ⟶ Word ⟶ Act

The Will of God is the before and behind of all creation. Thus our perfection and wholeness are bound up with the Will of God. We can press beyond the veil of creation into other dimensions only by His Will. Human beings need the Will of God to manifest their Divine destiny. Their true destiny is bound in it. We must learn to pray as the Lord prayed, "*Not my will but yours be done.*"

It is clear that man is not willing to relinquish his will. Those who have tapped into the power of God are those who learned to say, "*Not my will but yours be done.*" This is why Heaven was so open to the Lord Jesus Christ. He did not do just what He willed, He willed what the Father willed - even when it conflicted with the humanity He has taken upon Himself.

The question arises: If this Will of God is so good for humanity, why do human beings insist on doing their own will to their own hurt? What is wrong with human will? Why do human beings not live out this prayer for God's Will to flow into their sphere from some place called Heaven so that they may experience the bountiful, victorious life God has promised? Good questions. The reasons stem from the condition of the human will.

The Problem with Natural Human Will

St. Augustine, one of the African fathers of the Christian Church, wrote extensively on the natural will of the human being and its problem. In the "Confessions," Augustine states the natural man has **an infirmed will**:

> *For the will commands that there be a will - not another but itself. But it does not command entirely, therefore that is not what it commands. For were it entire, it would not even command it to be because it will already be. It is therefore, no monstrous thing partly to will, partly to be unwilling, but an infirmity of the mind. That it does not wholly rise, sustained by truth, pressed down by custom. And so there are two wills because one of them is not entire and the one is supplied with what the other needs.*[9]

Several things we grasp from Augustine regarding the infirmity of the human will. The will is not a cohesive force. The will is double-minded. It is not sustained by truth. That is, the human will rises by lying to itself because it is pressed down by human tradition. Augustine also states that the human will is perverted and bent aside from God. Augustine says he *"inquired what iniquity was and ascertained it not to be a substance, but a perversion of the will, bent aside from thee, O God, the Supreme substance..."* [10] The infirmity of the human will is the burden which humanity must bear until the will surrenders itself to the Will of God. Says Augustine, *"The virtue of that which makes the body, which becomes holy by virtue of the holiness of the **will**, the consent of the **will** to an evil deed makes it a sin."* [11] He suggests, *"In the supreme Will of God resides the power, which acts on all created spirits... [humans] are God's enemy not through their power to hurt him but through their **will** to oppose Him."* [12]

Becoming Universal Benevolence

This line of the Lord's Prayer goes directly against the deficiency of the will which breeds evil. The defect of the will is its misalignment or rebellious opposition to God's Will. The natural man's will can be deceitful and can harbor a subjective self-deceit in opposition to the life and ways of the Holy Spirit. Self-will can be carnal and often opposes God. Self-direction can be self-praising and can seek to dethrone God. This has nothing in common with the will that belongs to the Divine sphere, interwoven into the Will of God. The natural man's will fights with how and why the Will of God is expressed, and opposes the direction and purpose of the Divine Will.

As the Will of God is expressed in commandments, the will of the natural man influencing the mind requires the mind to be moral (which it was meant to be). But it cannot, because it sits in opposition to God's Will. Since the will in opposition to God acts only in its self-interest, it cannot enter into "the state of universal and disinterested benevolence." Since this is the foundation of true holiness, the will in rejecting Will, annuls the character of His heart. Since love is the fulfilling of the Law, and thus the conformity of will to God's intrinsic nature, the will of natural man fails because it does not choose love. In fact, it chooses to hate all - even itself in the end. The natural man's will does not choose divine things for their own sake. Instead, he wills them according to the temporal value they seem to have for him.

The issue of will is among the foundational distinctions between the Spirit-ruled life and the worldly life. The natural will stands contrary to the Will of God. It starts the carnality of the mind making one insincere in their relationship with God and men. This will has no confidence in the wisdom of the love of God. It does not believe that God is wise enough and good enough, and so is afraid to pray that God's Will be done universally. Because the natural will sits is on control over all the issues of it being blocked from submission to the Will of God, it has no right to pray, "*Your will be done on earth as it is in Heaven.*" It does not believe Him. Any such petition is mockery of the Divine Will. The natural will is replete with unbelief. It does not seek to depend on grace that makes provision. By doing its own desire it hopes to accomplish utopia on Earth. The natural will is like the builders of Babel seeking, by the power of the will, to accomplish what is done in Heaven on Earth.

Since the will of the natural man is undergirded by unbelief and not faith, its melody is out of tune. Human will, out of sync with Divinity, is downright rebellion in which man seeks to be God. The natural will thinks it is unfair for God to require people to surrender, heartily consent to and acquiesce to the Will of God. Since willing and doing are naturally connected, it means the natural man has **bad will**

> *The human will is so powerful; nothing can stand in its way when it is full of forcefulness. The will is a pervasive power over the soul which determines purpose and destiny.*

which results in acts that offer an insincere offering. This actually keeps Heaven from manifesting on Earth in their life! If the will is in sincere conformity and synchronized with the Holy Spirit, everything else that is under the control of the will - that is the body, the soul, and all the emotions and activities - must of necessity obey this state of the will.

Natural Man's Will is 'Will to Unbelief'

Natural man is inclined to disbelief and misbelieving, discrediting, discordance, infidelity to God, dissension, stubbornly held opinions, and passive inaction in the things of God. A powerful way to deal with this tendency of unbelief is to sincerely pray, "*Your will be done on earth as it is in Heaven.*" The Lord Jesus Christ, in speaking to the father of the young man who was epileptic said, "*If you believe, all things are possible to him that believes.*" The unnatural natural man's will is steeped in unbelief and, therefore, 1 Corinthians 2:14 (NKJV) states, "*But the natural man does not receive the things of the Spirit of God, for they are foolishness to him; nor can he know them, because they are spiritually discerned.*"

Deification of Will

There is nothing more pervasive and fundamental to the malfunction of the natural will than unbelief. When human will is not joined with the Will of God, it creates opposition to divine command and purposes. Unbelief is structured opposition to the Divine presentation of Himself. The will in opposition to God creates a situation where its presumption of God's lack of good will is emphasized. In fact, God's good intentions are overshadowed by man seeking to be god over God. This deification of personal will allows the self to act contrary to God. It believes itself to be greater bearer of a good will greater God!

> *It is in the human will that Wisdom finds itself concealed, waiting to flow out in Understanding, Knowledge and action.*

Despite its limitation in not understanding anything beyond its immediate context, natural will continues to believe itself to be more interested in its own salvation than God! One of the determining qualities of natural man's will is the insistence to walk by sight and not obey faith. One might argue that man's will is not so much infected by unbelief than it is seduced by misplaced belief - belief on self - allowing itself to be dazzled by the illusion of its self-importance. Unbelief comes as the unwillingness to trust God's power. Unbelief restricts the power and goodness of God by the power and goodness of fallen man. Its perception of God's power addresses itself to the perceived failure of God to act in good faith.

Rejecting The Son

The Scripture says, "*He who believes in Him is not judged; he who does not believe has been judged already, because he has not believed in the name of the only begotten Son of God. This is the judgment, that the Light has come into the world, and men loved the darkness rather than the Light, for their deeds were evil."* (John 3:18-19. KJV).

There is probably no more powerful place to see the power of man's will to believe or not believe than this acceptance of Jesus, His Son. This choice gives its assent or refusal to God's process, nature and purpose. Yes, even to God Himself. The will to unbelief does show itself as the denial of God as God. The refusal to assent and accept God's mode of salvation is in His Messiah Yeshua. Jesus is the stumbling block.

The will to unbelief also shows in the denial of God's power in practical situations such as the healing of the body, deliverance from our situation, reconciliation, forgiveness, and transformative involvement of God in the plain of human existence. Spurgeon puts it this way; unbelief is:

> *The Monarch sin, the quintessence of guilt, the mixture of venom of all crimes, the dreg of wine of Gomorrah. It is the A1 sin, the masterpiece of Satan, the chief work of the devil.* [13]

Unbelieving Believers

When we speak of the 'will to unbelief', we are saying that the natural man's will leans on human understanding. It bypasses Divine inspiration as expressed in Scripture and that which the Spirit of God calls to remembrance in the inner person. In the natural man, we find the will to unbelief in the refusal to believe God's revelation about himself. Instead he makes his tainted human experience the fulcrum on which he seeks to stand and rotate judgmentally the annals of eternity. What folly!

The natural man, of course, will not worship God fully. Rather, he feigns halfhearted worship to appease his conscience. The believer who is churched may think he is excluded from such a class of people. Unfortunately, unbelief is not the sole possession of the unchurched. Halfhearted worship and halfhearted commitment to the things of God are expressions of unbelief. For if we believed what the Lord says of Himself and us, how can we be less than passionate about the things which are in the heart of God. One place of course where this will to unbelief is manifest in believers is the area of witnessing for Christ. Lack of passionate posture for the things of God can be traced in this 'will to unbelief', even in believers. Of course, this will to unbelief breeds insensitivity to the Holy Spirit.

Another area of unbelief is that of worry. The will to unbelief says, *"God promised to take care of me, but if I do not do it myself, God will fail me!"* Of course, many believers will just say, "*I have to do something,*" but this worry about the future moves it to a denial of God as God. Unbelief says, "*I am my own god, I make my way in the universe; God cares not for my well-being, in fact, if He does, He only cares so superficially that I must augment His action. Otherwise, I will find myself left in the lurch by an uncaring god.*" Of course, we do not say it so clearly, but our mode of operation leads to this conclusion. Whether we accept it or not, worry and anxiety are the tendency of natural man's will to unbelief. Unbelief leaves man's well-being in its own power - and what a pitiable power it is!

Because this will of natural man to unbelief denies God His rightful place, man must try by his limited means to keep his heart. Being saturated with fear, he will have failed to take a courageous stand in God and is now threatened with annihilation unless he finds some refuge of lies in which to keep himself. The will to unbelief puts man at a disadvantage for he committed what is precious and of eternal value into the transient hand of a dying, carnal god-man. Lack of faith in the God - to whom every commitment is eternally secured - causes one to be perpetually unsafe, in his own hands.

Natural Man's Will Is 'Will to Create Bad Will'

The will in man is the key to the communicative process between the various dimensions of the human person. Where there is bad will, good dies and becomes evil, reason becomes arrogant, imagination becomes corrupted and action flows in the river of '*not-God*'!

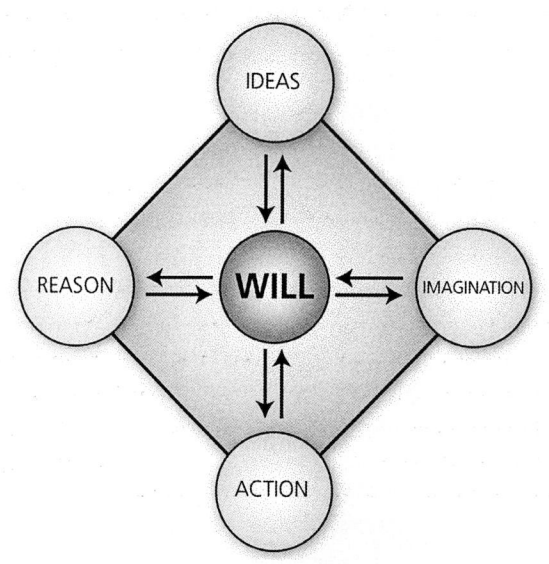

In the natural, the will distracts the mind, incapacitates reason, restricts action toward that which is good, and defiles even the best of ideas by its presumptive majesty. In so doing, it divides itself against itself - so that on the one hand it wills, but on the other hand un-wills! By this can *"the whole will may be bound which before was divided into many."* [14]

Life and Death

It is part of human will to rebel. It is from the corruption of the will of man that the works of the flesh flow. Romans 1 makes it clear that most, if not all of our sins, derive from our refusal to acknowledge God as God. When the will blocks the flow of the Divine Will, the flesh turns in on itself and works without the aid of the animating power of the Holy Spirit. The flesh then proceeds to balance evil with evil. It is unloving because God, who is love, is left out. This unloving nature is balanced not with good but with lack of mercy. Thus, on the one side, the fleshly person is not only unloving but unmerciful. The desires of the flesh go to the extreme where the will is shut God out. This flesh eating upon itself leads to the depravity of the mind, which then flows out in wickedness.

Because the Will of God is not there to serve as a closure valve, the desire of the flesh becomes greed and leads to evil acts. Furthermore, greed leads to envy and envy leads to strife - which ultimately leads to murder in some cases. In my opinion, every human war has underlying greed, not righteousness. Where there is strife, there is deceit. Where there is deceit, there is malice, and there also we find gossip and slander and insolence. Paul tells us that these are the results of God hating, boastful arrogance that leads to rebellion against God constituted authorities and the invention of evil. These all led to death. Finally, the understanding is darkened. This means that Paul is expanding his exegesis of corrupt human will which he began in Romans 1.

The will of man then is encapsulated in death and cannot give forth true life in its separation from God. The descent of the will of man into death infects the soul and body of man. The will of man denies not only the glory of God, but also its own glory. The will is the eye and, when it closes, it turns to infernal darkness. The natural will travels away from above and abandons everything that is available to it in God. When away from God, it penetrates the depths of ignorance and darkness. Wrapped in darkness, it is unable to perceive intelligently or to contemplate the beauty of Divinity from which it is hewn. The corrupt will is more than just bad, it presides over infernal ignorance and fleshly works. Though it may not embody absolute corruption, in denying God, it only finds its mystical ecstasy in sexual desires. It shuns the light and embraces destructive darkness.

Human will, in its natural state, cannot transcend its fleshly dimension. It is incapable of pure movement in the direction of Divinity. The natural man's will is filled with fear, not of God but of its own demise and disappearance, ever searching but never finding itself. The will that is subjected to the Holy Spirit of God brings joy, true happiness (in the Greek, **μακάριος,** *makarios*), and deep divine fulfillment. The will of this natural man penetrates the body, soul and thought with *not-God*. The natural will **is the will to death**. It must submit to the Will of God to receive life and to be life-giving.

According to the Lord's Prayer, there are two spheres in which the Will of God is to be done. The Kingdom of God is the necessary structure within which the human will acts and finds cohesion and meaning. However, the *coming* of the Kingdom depends on the Will of God being manifested through man on Earth. This prayer is so powerful because it opens our inner man to the dimensions of Heaven, allows us to peer into it, see the will of God being done and transfer that process into our sphere!

HEAVEN: THE SECOND MENTION

This Heaven (singular), where the will of God is done, is the Heaven which Jacob saw in his dream of the ladder connected Earth and Heaven (Genesis 28:12). This is the Heaven of the presence of the Lord, at whose feet we kneel to climb the ladder of faith. Our souls open up to that Heaven by doing the Will of our Father. Jesus told us that He is the Divine stairway - The Way. Because God is our Father, the passage is graciously opened for us to enter the realm where the 'Dominion Promises' of Genesis 1:26 is made manifest in our lives. Here, everything is opened to us. Through our Lord Jesus Christ, the city - where the angels serve and angelic commerce goes on between the upper and the lower kingdoms - shall be made more manifest to us.

Heaven Is Our Archetype

So when we pray "*on earth as it is in heaven*" in this second mention of Heaven, we ask that God, from whom Heaven proceeds, should be seen here on Earth. Since it is used in the 'dative masculine singular', it conveys the idea that Heaven is the means by which God's will is done on Earth. The wide varieties of activities which take place in Heaven serve as the archetype of what must take place on the Earth. Heaven must take personal interest and become the reference point for all Earthly activities. God uses Heaven as a means to move the Earth to do His will.

Heaven, according to this prayer and many other passages of Scripture, is the place where God is and where the Divine presence is clearly manifest as far as creatures can handle it. Heaven is regarded as the abode of God, the point from which God affects the world as a king form his throne affects his entire kingdom. Heaven is considered the habitation of YHVH in Solomon's prayer at the inauguration of the Temple. Seven times Solomon beckons YHVH to hear from Heaven, locating God in Heaven. We must be careful here to note that Solomon also says, "*behold the Heaven of the Heavens cannot contain you.*" This makes it appear that the use of Heaven as a location for God is metaphorical and is meant to give us the understanding that God's power is loftier than we can grasp. God's presence is unhindered in its manifestation, with no part of creation separated from God's holy presence (Genesis 24:7). He is called "*The LORD God of Heaven.*" The Scripture also states "*The Heavens declare your glory.*" Heaven is the arena of the manifestation of the declarative glory of God.

It is essential to know that in Heaven the glory of God is clearly manifest. Heaven represents the clear and unhindered brightness of God's glory. In the presence of that glory, celestial beings render to Him unfeigned reverence, worship, and adoration. There, the renown of God is proclaimed without injury to His character by the serpent's forked tongue.

> Heaven and Earth, life and death, center on two words: yes and no. This is the declaration of the will in its fundamental freedom.

From Heaven, God reveals and manifests His Will through the Kingdom (whose subjects have no more inclination to mutiny). To God's creatures, Heaven is the sphere which represents the ideal atmosphere that they all aspire to manifest in their temporal contexts - for us, Heaven on Earth. To lay open the Heavens is to have apprehended the place from which 'the fullness of all that is God' lays hidden. This is what Jesus came preaching and what was established by His life, death, resurrection, and the Pentecostal outpouring during the feast of *shvout (שבועות)*. The part of the prayer which our Lord taught us to pray which goes "*our Father which art in Heaven,*" is deeply relational and at the heart of why God gave His Son.

Heaven is Our Home

If our birth is by the Heavens, then our home even now is in Heaven - though not physically. In our spirit, we dwell there as often as the King, who is our Father, gives us access. So when this prayer is echoed in our soul, it is not just that God our Father dwells in Heaven, but that we ourselves have our home with Him (1 Corinthians 15:49). In His blessedness, God our Father through our Lord Jesus Christ, has blessed us not just with the Heavenly birth but located us in the Heavenly places in Christ. This is a choice which God makes by His sovereign Will and it is part of the foundation of the world. Until we find our location in the Heavens with our Father, the world "without" will remain in bondage. God loves us enough to place within us Heaven and yet to prepare a place for us to spend with Him in Heaven.

One who is adapted to sonship, as we have been adapted through Jesus Christ to himself, enjoys the pleasure of the Father's presence in Heaven though he remains on Earth. "*Who are in Heaven*" is a statement not only of where God is, but where we come to rest as those bought by the Blood and born by the Spirit. Our accepted location is in Christ who is in Heaven (Ephesians 1:3–6). This is a mystery, yet by the Scripture we know that spiritually we are located with God in the Heavens, not as equals but as sons and daughters of God's joy. For we read in Ephesians 2:4–6 (NKJV),

> *But God, who is rich in mercy, because of His great love with which He loved us, [5] even when we were dead in trespasses, made us alive together with Christ (by grace you have been saved), 6 and **raised us up together, and made us sit together in the Heavenly places in Christ Jesus**. (emphasis added)*

Our Father Is In Heaven

Our Father is in Heaven, therefore we who are now partakers of His nature have been made holy, and we partake in the Heavenly dwelling where we sit with Christ Jesus - our Apostle and the High Priest of our confession (Hebrews 3:1). When we confess Christ as Savior, we are translated spiritually to where Christ dwells. The mystery is that there is mutual relocation in which Christ moves into us and we move into Him. Where He is, there we are also! Being children of the Father, in prayer we are in the habit of tasting the Heavenly gift and partaking of the wine of the Holy Spirit. We are in fellowship with the Heavens. In Heaven, we are located beyond the veil which Christ, through the tearing of His body, had torn asunder. In fact, in describing our location, the writer of Hebrews says:

> *But you (we) have come to Mount Zion and to the city of the living God, the heavenly Jerusalem, and to myriads of angels, to the general assembly and church of the firstborn who are enrolled in heaven, and to God, the Judge of all, and to the spirits of the righteous made perfect, and to Jesus, the mediator of a new covenant, and to the sprinkled blood, which speaks better than the blood of Abel.*
> (Hebrews 12:22–24)

Jerusalem which is above is free and is the mother of us all (Galatians 4:26). Thus, Heaven is the place from which we came and are located and it is where we will go. From the original text, we see that the Hebrew הַשָּׁמַיִם (*hashamayim*) and Greek οὐρανοῖς (*ouranois*) are not what is used in the second mention in the Lord's Prayer. We have seen that its singular 'Heaven' is not the general concept of galaxies, but a wonderful idea, place and goal, high and holy, existing for those who have been liberated from the power of darkness and born as sons and daughters into the family of God. It is the peaceful and harmonious place where God rules without sinful interruption. It is the ultimate expression of the redeeming and preserving power of God. It is the τέλος (*telos*) - the end and the undeviating goal of God's goodwill toward man. It is a gracious patrimony, a chief part of God's purpose in redeeming man for Himself so that man might have a place and be in a place.

We consider ourselves being the habitation of God, where God lives. We can find that our inner identity flows from this eternal location called Heaven that is in God. There is a common confusion in the common parlance of 'paradise', 'Eden' and 'Heaven'. In the end, Heaven as we pray it, is the habitation of essential goodness. It would not be extreme to describe it as God, as God is in His internal relation as Father, Son and Holy Spirit. In every respect, Heaven is the summation of all that is beautiful, the culmination of sufficiency both for reason and for passion. It is that which is ever new and ever gives birth to the new Earth. It is the place where love and communion are a supreme principle. Heaven is fellowship with God in all its fullness. So true believers have intense feelings of being attracted and turned toward it. We pray *"who art in Heaven,"* that our whole being may bend toward that place of perfection, divine nobility, spiritual purity, continual godly delightful pleasure, and unending glory which flows from our Father, who is there.

In Heaven, there are no more:

- Processes, permanence instead
- Strivings, as beatific vision instead
- Separations, union with our Father instead
- Sorrows, eternal joy instead
- Rough seas, the sea of glass instead
- Tears, laughter and all tears are wiped away instead
- Manmade temples, for God Himself is the temple
- Days of burning hot sun, for God Himself shall be the light
- People suffering from mental illness, for God shall be the perfect sanity of the people
- Wars, for the God of peace shall be at the heart of the people

- Deaths, for the fount of life is there
- Lies, for the truth is the center there
- People wandering astray, for the Way and the destination are there

Our Father God is there in Heaven.

It is to that Heaven that we direct this line of prayer *"Your will be done, As in heaven so on earth."* God's Will is done in that sphere called Heaven, which is Eden, the birth place of the New City of God called the New Jerusalem. We know that place is different from the general Heavens because, in the general Heavens, stars eat up one another, chaos reigns and death is on every hand. The will of God is done in this particular Heaven, as we read in Psalm 148.

First is the sphere of the Heavens of Divine delight. Using Psalm 148, one may extract the specific topography of the Will of God as manifested in praise. The Will of God in the Heavens is done first in the heights, second by the angels, third by the hosts, fourth by great lights (sun and moon), and by the stars of light, fifth by the highest Heavens, and sixth by the waters above the Heavens. The Will of God is done in Heaven according to the prayer that Jesus taught us. In the Heavenly dimensions, God's Will is done perfectly. The Heavens and their occupants know perfectly what the Will of God is, for they gaze upon the glory of God's nature daily. In this knowledge of the glory, they do not seek to deviate from the nature of God or from the purpose of God. They combine the nature and purpose of God in an unbroken flow and submersion of their will to the Will of God.

> Divinity. Inside our will, this Divinity lies dormant. Dammed up in this reservoir is the Kingdom of Heaven, waiting to flow powerfully into the world.

The heights do not seek to be low. The angels seek clearly to manifest the nature of God and God's purpose, as far as we know. The hosts of Heaven do the same. The sun has never stopped ruling the day or sought to rule the night. It has remained constant in attachment to the nature and purpose to which God created it, not by will but by mechanical conformity to the laws of creation. The same can be said of the moon and the stars. Those among the Heavens that are sentient beings have the capacity to grow in their knowledge of God, because they do not know all of God as they are not God. In their expanding revelation of God, their good will and intention are continually conformed to do the Will of God. They have passed the point of continually choosing for they have arrived at the place of perfect conformity to the Will of God. But human beings must increasingly submit their will to God as God reveals to them greater dimensions of His redemption plan. They must choose continually to submerge their will into the Will of God. Charles G. Finney stated that *"the obedience of Heaven, therefore, must keep pace with their increasing knowledge, and therefore its inhabitants must continually grow in holiness."* Their whole being cries out *"Your will be done; They will alone is goodwill, O Lord of Hosts."*

GOD'S WILL IN THE SPHERE OF THE EARTH

On Earth, there are 24 spheres or locations of the Will of God which represents the sphere of Earthly creation. These 24 spheres of the manifestation of the Will of God are:

    1. Earth, 2. Sea monsters, 3. All deeps, 4. Fire,

    5. Hail, 6. Snow, 7. Clouds, 8. Stormy winds,

    9. Mountains, 10. Hills, 11. Fruit trees, 12. Cedars,

    13. Beasts, 14. Cattle, 15. Creeping things, 16. Winged fowls,

    17. Kings, 18. All peoples, 19. Princes, 20. Judges,

    21. Young men, 22. Virgins, 23. Old Men, 24. Children.

Of these 24, 16 are aligned with God's Will, eight are misaligned with the Will of God. The last eight involve Adam who needs circumcision of the heart and surrender of the will. Adam is king in the sphere of the Earth. He is cause of the 16 elements' movement from their original submission to the Will of God and, thus, distorts their divinely ordained purpose. People are the ones who stand in competition with the praise of the Lord. Therefore the psalmist ends the psalm with the command,

> *"**Let** them praise the name of the Lord, For His name alone is exalted; His glory is above earth and heaven."*
> (Psalm 148:13, emphasis added).

We as people must say *"Your Will ,not my will"* in order to open up the dimensions that are hidden within this Heaven. They must **"*LET*"**. In Heaven, the Will of God does not necessarily obstruct the will of angels, so on Earth we must understand that the Will of God is not intended to obstruct or destroy the will of man. It is the will of man that often stands in the way of the full implementation of the Will of God within the sphere, which God gave to man. The Will of God satisfies the requirement of fulfillment connected with the fact that the Will of God is good. In God, knowledge and action are intimately related. The will of man even stands against his own soul. So when we pray, *"Your will be done"*, we prophesy our submission to God and as a result prepare our body to shift dimensions.

God's Will Is Always Good

Will and knowledge are connected in God because they serve as a fulcrum for the turning of the wheel of Divine goodness, mercy and justice. Thus, God's Will is always **GOOD WILL**. The Will of God, being good will, cannot allow for a mere imaginary and partial process, lacking authentic and transformative acts. It must work itself out in full Kingdom manifestation and can only do so in the interim by the alignment of human will with the Eternal Will of God. If one claims to be in the Will of God, one cannot act in such a way that the interest of the Kingdom of the Lord God is denied or betrayed. Non-Kingdom acts that claim to be in the Will of God must be rejected as falsities and demonic usurpation of the Divine right by archetypal evil.

Where the Will of God is present, the Kingdom of God comes. Certainly no secondary will can serve as substitute for God's Will, yet the obvious denial of the Will of God within any context can be evidenced by the absence of the signs of the Kingdom of God. We need to know God's Will. The knowledge of the Will of God makes possible the manifestation of the Kingdom in our daily lives and in our families, communities and world. The Will of God should not be confused in any way the ritualized formula so common among religious people. Far from it, many of the formula avoid the Will of God and do not seek to manifest the Kingdom of God but the emotional and sentimental kingdom of man.

It needs to be mentioned that though there are similarities between the Will of God and the will of man, there ought to be no confusion about the infinite gap that divides them. The Divine must Himself come to bridge them. Of course, the Will of God, as has been noted, is the basis of God's absolute sovereignty over all creation. Here, we enter not into the philosophical **why** of *theodicy* - understanding Divine providence in the presence of evil in the world. Suffice it to say that evil has its origin in will. Not the immediate Will of God, but secondary will over which God has willfully given to free agents. The Will of God is intrinsic to God's nature from the fundamental goodness, holiness, compassion, creativity, and all that may rightly be attributed to His character. As motivation, Will in God motions in the direction of God's glory and good pleasure (Ephesians 1).

The problem we, as human beings, have is that our wills can never be stopped when it is in one's intrinsic will to do something. Yet there seems in our world to be many troublesome things which we suppose God does not will that are being forced upon God as His weakness or carelessness. Please note, even though these issues may appear to human beings as the weakness of Divine Will, that man's will seems to supersede God's, yet it is intended willfully by God to put to shame the strong (1 Corinthians). Furthermore, as believers know in some cases, God allows

His Will to be influenced or affected by the prayer of His human beings, as in the case of Moses and the Children of Israel, Nineveh, and other instances. Yet it must be remembered that this is not a forcing of God by an external force to change, but an intrinsic will to will influence by God, in God and through God. The Will of God carries with it purpose, and this is summarized in the eternity of God in which God knows everything at once and not in succession.

The Will of God is always accomplished; that of man is often defeated. His Will does not change because of the flux of time. Since God knows everything in advance, God is in the best place to deal with our confusion in time and flux and failure which our weaknesses will causes us. He sees all at once.

DIMENSIONS OF THE WILL OF GOD

It is the Will of God for us to be delivered from this present evil world. According to Galatians 1:4, Yeshua the Messiah *"gave himself for our sins, that he might deliver us from this present evil world, according to the will of God and our Father,"* (KJV). Undoubtedly the Will of God is to deliver humanity from sin and evil. The story of the bondage of humanity to the shackles of evil is written on every page of Scripture and upon the scroll of history - it needs no rehearsing here.

Deliverance Is God's Will

Deliverance from evil is so vital to the Will of God that the Lord Jesus taught us to pray *"deliver us from evil."* The Hebrew word **hawvy** (pronounced "yeshuw'ah") is something that happens to one, from the exercise of another, meaning to be saved or to preserve something from negative influence. This deliverance leads to health and provides help by saving one. The other implied meanings derived from it are: to be delivered from a corner, to give to someone in times of need, and give victory over difficult circumstances. This is no partial victory but a victory that is total and complete. It also implies prosperity or a deliverance from poverty and lack. So when John says, *"I wish that you prosper and be in good health even as your soul prospers,"* he is drawing from the Hebrew idea of salvation as a Divine event affecting the physical and spiritual sphere of human lives.

> *Our will, content with unrestricted freedom of choice, stands as gatekeeper over all other faculty of being, owning none yet controlling all by its majesty. Accordingly, we must flee to a greater will.*

So if deliverance is the Will of God, why is everyone not delivered? Rightly asked! The key lies in the alignment of the human will and the Will of God which we have considered at length in this chapter. If sin is a dealt issue, as Paul and Augustine argued, why not will? Part of the lack of deliverance in the world can be attributed to the fact that human will is not united in alignment with the Will of God. When God speaks in the Scripture of His people, there is an emphasis on the unity of that body - this unity must be a spiritual unity which leads us to the idea of unity of will. That is why Jesus Himself says, "*If two of you shall agree.*" At another place, He says, "*...where two or three.*" The human will, in its fallen natural state, is self-seeking, self-deifying and antagonistic to one anothe. What God intends is that the good Will of God pervade humanity in such a way that all humans will join as one. They then begin to manifest God's good intention and purpose in the world. In Heaven, there is a seamless flow of the will of its inhabitants into the Will of God. There is now no friction between the Will of God and the will of the angels, hence, David says, "*You angels who do His will.*"

Deliverance is for The Community

God uses individuals to activate deliverance but the target of that deliverance is very seldom an individual. In a sense, it is the will of human beings coming in submission to the Will of God, for the Will of God is deliverance that calls for the deliverer. In Exodus 3, God (Elohim) says to Moses, "*I have seen the suffering of my people and their cry has come before me.*" The will of the people (at least a majority of them) was united in the direction of deliverance, thereby aligning with the Will of God. Deliverance is a communal and Kingdom principle. The target has always been the community. For the deliverance of the individual to be truly secured, there must be a community of delivered persons standing with the person. When God delivered Joseph, the goal was the preservation of people. "*God sent me before you to preserve for you a remnant in the earth, and to keep you alive by a great deliverance.*" (Genesis 45:7).

> *All that comes in time and space and passes through the channel of the will is not necessarily good for us. So we must submit our will to God by praying "Your will, not mine, be done."*

In Judges 15:18, when God uses Samson, He does so for the deliverance of the people. When Samson prays, we see the has already began to misunderstand the purpose of God for his life and was using his deliverance as an opportunity for a personal vendetta. "*Then he became very thirsty, and he called to the Lord and said, "You have given this great deliverance by the hand of Your servant, and now shall I die of thirst and fall into the hands of the uncircumcised?*" Joseph's deliverance from prison would have been empty had Israel not been delivered also. In Second Kings 5:1, the purpose of the LORD's use of Naaman was to bring great deliverance unto Syria. The arrow of the Lord's deliverance which Elisha orders the king of Israel to shoot eastward is directed at deliverance of Israel as people (2 Kings 13:17). The deliverance from enemies in the Old Testament is never merely the enemy of an individual. In most cases, what was at stake was the survival of Israel as the paradigm of the Kingdom of God. Individuals come as deliverer, but their act of deliverance is always geared to the people as a whole, as we find in Esther 4:14, *"For if you remain silent at this time, relief and deliverance will arise for the Jews from another place and you and your father's house will perish. And who knows whether you have not attained royalty for such a time as this?"* When we read in Psalm 18:50, *"He gives great deliverance to His king, and shows lovingkindness to His anointed, to David and his descendants forever,"* it is to the king as the embodiment of the community.

We read in Joel 2:32, *"And it will come about that whoever calls on the name of the Lord will be delivered; for on Mount Zion and in Jerusalem there will be those who escape, as the Lord has said, even among the survivors whom the Lord calls."* In Joel, where the deliverance starts from the individual, it ends in its perfection by being in the holy city and ending in the remnant which is the community of the preserved. Here is deliverance as described by Obadiah 1:17: *"But on Mount Zion there will be those who escape, and it will be holy. and the house of Jacob will possess their possessions."* This is territorial deliverance, resulting in territorial holiness leading to kingdom possession. The essential task of the Messianic process is the complete deliverance of the people who enter into the Messianic community. The ten sets of acts which the Messiah carries our for the establishment of the Kingdom are all about deliverance (as narrated in Isaiah 61).

APOSTOLICITY IS BY GOD'S WILL

Apostolic ministry is the Will of God for the church, so by praying "Your will be done," we activate apostolicity. And one cannot be an apostle except by the Will of God, as Paul so often states it in the New Testament. At least five times Paul mentions apostolic calling and the Will of God in the same breath:

> *Paul, called as an apostle of Jesus Christ by the will of God, and Sosthenes our brother.*
> (1 Corinthians 1:1)

> *Paul, an apostle of Christ Jesus by the will of God, and Timothy our brother. To the church of God which is at Corinth with all the [a]saints who are throughout Achaia.*
> (2 Corinthians 1:1)

Paul, an apostle of Christ Jesus by the will of God. To the saints who are at Ephesus and who are faithful in Christ Jesus"
(Ephesians 1:1)

"Paul, an apostle of Jesus Christ by the will of God, and Timothy our brother"
(Colossians 1:1)

"Paul, an apostle of Christ Jesus by the will of God, according to the promise of life which is in Christ Jesus"
(2 Timothy 1:1)

SANCTIFICATION IS THE WILL OF GOD

The idea of sanctification is often confused with the idea of holiness in the body of Christ. But there is a difference, based on the spelling in the Old Testament. The word *"sanctify"* is often translated in the Hebrew Scriptures of the First Covenant from the word קָדַשׁ *qadash* (pronounced "kaw-dash' "), which is a sense of causation. In many cases, a human being can sanctify, or make it so, by pronouncement or by ceremonial cleanliness. Sanctification can even be abstractly considered, though it does involve a sense of 'set apartness. It is 'set apartness' in which human beings can participate. It often grows out of the free will of the persons in setting themselves or something apart to God. God can also sanctify something by dedicating it Himself. The KJV is probably more accurate in this instance when it suggests that one can, by appointment, consecrate and dedicate a particular thing to be kept as holy or, by mere proclamation, purify a thing or an entity. While there is no absolute distinction between this, there is separation often made between this word and the other Old Testament word which is its derivative קֹדֶשׁ *qodesh* (pronounced "ko'desh"). Note the difference in spelling. This can refer to nouns, a sacred place or thing. It is never merely proclaimed upon a thing, but it is what a thing or one *is* by reason of its nature. The consecrated thing that is dedicated carries holiness because the God to which it is dedicated comes to take abode in it, transferring His intrinsic nature into the thing or person.

Sanctify Yourselves

In a sense, 'sanctification' is the process by which we separate unto God and 'holiness' is who we are as separated persons who now belong to God. I believe I am warranted in this interpretation by the phrasing of the verse from Leviticus 11:44:

For I am the Lord your God: ye shall therefore sanctify yourselves, **and ye**

shall be holy; *for I am holy: neither shall ye defile yourselves with any manner of creeping thing that creepeth upon the earth.*
(KJV, emphasis added)

In 1 Thessalonians 4:3 Paul says, *"For this is the will of God, your sanctification; that is, that you abstain from sexual immorality"* Our deliberate separation and removal of ourselves from immorality is in God's Will. In some cases, it is us who must separate ourselves from the context of this particular evil. In this case, our sanctification exemplifies the alignment of our will with the Will of God. In Exodus 13:2, God shows Israel this by asking them to *"Sanctify to Me every firstborn, the first offspring of every womb among the sons of Israel, both of man and beast; it belongs to Me."* Though they are God's, yet it is the act of sanctification by the parents and the owners of the animals that set them apart for God's use. The principle of sanctification as the Will of God is also revealed in Exodus 19:10 when we read, *"The Lord also said to Moses, "Go to the people and consecrate them today and tomorrow, and **let them** wash their garments."* In Exodus 19:22 we read, *"Also let the priests who come near to the LORD consecrate themselves, or else the Lord will break out against them."* It is interesting that the burden is placed on the human persons in these passages to sanctify them. The '***let***', as I have pointed out, is a call for the recipient to release their will for the designated purpose of God for a particular item or task.

In Exodus 19:23, Moses sanctifies the mountain. In Exodus 28:41, he consecrates and sanctifies Aaron and his sons to minister unto the priest's office. Upon their consecration, as we read in Exodus 29:27, Aaron sanctifies *"You shall consecrate the breast of the wave offering and the thigh of the heave offering which was waved and which was offered from the ram of [b] ordination, from the one which was for Aaron and from the one which was for his sons."* There is nowhere in Scripture where

His Will is the most universal characteristic manifestation of who God is. It expresses the very essence of God as God.

the involvement of a human agent in sanctification is more obvious than in the command which God gives in Exodus 29:36, *"Each day you shall offer a bull as a sin offering for atonement, and you shall purify the altar when you make atonement for it, and you shall anoint it to consecrate it."* The human being, in this case Moses, sanctifies the altar and God makes it holy. God transfers Divine holiness to the altar after man deliberately and speaks to him about voluntary setting himself apart to God. We also find this process in Exodus 29:37 where God says to Moses, *"For seven days you shall make atonement for the altar and consecrate it; then the altar shall be most holy, and whatever touches the altar shall be holy."* Exodus 40:13: *"You shall put the holy garments on Aaron and anoint him and consecrate him, that he may minister as a priest to Me."*

We read in Leviticus 8:11–12:

He sprinkled some of it on the altar seven times and anointed the altar and all its utensils, and the basin and its stand, to consecrate them. Then he poured some of the anointing oil on Aaron's head and anointed him, to consecrate him.

It is not oil that sanctified Aaron, but the act of obedience activating the oil and therefore activating Aaron. Because sanctification is the Will of God, when we pray *"Your will be done,"* we call upon God to sanctify us and our world. As we read in Exodus 29:44, God sanctified the tabernacle and the altar and the priests that ministered on that altar: *"And I will sanctify the tabernacle of the congregation, and the altar: I will sanctify also both Aaron and his sons, to minister to me in the priest's office."*

Separation is Continuous

The idea of separation is both singular and continuous. In several places in the Torah, God insists that Israel is continuously being separated by God unto God. Thus, there is continual affirmation of the holy status of Israel in the sight of God. For example, the Sabbath which Israel is commanded to keep continually is a reminder of this continuous set-apartness in which the Lord of the universe engages perpetually on behalf of Israel. Thus, it says in Exodus 31:13, *"But as for you, speak to the sons of Israel, saying, 'You shall surely observe My sabbaths; for this is a sign between Me and you throughout your generations, that you may know that I am the Lord who sanctifies you."* Though many times God says to Israel, *"Sanctify yourselves"* (Numbers 11:18; Joshua 3:5; 7:13; 1 Samuel 16:5; 1 Chronicles 15:12), yet in other places He says, *"I am the LORD which sanctify you"* (Leviticus 20:8; 21:8). In several other places especially in Leviticus He insists, *"For I the LORD do sanctify..."* (Leviticus 21:15; 21:23; 22:9, 22:16). When God sanctifies, He does so by His truth which is His word (John 17:17). The Lord said, *"Sanctify them in the truth; Your word is truth."*

If we consider it further, the Word and truth refer to the Messiah. We also know that it is the Will of God, because Jesus sanctified Himself to release truth for our sanctification. *"And for their sakes I sanctify myself, that they also might be sanctified through the truth"* (John 17:19). This is reiterated in Ephesians 5:26, *"That he might sanctify and cleanse it with the washing of water by the word."* The Will of God in this regard is so strong that Jesus also sanctified us with His own blood, suffering outside of the structures of this world. He was crucified outside of the gate of Jerusalem, putting Him beyond the judgmental structure of the present age.

Peter makes clear in 1 Peter 3:15 that this sanctification is directed at *"our hearts"* in such a way that it affects our willingness to respond to those who question the hope that is in us. If the way of the Kingdom of God has become our structure of consciousness, and the Will of God has been manifested in us, then the will gives forth meekness and fear in honor of God.

The Will of God for us is tied directly to service to the generation in which we live. It must be our prime goal that, before we die, we have done what God wills for our generation. Acts 13:36 says, *"For David, after he had served the purpose of God in his own generation, fell asleep, and was laid among his fathers and underwent decay."* But remember that though David saw corruption, his "seed" never saw corruption. Our serving God in accordance with His Will for us, as it relates to our generation, is "seed faith" (if I may borrow a term). The length of this mighty journey and its prosperous nature will depend on the alignment of our will with the Will of God concerning the generation to come. In walking in the Will of God for future generations, our own will must be open to the one who searches hearts, knows the pathway of the mind of and is able to tame it by the Spirit - aligning its processes according to the Will of God.

SALVATION IS THE WILL OF GOD

When we pray *"Your will be done,"* we invoke salvation. We must not fall into the temptation of thinking that praying the Will of God is a philosophy of practical fatalism. Rather, it is the most freeing act and creative place to be, because we know that God has good will. How do we prove the Will of God? In the Old Testament, the Will of God was proven in several ways. (It must be remembered that it is revealed Will of God that was to be proven by the means, which is under discussion. The written Will of God, which was the Torah, was not to be sought by any other means except the reading and interpretation of the text).

Proving God's Will

Where the Will of God is sought regarding individual or communal direction (which are not explicitly commanded within the Scripture) then other means were used. For example, the Will of God was never sought as to whether a murderer should killed. But in the case of David, in the pursuit of the Ziklag murderers, there was no clear direction and God was to be sought for directions.

The Will of God can be proven. Read Romans 12:2, *"And do not be conformed to this world, but be transformed by the renewing of your mind, so that you **may prove what the will of God is, that which is good and acceptable and perfect.**"* The

Will of God regarding temporal matters is not usually known immediately, yet by persistent pressing in on God, we may be able to ascertain what God wants from us in particular situations. When Paul sought the Will of God to Christians in Rome, he sought specifically to go in the mood of joy: *"That I may come unto you with joy by the will of God, and may with you be refreshed,"*(Romans 15:32). James is even clearer about how we ought to approach temporal situations as it relates to the will of God. *"Instead, you ought to say, "If the Lord wills, we will live and also do this or that."* (James 4:15).

Doing the Will of God when we know it is non-negotiable: We neither do the Will of God based on whose eyes are on us or for the pleasure of men, but us as the servants of Christ. Do the Will of God from the heart, not fearing what it will cost. This line in the Lord's Prayer calls us as believers to pray for the ability to do the Will of God our Father. James 1:18 tells us that seeking to do God's Will is consistent with the fact that it is this will that gave birth to us: *"In the exercise of His will He brought us forth by the word of truth, so that we would be a kind of first fruits among His creatures."* Hebrews 13:21 states it this way, that the Lord may *"equip you in every good thing to do His will, working in us that which is pleasing in His sight, through Jesus Christ, to whom be the glory forever and ever. Amen."*

One can suffer according to the Will of God: Hebrews 10:36 says, *"For you have need of endurance, so that when you have done the will of God, you may receive what was promised."* In 1 Peter 2:15 we read, *"For such is the will of God that by doing right you may silence the ignorance of foolish men."* In 1 Peter 3:17 we read, *" For it is better, if God should will it so, that you suffer for doing what is right rather than for doing what is wrong."* We read in 1 Peter 4:19, *"Therefore, those also who suffer according to the will of God shall entrust their souls to a faithful Creator in doing what is right."*

Doing the Will of God is the key to living an abiding life forever: In 1 John 2:17 we read, *"The world is passing away, and also its lusts; but the one who does the will of God lives forever."*

Prayers are answered by God only if they are according to the Will of God: 1 John 5:14 tells us, *"This is the confidence which we have before Him, that, if we ask anything according to His will, He hears us."*

Prophesy is the Will of God: We read in 2 Peter 1:21, *"For no prophecy was ever made by an act of human will, but men moved by the Holy Spirit spoke from God."*

Prayer and Human Will

We need to know that by praying this line of prayer taught by the Lord, we transmute the straw of the decaying effect of human will into the gold of the glory of God's Will. We see then the importance of giving ourselves entirely over to God's Will. If our will is malformed or corrupt, we are in danger of being far removed from the Will of God and carrying out that which is contrary to God's purpose. Therefore, our will needs to be formed and trained to submit and conform to the Divine Will. The human will cannot transform itself. It has no power to do so. There must be a commitment to something greater than it. Thus, Romans 12:1–2 reads, "*Therefore I urge you, brethren, by the mercies of God, to present your bodies a living and holy sacrifice, acceptable to God ...*" How then do we renew our mind? By training our will to say without reserve, "*Your will, O God, be done not mine.*"

By practicing submission to the Holy Spirit in all things, we can turn our will over to the Will of God. The first act leading to transformation and training is that of the unequivocal submission of the will of man to the Will of God. This submission of the will illuminates it and draws it into the Kingdom process and

> *Will in God is indeed the creative universal element which gives purpose and fulfillment to all which exists. As there is one God, so there is one absolute WILL.*

the will of human being is formed, transformed and trained. The formation of the will is based on reflection on the information provided by the Divine concerning Himself. There is a constant of flow of communication that allows for the Divine Will to saturate the will of human beings - and this is done through prayer. Prayer, being a consistent exchange between God and the believer, creates a cross-flow of the Kingdom by aligning Will to will. Thus, the believing community becomes the communicative community, carrying with it the communicative action whose content is obvious to the believer - the Word of God who is the Messiah.

Kingdom Imagination and Manifestation

By contemplating the greatness of God, our will is released to trust the Will of God. The Will can be formed also by contemplative posture. Only in being a people whose will and acts are deeply influenced by contemplative will, can we reach into the future and determine it rightly. Rightly by that will which has been intertwined with the Will of God. Such people can know not only history but can produce and change history! The Kingdom of God radiates from transformed will, which is also a contemplative will. From the will having a contemplative posture, there is reoccurring interweaving of the Heavenly and Earthly, God and human, which reaches out in a productive imagination that can also be called Kingdom imagination.

By developing a visionary symbolization of how our situation can be like Heaven, we bend our will to simulate Heaven. The living impulse of the will is as a symbolizing instrument within a human being, able to capture and take hold of the future in the present. Will is the principle of unity, cohesion and continuity. However, *"The performance of an action may be impaired by an error of the will resulting in the faulty planning and insufficient idea or else the plan maybe adequate, but when the will attempts to carry out the plan, some part of the body may fail to obey its command."* [15] In a failure of will, or its entropy, the failure is manifested in the movements that are made related to the desired action in the order of the Kingdom of God and its manifestation.

Surrendered Human Will is the Instrument of Divine Will

To develop a will conformed to the Will of God, we need to of course go beyond the purely sentimental, entertainment-driven, materialistic Christianity that is common in post-modernity. It is the transformation of the will that enables us to participate as God intended us - in the manifesting Kingdom! It is not so much our willed effort that causes the Kingdom to manifest, but the subjection of our will to the Will of God that causes an unhindered flow of Kingdom action. The impotence of unregenerate human will or carnal power is seen in the fact that man cannot bring forth pure relationship.

> *The natural will is replete with unbelief. It does not seek to depend on grace that makes provision.*

Will can become old, decayed, dilapidated and even fossilized, so that it gives forth mainly death and destruction. But God's Will is actualized in its highest form in humanity's choice to connect with God. It is amazing to me that God deems it important that the Will of God shall be manifested by connecting with finite human will. God's Will serves then as freedom and constraint to the human tendency to annul boundaries and pervert righteousness. God's law is to curtail humanity's unregenerate will in its rampant, sinful, self-imposition upon God's world.

If a person wishes to flow in the Kingdom of God and to actively abide in its sphere, the person must develop a will bent toward transformation. The development of the will that reflects the Will of God takes disciplined spirituality and consistent practice. The training of will is more important than the training of logic. One whose will is trained to submit is ready to hear God and see beyond the rational sphere and is able to act from a supernatural place. It is by conformity of the human will to the Divine Will that we come to sit in the Heavenly places with Christ! Decision, deliberation and discipline of the will are prerequisites for manifestation of the Kingdom of God. The will and the mind have a connection. The atrophy of the will leads to the darkening of the mind. The believer is told *"be transformed by the renewal of your mind."*

The presentation of the body and the renewal of the mind are carried out by active involvement of the will. When the will is committed to anything, the whole life begins to change to accommodate it. When the will is connected to the Divine, the foundation of former actions begins to be transformed and structures itself in the direction of the Divine. Here is where believers are different from non-believers, their wills are directed toward opposite ends. The law of God hidden in the heart serves as a bridle that tames the will and brings it into subjection to the Will of God. So we choose what we see by conforming to the beauty of the Lord, so that our inner eyes may not be deformed.

The human will can be trained by hearing from Heaven. The ear is a spiritual gateway by which others enter into the recesses of our being. The Bible even tells us that faith comes by hearing and hearing by the Word of God. Major attacks used by the enemy to infiltrate the souls of men are in the audio dimension. In prayer, we can form our will by causing ourselves to hear affirmation of the Word of God. Self-talk that puts God's positive Word into our souls can help form our will. The Scriptures tell us that *"faith comes by hearing and hearing by the word of God."*

THE GOAL OF WILL FORMATION AND TRAINING

When our whole being says, *"Your will be done on earth as it is in Heaven,"* we are ready to see wonders and signs. In this state of mind, we will every good for its own sake and according to its eternal value. Nothing more or less than this state of mind, *"Your will be done,"* can be called true virtue. The goal of human beings, as this prayer suggest, is to completely release our will so that God's will swallows up our will.

The "I" that stands in rebellion against the Most High must bow. If will, as the instrument for our decisions, reveals our power to choose and expresses what "we will" or "we won't," then the will becomes the power over all areas of human thought life. We know that, without the will, a person is reduced to being a mere machine. The will is the instrument for thoughts. It can, if it so chooses, impede our intellectual power and subvert the imagination of the soul, holding back the flight of the spirit to the Heavens. So we must choose a will from where flows perfect wisdom, knowledge and action.

Lack of understanding and submission to the Divine Will makes a man foolish and dull. The instrument for our likes and dislikes in the faculty of emotion distorts our will. So when we say *"will of yours be done on earth as is in Heaven,"* we are calling for God to take over our ability to express love, transform hate to joy, anger to tranquility, and all that we may call emotion. We call for His Spirit to determine its ebb and flow. It is not so much its shortage of will that renders man as insensitive as wood or stone but its fullness apart from the Spirit of God.

> *"It is, in a word, the obedience of the will or heart to the law of God as this law lies revealed in the intelligence. I have just said that sin consists in the supreme devotion of the will, and consequently of all the powers of the mind to self-gratification. On the contrary, holiness consists in the supreme devotion of the will, and consequently of the whole being to the glory of God, and the good of the universe."*
> (Watchman Nee)

Two Wills Become One

> The will to unbelief says, "God promised to take care of me, but if I do not do it myself, God will fail me!" Whether we accept it or not, worry and anxiety are the tendency of natural man's will to unbelief.

According to Charles Finney, *"This entire consecration of the will to the glory of God and the good of the universe is the whole of virtue in any being, and in every world."* Finney also reminds us that we cannot even be submitted to the Will of God nor do His Will in any moment unless, *"especially in difficult times, we must first be practicing the remembrance of God in our lives."* He insists that the human will must be trained to remember God with consistency in today's noisy world where the physical ear, spirit and emotion are continually bombarded with distraction from devotion to God. Unless the Will of God takes supremacy over the will of man so that the Will of God becomes the will of man, the whole process is futile. Jesus tells us that His whole purpose on Earth was to do the Will of the Father, not His own will:

> *For I have come down from heaven, not to do My own will, but the will of Him who sent Me.*
> (John 6:38)

He that will do the Will of God will know! One is not qualified to know the Will of God who is not already doing the Will of God. The Will of God is known where it is incarnated in the flesh of everyday action. The goal of the discipleship of the will is to make the two wills one. The two wills which are fighting in man can be made one by confirming them to the Will of God. One soul fluctuating between conflicting wills. I do not mean to say that the Kingdom of God will not come if men do not will it so, but that its manifestation in their life, their circumstance and sphere of being is limited and they live outside of that abundant life.

THE HOLY SPIRIT AND THE WILL OF THE BELIEVER

The fruit of the spirit buds through the instrumentality of the will submitted to God's Will. In Galatians 5, we see the difference between a will submitted to God and working in Divine efficiency and a will working from the deficiency of the human self held in the bondage of sin. Charles Spurgeon says:

> *The work of the Spirit, which is the effect of the Will of God, is to change the human will, and so make men willing in the day of God's power, working in them to will to do his own good pleasure. The work of the Spirit is consistent with the original laws and constitution of human nature.*

In the Lord's Prayer, there is a line that reads "*Your will be done on earth as it is in Heaven.*" There is also a line in an old song that reads "*and my will be lost in thine.*"[16] The principle of will argues, thus, "*that unfathomable something*", the principle of cohesion, the sufficient reason of all is the will. It is the inscrutable and deep secret of all causes in Heaven and in Earth. It is the basis of the transformation of matter and spirit. Behind the flow of all that becomes is the will, whether it is the will of God or that of creation. It is the alignment of the will that is necessary for the manifestation of the kingdom. All the inner and outer workings of the kingdom of God are grounded in the Will of God. But the question becomes what is the Will of God?

There is nothing more pervasive and fundamental to the malfunction of the natural will than unbelief.

HOLY SPIRIT

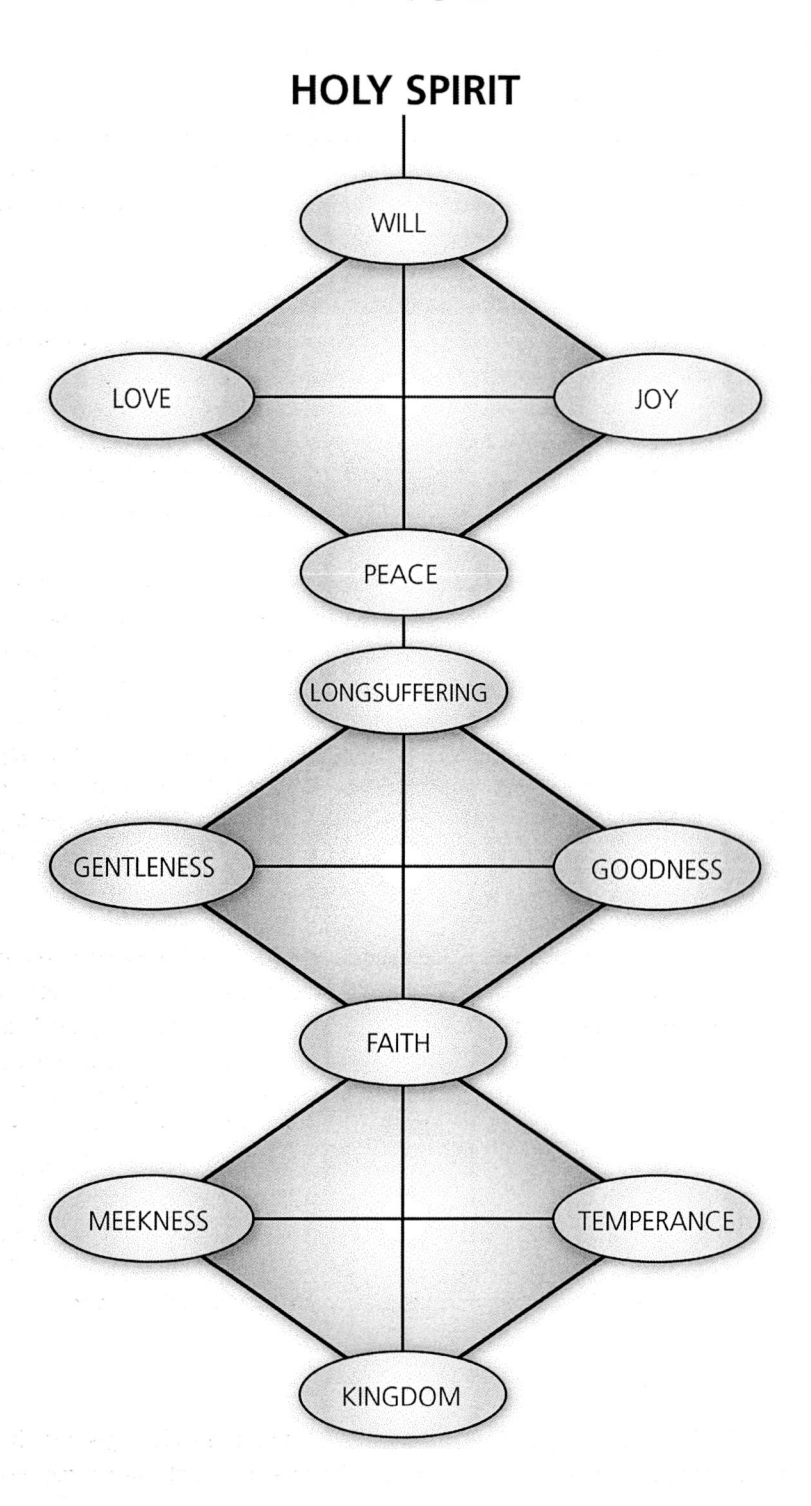

- WILL
- LOVE
- JOY
- PEACE
- LONGSUFFERING
- GENTLENESS
- GOODNESS
- FAITH
- MEEKNESS
- TEMPERANCE
- KINGDOM

What Is The Will of God?

The question demands that we define will as it occurs, both as an intrinsic nature of God and as it works in God's creative outreach. In Ephesians 1:11 we read, "*also we have obtained an inheritance, having been predestined according to His purpose who works all things after the counsel of His **will**,*" (emphasis added).

Will raises the question of faith at its most foundational level. There is a sharp distinction between knowing the Will of God and doing the Will of God. There is a distinctive difference between the intrinsic Will of God as known by God, and the Will of God as man sees it and seeks work within it. In most instances the two wills are incompatible, seeing that the profound nature of God keeps man always at the minimalism of knowing God and God. But there is an incompatibility of will which results from the stark opposition which flows from man's degeneracy and natural deficiency resulting from the Fall. Our fall away from God places our will in opposition to the Divine Will, until it is regenerated by the infusion of the Divine Will activated by the indwelling presence of the Holy Spirit. Man cannot know that Will of God and still believe that anyone other than God does the perfect Will of God. There is no human will strong enough to will the Will of God! However, that does not mean there is no communicative possibility between the Will of God and the will of man. In fact, God seeks to communicate His Will to human beings in such a way that the human will becomes the Will of God - not vice versa. When anyone insists that their personal will is the Will of God, they have crossed the line from humility to self-deification. The recognition of how far our will is from the Will of God is the beginning of Wisdom, and sets us on the path of Divine Knowledge.

I have a growing impression that many people who mouth the Will of God do not really mean to know the Will of God or to do it. Instead this is their way of imposing their own will upon the will of others. In fact, in so many lives, including the lives of those of us who claim to be followers of Jesus Christ, the Will of God is nothing more than 'shibboleth' tool for dividing us from those whom we dislike and wish to do away with as an excuse for our rebellion. If the Will of God is as important as we have claimed it to be, and as I believe the Bible teaches, knowing and doing it becomes the primary priority of the church and of all human beings who claim the name of Yeshua our Messiah. On the other hand, if the Will of God is not important to know or to do, it has no priority in human life, then the world simply is a tragic place and there is no higher place from which human transformation can come.

Life or Death

If the Will of God is merely something that we use to make us look good in the face of others' accusation, then it fails to meet the criteria for that which is the Will of God. Will belongs to the very essence of what it means to live, move and have being. For God and for man, it is the ground of the recognition of the true nature of a being. It is a necessary condition for the ideation, formation and manifestation of whatever is spiritual in the material world. It is the principle by which nature expresses itself and finds inner and outer fulfillment.

God's Will offers the only way to stand against the distortions of thought and action so common among human beings. In a world of flux and impermanence, will offers conditions of stability and truth here and now. By will, man in the world in which he lives, is sustained and comforted through heartaches and disappointments. By will, control of nature is set and escape is possible from the cycle of bondage into which human beings are caught. There are two ways to approach the discussion of will. We can either approach from the perspective of what the Bible teaches about God or we may approach it form the dimension of man. We can choose life or death!

References

8 My viewpoint on the will is strongly influenced by Schopenhauer's treaties on the will though I do not subscribe to some of his tenets on the human will. In this chapter, I use the uppercase "Will" to refer to the Will of God and the lowercase "will" to refer to the human will.

9 Aurelius Augustine, "Confessions," Nicene and Post-Nicene Fathers of the Christian Church, Vol. 1 (Grand Rapids, Eerdmans, 1979), p. 21.

10 "Confessions," p. 21.

11 Ibid.

12 Ibid.

13 Charles Spurgeons, "The Sin of Unbelief." In Spurgeon's Sermons: Memorial Library (Grand Rapids: Zondervan, 1952).

14 Book viii, 19:24.

15 Ernst Cassierer, p. 263.

16 Frances J. Crosby, "I Am Thine, O Lord," 1820–1915, Melody by William H Doane.

Chapter Twelve
Key #6: Access to Provision

> *"Give us this day our daily bread"*
> (Matthew 6:11).

Whenever I have been I dire need, I have taken this line and meditated on its many possibilities. Often I have received miraculous provision as I have focused on this simple line. Once I was caught up in the other realms and saw the immense provisions. Upon returning to myself, within a few hours I had the provision I needed for the work to which the Lord had called me.

Activating Heaven's Manna

Praying this line opens dimension of provision. "*This day*" from the Greek word *σήμερα semeron* (pronounced "say'-mer-on") is seen as a neutral adverb meaning "*this day*" and sometimes might refer to the night from which the day is birthed. It can also mean *now*, this present moment. This provision is birthed from the dark of the night. This idea seems to grow from the fact that, as God called the light from darkness, so now out of the night of need, the light of provision is being birthed. "*And I will give thee the treasures of darkness, and hidden riches of secret places, that thou mayest know that I, the LORD, which call thee by thy name, am the God of Israel*" (Isaiah 45:3, KJV). "*Give us this day our daily bread*" recalls the manna in the wilderness which came in the night and was manifested in the morning:

> And the Lord spoke to Moses, saying, "I have heard the grumblings of the sons of Israel; speak to them, saying, 'At twilight you shall eat meat, and in the morning you shall be filled with bread; and you shall know that I am the Lord your God.'" So it came about at evening that the quails came up and covered the camp, and in the morning there was a layer of dew around the camp. When the layer of dew evaporated, behold, on the surface of the wilderness there was a fine flake-like thing,

fine as the frost on the ground.
(Exodus 16:11–14)

Though this was a response to murmuring and not a prayer, yet it serves as the archetype for divine provision for a person or people in need.

Kingdom Provision

When God moves in provision, He allows us to see through our circumstance in the night. Such provision is meant to call us to speak to one to another in praise to praise. This bread which the LORD gives us is more than what we need to eat. We receive this in order to resource the Kingdom. This supernatural provision is more than drops of blessing, it is showered on everyone according to need for their influence and effect on the Kingdom of God. This Divine provision is prepared in the secret place of God according to the number of your days. Everyone involved in the Kingdom of God - for God and His glory - will have their tents overflowing with supernatural provision. It would not be just for you. *Even your children, oh Israel of God, will gather more and not less. You shall mete it with a Heavenly measure and even that which you have not gathered, much and over-abundance shall flow from the supernatural provision to you. Those who gathered little shall remove all lack; everyone shall eat and have more to give away!*

> This is not a cry for provision, but an affirmation of the willingness of God to meet us at the point of our need.

The word *day* is used in Scripture to represent an age or a particular generation. Supernatural provision can be generational. God causes supernatural provision to flow from one generation to another for those who are positioned for it by the Covenant. It can also mean 'always and forever'. In this line of prayer, we place our provision out of time, unaffected by seasons, wars or physical geography. If this prayer is a Kingdom prayer, then all that is written within it must be connected to the longevity of the Kingdom. We read *"and of the increase of his kingdom and peace there shall be no end"* (Isaiah 9:7). The idea then is that there is a continual birthing of provision from the fertile womb of eternity for those who are in the Kingdom of the Lord of God.

Supernatural provision is always new and is not tied to past considerations of need. Occasionally, it may seem that Divine provision has been depleted because our need is so acute. But the logic of Divine provision is that Heaven's resources are superior and do not suffer the fate of time and flux in which our perceived need appears. Our inner tensions regarding supernatural provision, pseudo moral uneasiness and self-rejection, all yield to futility. They must give way to a sense of the adequacy and limitlessness of Divine provision laid up for us in Heaven's storehouse. And by

"Heaven," I do not mean a location out of reach in this life, but a realm concurrent with this one into which the child of God can reach for God's provision. This is not a cry for provision, but an affirmation of the willingness of God to meet us at the point of our need. There is not a place of more intense self-doubt for many people who do the work of God than the area of material resources for the work. Note that I did not say God's doubt, but self-doubt. Supernatural provision, as we have seen in the case of Israel, can and does bypass our stubbornness, self-rejection and self-doubt to create an immediacy of hope and to materialize in the now. This Heavenly provision we have so often pushed into the future because of our misguided false humility.

Evening and Morning

At this moment, God is seriously committed to our progress and adequacy and wants it reflected in our life daily. The Divine provision that flows from this Kingdom prayer, as we see from Israel's supernatural provision in the wilderness, are evening and morning manifestations. That is when we have the strength (in the morning) and when our strength is weak (in the evening). Evening represents the closure of the day. It is our entrance into a time in which we cannot naturally see, because we are not awake enough to fight or fend for ourselves. It is a time in which one may be haunted by an imminent sense of emptiness. In that season, God reemerges riding on the wind of supernatural provision. God perceives the confines and the limit of our ability at such times. Rather than judge us, God opens up the flow of eternal possibility, invigorating and inspiring new vistas of providence that remove the deadening effect of want and need which has attempted to limit the progress of our redemptive history. When we pray "give us this day," we include all that has been said above and more!

Now this provision is not just for some of God's children and is not dependent on the mood swings of man or woman, It is given to all flesh, because of what happens in eternity and made flesh in the life, death, burial, resurrection, and advocacy of Jesus Christ our redeemer. Provision grows out of the eternal, enduring mercy of God.

In blessing Asher, Jacob say in Genesis 49:20, "*Out of Asher his bread shall be fat, and he shall yield royal dainties.*" So the idea of bread is not just so that one fills one's belly with the husk as the prodigal in the swine pit, but that one will become royalty before God who causes there to be an overflow. This supernatural provision symbolizes not just the visit of God to His people in times of need, but the dwelling of God among His people perpetually. By this provision, we arise and return from the far country of our resource exile. Supernatural provision is the LORD visiting the people with the release of Heaven's resources. It is a sign to the believer of God the Father, mercifully lending eternity's fruitful bow into his/her life. This supernatural providence is directed to the heart of God's people to make them drunk with the wine of gladness. It is meant to cause their faces to shine with the oil of the Lord's anointing. This supernatural bread strengthens the believer's heart. This provision is not because we are so wise or so strong, not because of our depth of understanding and not because of our righteousness - it is the favor of God freely flowing to us!

Accessing "Over Provision"

The next part of the Lord's Prayer, "*our daily bread,*" offers us insight into the principle of provisional grace for which this prayer is intended. The word "daily" from the Greek ἐπιούσιον *epiousios*, (pronounced "ep-ee-oo'-see-os") could mean "*tomorrow's.*" This is not so much a prayer for tomorrow's provision, but the acknowledgment of the future as already manifest in God. With God, all that every day holds is already perfected. However, what is interesting is that Greek scholars seem to think it is derivative of the 'present participle feminine'. This will then mean that we speak forth in the belief that every day, today and tomorrow are pregnant with all that we need to thrive!

The solutions to our need are pregnant and waiting to be birthed into whatever day we enter. The idea is that of the primary presupposition of Divine superimposition of provision in all of the time, place and relation. Because of the relationship with God, providential distribution flows from Father over us so that we can find full rest. The enemy finds no point with which to point an accusing word toward God. So if this text is read in that way, then what we speak into existence in this prayer is the provision of God, above and beyond what we think, ask or even need. The exemplification of this prayer in its fullness seems to me to be the miracles that Jesus Himself did. We read:

> But Jesus said to them, "They do not need to go away; you give them something to eat!" They said to Him, "We have here only five loaves and two fish." And He said, "Bring them here to Me." Ordering the people to [b]sit down on the grass, He took the five loaves and the two fish, and looking up toward heaven, He blessed the food, and breaking the loaves He gave them to the disciples, and the disciples gave them to the crowds, and they all ate and were satisfied. They picked up what was left over of the broken pieces, twelve full baskets. There were about five thousand men who ate, besides women and children.
> (Matthew 14:16–21)

In the passage, we see that the times is important because it was evening, which is the extreme of the day. We also note that they were in a wilderness where they could buy no food. It is interesting that Jesus lets them follow Him into the wilderness where they would have to look to Him for sustenance. But what is important here for our point is the fact that there was an overflow - enough for the next days.

From The Father

This provision stands strong against attacks of the enemy who comes to steal, kill and destroy. As long as this provision stays tuned with the realm of God's glory, nothing touches it other than the ones who have charge of it. This bread must come from the Father. He provides it, who must give us this day.

Note in the Lord's Prayer, it says not "this night" but "this day." The simple indication is that it must be bread received in the light of God's presence and not from human avarice or selfishness. If you will recall, the first temptation of Adam and Eve was the temptation of bread, and they fell. The first temptation of the Lord in the wilderness was to receive bread apart from the generosity and kindness of the Father. The bread must be given by the Father and not taken from another by force. It must not be conjured up magically from hell or by violence. it must come from the hand of the Father of light from whom all good gifts come.

> *This Heavenly provision we have so often pushed into the future because of our misguided false humility.*

> "For this reason I say to you, do not be worried about your life, as to what you will eat or what you will drink; nor for your body, as to what you will put on. Is not life more than food, and the body more than clothing? Look at the birds of the air, that they do not sow, nor reap nor gather into barns, **and yet your heavenly Father feeds them. Are you not worth much more than they?** And who of you by being worried can add a single hour to his life? And why are you worried about clothing? Observe how the lilies of the field grow; they do not toil nor do they spin, yet I say to you that not even Solomon in all his glory clothed himself like one of these. **But if God so clothes the grass of the field, which is alive today and tomorrow is thrown into the furnace, will He not much more clothe you?** You of little faith! Do not worry then, saying, 'What will we eat?' or 'What will we drink?' or 'What will we wear for clothing?' For the Gentiles eagerly seek all these things; **for your heavenly Father knows that you need all these things. But seek first His kingdom and His righteousness, and all these things will be added to you."**
> (Matthew 6:25–33, emphasis added)

Note the passage above says, "*your Heavenly Father feeds*" and "*your Heavenly*

> It is interesting that Jesus lets them follow Him into the wilderness where they would have to look to Him for sustenance. But what is important here for our point is the fact that there was an overflow - enough for the next days.

Father knows." That is a key for belief in God's ability and desire to meet the needs of even the least of His creation. Releasing himself to pray, "*give us this day our daily bread,*" the believer transports himself to stand on the holy hill of God where the streams of provision are in constant flow. Our security and safety from the dread of lack and famine are assured in the Kingdom's hills. Let the world worry about drink, food and clothing; our thoughts and our will remain focused on the structure and flow of the Kingdom of God. Even when the warriors and chariots of incessant need come charging through the valleys and hills of our lives, we will simply take a firm stand and focus our whole being on the Kingdom of God. In the focus of my thought to the Kingdom, whose eternal content is the righteousness of God, I align myself with the flow of supernatural provision. In this way, when things increase, one's heart is not set on it, but the Kingdom and the Father.

God's Righteousness (Jesus) Is The Key

The source of provision is God and its location is the Kingdom and the key to unlock it is the righteousness of God. The righteousness of God, which we seek, that unlocks the provision is Jesus Christ our Lord. He is the key of the Kingdom. He is the very righteousness of God we are commanded to seek. As He said, "*I am the door: by me if any man enter in, he shall be saved, and shall go in and out and find pasture*" (John 10:9). The ordinary principle of daily provision means more than just food to eat. It is the flow of abundance in which God secures our whole life in the Kingdom's reality. Really, in the flow of abundance, we do not need to raise chariots of war to go and get what God has given us. The sample of God's continuous provision, based on the absolute move of God and not merely on the sword of man, is revealed in several provisional miracles of the Bible. It is not that we come charging through hills, fields, and valleys with our swords and spears to take our provision. God simply asks us to take hold of Him and come to the hills of His provisions. He tells us that He prepares a table even in the presence of the enemy. When the enemies of our provisions come, God will return and re-supply our troughs with His abundance. He has lifted up His voice and His hands to Himself and has said many things regarding what He provides for us, as exemplified in the Scriptures. When the Children of Israel went out to gather their provision or increase, it had nothing to do with their physical ability to gather much. In fact, God made sure that they got this as clear as possible.

> *When they measured it with an omer, he who had gathered much*

> had no excess, and he who had gathered little had no lack; every man gathered as much as he should eat.
> (Exodus 16:18)

Before entering the Promised Land, God takes the time to let the people know that He will be the security of their provision and they must understand that the abundant overflow they we about to experience was not the result of their own power:

> For the Lord your God is bringing you into a good land, a land of brooks of water, of fountains and springs, flowing forth in valleys and hills; a land of wheat and barley, of vines and fig trees and pomegranates, a land of olive oil and honey; a land where you will **eat food without scarcity, in which you will not lack anything**; a land whose stones are iron, and out of whose hills you can dig copper. When you have eaten and are satisfied, you shall bless the Lord your God for the good land which **He has given you.** "Beware that you do not forget the Lord your God by not keeping His commandments and His ordinances and His statutes which I am commanding you today; otherwise, **when you have eaten and are satisfied, and have built good houses and lived in them, and when your herds and your flocks multiply, and your silver and gold multiply, and all that you have multiplies.**
> (Deuteronomy 8:7–13, emphasis added)

Remember The Lord

So, why pray this prayer? Is it to remind God of the need for supernatural outflow? Absolutely not. Rather, it is to keep our hearts in check and remind us of God as our eternal source. No matter how resourceful we are, we cannot give ourselves life, nor can we provide ourselves with the strength to get wealth and provision. So this prayer is not begging God but a placing of fence around the heart so that we do not fall into self sufficient pride, as God warned Israel about. Guard your heart so that you do not get to the place where:

> Otherwise, you may say in your heart, 'My power and the strength of my hand made me this wealth.' But you shall remember the Lord your God, for it is He who is giving you power to make wealth, that He may confirm His covenant which He swore to your fathers, as it is this day.
> (Deuteronomy 8:17–18)

When it comes to provision, we should not be just ordinary men and women and look at things from the material perspective alone. If we are going to enter the dimension of supernatural provision, we must see with the eyes of the Spirit. We ought to be aware of the weakness of trusting in our natural resources and concluding that our provision is a result of our physical strength or even our spiritual qualities. Truly our help in the time of need is not us but God, who is in His grace and His indescribable love pours them out as He wills. God wants us to taste and see. "*O taste and see that the LORD is good: blessed is the man that trusteth in him*" (Psalm 34:8, KJV). We need to know that loving and serving the Lord is not in vain no matter what things may look like. The Lord has not called us just to suffer with Him but also to reign with Him. Thus, the plea "*O fear the LORD, ye his saints*" (v. 9a) is followed with "*for there is no want to them that fear him. The young lions do lack, and suffer hunger: but they that seek the LORD shall not want any good thing.*" (v. 9b–10, KJV). "*There is no lack to them that fear him*" is then qualified by the fear of the Lord and the goodness of God. Again, this is why the Lord's Prayer begins with "Our Father" and then proceeds to speak of His Kingdom at its very inception.

The idea from the beginning of this prayer is that we approach God as loving Father but also fear Him as the King who wills to protect His domain from the impact of the negative influence of unrighteousness. He will go to war for the citizens of His Kingdom. He does not withhold from those that fear Him. Not just any thing, but "good" things. The very idea of good is God. Thus, what we ask for when we ask for bread is not merely material provision (even though God will give material things to their fullest). When we ask for "bread," we ask for God in all of God's fullness. The daily bread as supernatural provision is truly good. It is a manifestation of God in our life's circumstance. Even material provision is a physical taste of the goodness of God.

Rest

Provision to the believer is the bread that comes down from Heaven. It is a gift given from God. There are two parts to provision as there are two parts to the week in Hebrew calendar. The first part involves six days of creation and the second part is the seventh day. The six days are the days of human labor, but the seventh day is the day of Divine Rest. It is a day in which we receive from the flow of eternal satisfaction. Provisions for the six days have to do with the labors and sweat of man mixed with the grace of God. The seventh day is God's alone. In Exodus 23:12 we read, "*Six days you are to do your work, but on the seventh day you shall cease from labor so that your ox and your donkey may rest, and the son of your female slave, as well as your stranger, may refresh themselves.*"

It is the day of that bread which man, no matter how much he labors, cannot receive unless it is given to him from Heaven. It is bread eaten for the refreshment of the soul. In this Sabbath of provision, God reveals the equality of all. This Heavenly time, called Sabbath, is the place of the release of your abundance. In restful trust, you and I open the gates of supernatural provision. In this dimension, there is ample supply for our need. Supernatural abundant supply for our needs in that day is equally present for all human beings. "*As it is written, He that had gathered much had nothing over; and he that had gathered little had no lack*" (2 Corinthians 8:15; Exodus 16:18).

Fall back on God for your provision in these times of need. Fall back on the Blood for protection in this period of turmoil. Rather than being afraid of the menacing winds of our time, stay constantly in His presence and you will receive into your life the infinite flow of this supernatural provision and power. Whether afternoon, evening or morning, the good news is that everything is provided for you.

Bread: More Than Bread!

This provision is all-inclusive. This prayer is not just for the bread that goes into the mouth. God is faithful to give full provision in all areas. "*Give us this day our daily bread*" includes also the provision of healing. Our Lord Jesus intimated that healing is bread for the children of God. Said He, "*It is not meet to take the bread of the children and to cast it to dogs.*" Many times, the bread of the mouth is not sufficient for the soul of man. God has proven faithful in meeting the needs of His children, be it physical, psychological or spiritual. When we are sick, we have an emergency room for our healing in the presence of the Father.

For a long time, I tried to separate this provision of bread from bread. In other words, I did not see the bread is all-inclusive. The essence of this bread is that it brings with it the healing of our physical body. The fact that God wants us healthy must be taken seriously. For some time, many in the church did not reach out in faith for healing. But God is provider both of meat and perfect wholeness. The prayer taps into the possibility of immediate change by the power of God, in the life of the person who prays. Praise the wonder of such a God whose name many times meets us with the bread of life.

When we pray "*give us this day*", we immediately cause our inner being to turn its gaze from the natural to the supernatural, and to depend entirely on God as our source for bread that sustains the physical strength and health in all dimensions. Bread (all bread) is the heritage of the Son of God who said, "*I am the door: by me if any man enter in, he shall be saved, and shall go in and out, and find pasture*" (John 10:9). In this prayer for bread, we have an extraordinary entrance into an extraordinary sustenance. It is a call to have open eyes in the realm of the Spirit. While this may lead us to the recognition of our weakness and our inability to use our natural resources to overcome the vicious cycle of famine and loss and locust, grasshoppers and cankerworms, it is not meant to place us merely as helpless victims in the face of our need. It is meant to secure our sense of God's all-sufficiency toward us.

THE BREAD AND MANNA SYMBOLISM

When Moses was admonished to build the Tabernacle, he was instructed to gather a pot of the manna that fell from Heaven and put it into the Ark of the Covenant in the Holiest Place. This was a symbol and reminder of God's supernatural provision for the Israelites throughout the wilderness journey. Praise God!

From Natural To Spirtual

When God trains us for a particular work, we may find ourselves often where we are forced to trust God alone for our daily provisions. In this way, God gets us acquainted with the keys for entering the dimensions of supernatural provision. When the terrible day comes, we must be able to tap into a greater realm for our provision. It would not do to hoard earthly provisions, as has been the custom of men in times of famine. There is a lesson to be learned in the way God provided for Israel in the wilderness, for Elijah in the days of famine and how the Lord Jesus provided for the people in the desert. It is not those who gather much who will be protected, but those who through it all purpose in their hearts to trust the Lord. It is those who choose to walk by faith and not by sight that will thrive. Pray this line as an acceptance of the grace of God. Pledge to depend on God not on natural resources and abilities.

> When God trains us for a particular work, we may find ourselves often where we are forced to trust God alone for our daily provisions. In this way, God gets us acquainted with the keys for entering the dimensions of supernatural provision.

Those who have not learned to pray "Give us this day our daily bread," and make it part of their daily meditation, find themselves buffeted by the forces of worldly anxiety. Being filled with anxiety and fear, they put pressure on God's people to walk by sight. They become concerned about personal survival and protection of their excessive lifestyle, instead of building faith and trust in God. As you pray this line, your inner self will become more aware of God's Divine provision and goodwill to you. You will seek Mount Zion, the city of the living God, the Heavenly Jerusalem, and not Edom, for your provision. It is not coincidental that this line of prayer comes after the line *"Your will be done on earth as it is in Heaven."*

It is God's will that Heavenly provision be made manifest on Earth for God's children. It is also not an accident that one of the major temptations of Jesus in His wilderness training was about bread. Heaven's provision is always bent toward us but must not be forced by carnal processes. The question is: "*Have we developed the discipline necessary for God to put them into our hands?*" This part of the prayer is a check on greed and our often misguided attempts to use God's resources to lift ourselves over others. The fact that "day" is used twice in this line means that provision is about human intimacy with God. During the first 12 hours of a day, man pretends to be his own provider. During the second 12 hours, at night most men are asleep, unaware of their earthly possessions. Even men who do not believe in God must depend on providence to keep them safe during the latter half of the day. This could be the reason the manna came by night when Israel was asleep, to show that God is the one who gives this day, the bread for the day.

Today we are being called to transition from the six days of human labor to the seventh day of Divine rest. In this Sabbath, we cease from materialistic strivings and enter into the rest of our God. In this rest, our daily bread becomes the responsibility of the one we call Father. Our food and clothing are the responsibility of this one whose image and likeness we bear, whose dignity, honor and glory we worship and adore. For us who are God's children, there are different types of bread available to us.

THE BREAD OF LIFE - JESUS CHRIST AS BREAD

When Israel was in the wilderness, they ate manna which God gave them - bread form Heaven. Jesus insists that He is the bread:

> *Jesus then said to them, "Truly, truly, I say to you, it is not Moses who has given you the bread out of heaven, but it is My Father who gives you the **true bread** out of heaven. For the bread of God is that which comes down out of heaven, and gives life to the world." Then they said to Him, "Lord, always give us this bread." Jesus said to them, "**I am the bread of life**; he who comes to Me will not hunger, and he who believes in Me will never thirst.*
> (John 6:32–35, emphasis added)

He says that Moses did not give the bread from Heaven. It must have been shocking to the people that the bread which their fathers ate did not come from Heaven. It was a shadow of the true bread. God is the one, not Moses, who gives the true bread, the Son, to Moses. The Master insisted that if that bread was from Heaven, the abode of the Father, they would not have died in the wilderness in disobedience as they did.

> *I am the bread of life. Your fathers ate the manna in the wilderness, and they died.*
> (John 6:48–49)

This line also calls up participation in the life of Jesus Christ. Jesus is

> *… the bread which comes down out of heaven, so that one may eat of it and not die. I am the living bread that came down out of heaven;* ***if anyone eats of this bread, he will live forever;*** *and the bread also which I will give for the life of the world is My flesh.*
> (John 6:50–51, emphasis added)

When He taught us to pray *"give us this day our daily bread,"* Jesus was placing us in a position to have access to His life as our sustenance for eternity. In this phrase, we activate our access to the life of God within our own being. This bread keeps us from falling into death, as the Israelites did in the wilderness. It empowers us to faith and obedience. He is the bread of healing. He is the bread of fellowship that binds the brethren in Divine unity. He is the bread of forgiveness. In communion, He is the physical bread which sustains our natural body. Whatever Christ is as the living Word, He is also **the Bread of the written Word of God,** which carries revelation for our daily journey. In Jeremiah 15:16 we read, *"Your words were found and I ate them, And Your words became for me a joy and the delight of my heart; For I have been called by Your name, O Lord God of hosts."* So when I pray *"give us this day our daily bread,"* I reach for the internal life of God and the revelation that is seeded in the written Word.

Chapter Thirteen
Key: #7: Forgive

"And forgive us our debts, as we forgive our debtors"
(Matthew 6:12)

The crisis of offense has saturated the body of Christ. A 'Gordian knot' is a metaphor for a highly intricate, extremely difficult problem (knot) that needs to be cut through with a sword. Offense has become the Gordian knot that has wrapped up believers in many arenas. Everybody seems offended by someone.

More Than Words

Jesus addresses this issue in many passage of Scripture. This prayer of forgiveness is not concentrating on our own failings, but focuses on a **perception** of the failings of others and their effects on us. The formula, the 'sword', for untying this Gordian knot is given in the Lord's Prayer. The measure of forgiveness is not the infinite nature of God, but the context of human beings in our own act of forgiveness. The prayer of forgiveness is not just us *asking* God to forgive our sins or daily failings. It is more than speech - *it is action*.

Here, prayer becomes action and being, not mere words. We are answered, as this relates to forgiveness, according to our action, not according to our request. There is a measure and it is us. While man may not be the measure of all things, "*he is the measure of his own forgiveness.*" The act of forgiveness is in itself a prayer which resolves this crisis of a person's failings and conflict with Divinity. In this act of forgiveness as prayer, we bring to God our understanding toward our brothers and sisters' wrong in the presence of God. He measures our act back to us as harmonic resolution or disharmonic condemnation to our own dilemma. This acting toward our brothers and sisters, neighbors, friends, and enemies (as embodiments of ourselves!) is the answer to our own prayer for forgiveness at all times in the eyes of Heaven. It is as though the brother who offends us is the context in which the loaf of bread, that becomes our life, is baked. Our basic instinct is to tear into our sister, friend, enemy in such a way that their longing for life is cut short, ending in the eradication of their hope and possibility. In this simple prayer/act of forgiveness, the person is presented to us *as ourselves* (!) - *"for with what measure we measure, the same shall be measured back to us."*

You are definitely not the measure of your salvation, however you are the measure of your own forgiveness.

Chemistry Of The Heart

You are as free as you let your brother be, you are as released as you release your sister - you are the measure, not God. How deeply you can continue to experience the forgiveness of God depends on how many people you are willing to release from the grip of your inner shackle of un-forgiveness. The release of power, true godly power in our lives, is very much dependent on the aphekemical (from the Greek *aphikemi*, "chemistry of the heart") disposition of our hearts. Our capacity to forgive gives birth to real transformation, which allows the supernatural resolution of our own inner crisis.

> The act of forgiveness is in itself a prayer which resolves this crisis of a person's failings and conflict with Divinity.

Now, we each know as believers what forgiveness is, because our Father in Heaven has placed before us the Son, Jesus Christ, as our mark of what it means. Our act-prayer of forgiveness deals with the imperceptible inner influences where our criticism, judgment, condemnation, and hurt churn and clutter our perception. We struggle to see the person as one who God loves and for whom He gave His Son as sacrifice. By the act of forgiveness, we unmask the false covering under which the enemy hides in order to attack us and make us vulnerable.

Self-Enclosed Hell

Forgiveness is redemptive. It is the supernatural resolution of what can become an eternal crisis. It redeems the one against *"whom we have an issue."* It sets us free from our self-enclosed hell, forming a bridge for reconnection with the other. We cannot exclude the possibility of forgiveness if we are in Christ and are truly conscious of how God redeemed us from bondage. In forgiveness, we embody God for the world, so that God can see His true reflection in us.

Many use anger and hurt as an excuse to control and hold others in place of subordination. However, if we look carefully at this act-prayer, we realize how seriously God takes this act of offering ourselves as prayer in forgiving one another.

Forgiveness is the act of prayer that deconstructs and recreates situations. It allows us a new visional power to see ourselves from God's perspective and, therefore, reverse the headlong plunge of our baser nature into chaos. In the prayer-act of forgiveness, we choose to see God in the other person, no matter how far they may seem to be from Him. Forgiveness is a practice of participation with God in the healing of another - and ultimately in our own healing. What we cannot achieve through vast accumulation of knowledge, we can accomplish in one moment of prayerful forgiveness.

The process of forgiveness should be understood as an act in which God heals the situation through us. It is related to the act of judging righteously, but its structures allows us to resolve the antithesis of wills into synthesis of being. Forgiveness is a revelational move, as it identifies us with Christ and allows Him to be manifest to others through us. We are bearers of God and, as such, we dispense Him to our brethren and open them up for wholeness. When we forgive, we see, live and speak Divinely. Forgiveness must occur, as the prayer states, because we ourselves are in desperate need of it. As we forgive, our vision is expanded. Heaven and Earth nudge closer toward each other in us.

Forgiveness is not the same for everyone, for everyone is not hurt the same way nor does everyone hurt the same way, but by intending and acting upon the Divine command to forgive, we all expand our horizon. God's forgiveness of our daily errors and our forgiving of our brethren's daily faults against us are made interdependent in the Scriptures. "*Forgive us*" cannot be separated from and cannot be said apart from "*as we forgive.*" In the Cross of Jesus Christ, we find forgiveness, but in our forgiveness, we carry the Cross.

Forgiveness is a spiritual attitude held in relation to God, self and others. Things that people do are allowed to impress themselves so strongly on our consciousness that they dictate our responses to other things - things which are not even remotely connected to them in real life! We walk, talk, reflect on it until it enters deep into us and seeps into our subconscious and, from there, informs our instinctive responses. Our spiritual atmosphere becomes charged with the energy of the person who hurt us in the first place. When we think of them, their actions, voice and appearance vibrate through our whole person, raising the negative force to a higher octave of anger, disgust, shame, hate, and the like. This clogs our soul and spiritual pathways and distorts channels to our movement in God. We cannot get to God and, most importantly, God cannot get to us. We remain in the cube of unforgiveness. This can become so toxic that those who come in contact with us and even seek to help us are repelled without knowing why.

An Atmosphere of Personal Breakthrough

I must urge you to know how important a forgiving spirit is for creating an atmosphere of personal breakthrough into other realms - especially the realm of the true power of God. Sometimes being able to break through into dimensions of which we dream or envision is simply to take hold of forgiveness. A knot in the cord in this area will keep us from crossing over into Heavenly dimensions. It will keep us tied into knots in our body and soul. Lack of forgiveness can hinder our physical body's healing ability. It is true that lack of forgiveness in many of us is fueled by beliefs, opinions, views, and ideals - many of them justified by our religious outlook. But forgiveness has very little to do with these. It is meant to release Divine dynamism into our spiritual walk. Our good intentions, godly ambitions and desire to change the world for good can be blocked not by the devil or others, but by a knot of unforgiveness on the Heavenly cord of prayer.

I encourage you then to cultivate a spiritual attitude of forgiveness so that you walk constantly in an atmosphere of openness to other dimensions with the ability to see and hear from Heaven. When this is done, you will find that you will attract good toward you more often than evil. The leaven of forgiveness will leaven the whole lump of your life. Conversely, the leaven of unforgiveness will leaven the whole of your life in the negative direction.

Forgiveness	Unforgiveness
Loose	Knots
Joy	Anger
Trust	Distrust
Faith	Fear
Love	Hate

We can list many things like these, but you get the point. Building up a spirit of forgiveness will free your being to forge into other dimensions. Train your heart to forgive and train your mind to release the pain so that new thoughts, idea and visions may flow freely into you.

Defeating The Dragon

I personally believe that Jesus won victory over fallen humanity. He has taken it all upon Himself on the cross, specifically at the moment when He said *"Father, forgive them"* (Luke 23:34). Wow! The first cry that reached Heaven from fallen humanity was that of unforgiveness: Abel's blood crying out against his brother. Since then we have fought, maimed, decimated, and attempted to destroy each other because of this beast called unforgiveness. When Christ asked the Father to forgive those that hurt Him, He won the battle over that sinister dragon that has wrapped itself around the neck of fallen humanity since the fall. One way to deal with this is make a list of all those against whom you have something (yes, especially the one you keep talking about and every time you think about it, you re-experience the pain). Now intentionally release them and symbolically burn the paper. Speak healing to the situation in the name of the Lord. As you forgive and let go, you will experience the combining of the forces of Heaven and Earth propelling forward to affect and influence your environment toward Divinity for good!

How many of us are like Peter in Matthew 18:21–22:

> *Then Peter came and said to Him, "Lord, how often shall my brother sin against me and I forgive him? Up to seven times?" Jesus said to him, "I do not say to you, up to seven times, but up to seventy times seven.*

Peter really must have thought, *"Boy, I am doing so well,"* but Jesus blew him out of the religious water. The Lord said 70 x 7 = 490; (By certain mathematical standards, we could say that it is closer to 144 which is the number of New Jerusalem, the new Israel. So if Peter is going to measure forgiveness, he must measure it by how many times God forgave Israel). So if you are counting, you have missed the point.

Manifesting Your Heaven-Born Self

Forgiveness is the harbinger of Divine creativity. Forgiveness produces tangible transformation in the one who forgives as well as one who is forgiven. Only the one who has experienced hurt can forgive. No one else can forgive for you. You must do it yourself. God cannot do it for you without you. You cannot hold onto the pain and ask God to forgive the person. It does not work like that. It is seed you must sow, because you are going to need its harvest for yourself in the future.

Forgiveness is not restricted to the act committed against you but it extends to yourself as the recipient of the act, as a willing or unwilling partaker in the act. Forgiveness does not co-habit with judgment in the same person for the same act. This does not mean that the act may not turn around and bite the doer. It means that forgivers must free themselves from being the judge of the act and release their minds to love as God the Father loves. This is difficult. Yet this is what God asks of us in order to create new forms for the manifestation of our Heaven-born selves. True forgiveness flows from intimate knowledge of the Christ whom we follow. It is not just therapeutic, but redemptive in that it reaches to the eternal point within us and there touches the heart of God. Jesus did not just teach this prayer, He practiced it at the most inopportune time - on the cross. By so doing, He took away from me any reason to hold onto my hurt.

God has given us the capacity for self-expansion into so many dimensions. Our capacity to move in these dimensions are buried deep within us and can only be activated by God's love. The more hurt we harbor, the more this possibility for self-expansion is pushed further away from our conscious reach. If we can reach deeper through the Holy Spirit and activate this capacity by letting go of the hurt and forgiving, our Divine creativity can burst forth.

> *If we can reach deeper through the Holy Spirit and activate this capacity by letting go of the hurt and forgiving, our Divine creativity can burst forth.*

Forgiveness is the only original act left for humankind. It is the only originality left for us in a world of hurt and sin. It is our only creation out of nothing. By it we become new and by it we move the hand of Heaven to make all things new. It seems clear that there are no easy steps on the way of forgiveness. But here is where our Divinity is hidden and our Divine likeness still shines forth. A flood of constructive creativity can overcome the pessimistic bitter waters of life, re-igniting God's awareness and gracing the darkened night with its glimmering ray - that's forgiveness. Here on Earth, the worlds wait for the moon of man to reflect the sun of God's eternal light by simply letting go and releasing the hurt. *"Father, forgive them."*

THE TWO-LETTER MILLION DOLLAR WORD: AS

When we learn to pray *"Forgive us our sins AS we forgive,"* then we have unknotted the golden cord in its most knotty section. We cannot just pray *"forgive me"* and leave it at that, for that is not a prayer but a weighing down of the soul on the scale of Heaven's justice. *"Forgive me"* cannot be the first. *"AS we (I) forgive"* is the first act which puts me in place of being able to ask *"forgive me (us)."* This is putting my brothers' error in my presence so as to feel it again. Then to release it lets me know that depth of what I am asking the Father to do for me, at least in terms of my finite human ability. *"I forgive you"* must be the primary orientation of my being if I am ever going to reach the depth of the being I desired by calling *"Father."*

How do I forgive? That is the question! By what process do I arrive at forgiving another? By what tortuous road of twisted human logic do I travel to forgive those who have hurt me? "AS" scares the daylights out of me. For when I look at the *"as*

I forgive," I tremble before the majesty of the King before whom I have come for forgiveness. If I must cross the threshold of Heaven and reach into the Throne, I must be willing even from the cross to say, *"Father, forgive them."* For me to say *"Father, forgive me,"* I must first of all from the depths of my heart forgive, for I cannot lie to the one to whom I come for forgiveness.

Restoring Breaches

Forgiveness plays a considerable role in training our will to submit to God's Will and helps our soul to break through to submission. In performing acts of forgiveness, we set in motion processes by which a human being goes back into a taste of Eden's grace by doing the Will of the Father. In forgiveness, the voluntary action of our will is initiated and works independently to run the course of love. We extend our soul to abduct another person redemptively into peace and joy from an act that has served to limit their Divine nature. The thing about forgiveness is that it does not need superhuman strength or even acceptance from the person to whom it is offered to be powerful; it merely needs the conjunction of the human will with the Will of the Father. In this seeming weakness, the will is stronger than physical force and can bridge distance and time, restoring breaches.

The forgiving person leaves an impact in the world that is eternal by extending goodwill to all. His own abduction from the abyss by God's goodwill propels his will. If another reaches for the forgiveness which has been offered to him, he willingly gives it. He wills the eternal hand of God to reach through him to abduct them from their encircling darkness. This stretching out of the self to another is so clearly seen in our Master and Lord as He hung dying on the cross. Forgiveness is the result of the will of man trained to conform to the Will of God. This move to forgive is grounded in the surrender of the will of the inner man, as well as the world, to the Will of God. The one who forgives has formed a flow of will in the stream of Divinity - and stands firmly contrasted with the world. They have overcome the influence of the egotistic factor that rules the world. They have apprehended the spiritual world and the emancipative possibilities which free men from a constant debt owed to the cycle of anger and revenge. They have a free will, because their will is interwoven with the absolute free Will of God. By conjunction of will to Will, they have forgiven others. Therefore, they can cry *"as we (I) forgive."* This bending of the will toward forgiveness releases one from the grasp of the materialistic mindset of the world. By willingly letting others be released, one is not submerged into the present cosmos but transported through the gates of love and mercy into the Throne Room in the presence of the Mercy Seat.

New Dimensions

Lack of forgiveness is a dangerous impairment of the spiritual faculty in any human being - but worse in the Christian, because it blurs the image and likeness of Christ. It affects his/her ability to be a witness for Christ who, while hanging on the cross, said *"Father, forgive them."* The pattern set in this line of prayer, and illustrated at that moment on the cross, sets the galactic traveler apart from those who wish to go nowhere beyond their present cosmos. The forgiver may be termed excessively indulgent, compromising, or in common sarcastic language, "touchy-feely." Yet, in truth, what the forgiver does or does not do is not based on sentimentality, but based on the objective measure of Divine Will in Christ - notwithstanding feelings, moods or need. The forgiver does not lose sight of Christ's reality which has been experienced. When we lose sight of *"As we forgive,"* we become judgmental and destructive and tend to use the law of God as weapons for our own vengeance and presumed righteousness.

Forgiveness can help organize our life, center it, and allow it to manifest its ultimate purpose which is to be like God. Here, in forgiveness, freedom and meaningful actions springing from God's heart produce its fruits and force shifts in the landscape of our conscious and unconscious. We become no mere persons. Here is the key to expansiveness, modification, redirection and renewal. The greater the move to forgive, the stronger the spirit and the higher the consciousness of God and the more open the channels of movement in various dimensions of life.

Forgiveness is Divine radiance which moves us into deeper places in God to which we would not have gone had we allowed our hurt to calcify and become an underlying root of bitterness. It is valuable in itself and brings more good and causes growth. The very definition of forgiveness implies growth and progress in the quality of our spiritual walk. It changes the environment for the release of God's dynamism and repairs pathways to the realms of the spirit. The practice of forgiveness helps us to increasingly adapt our spirit and mode of thought to the mind of Christ. Concepts which are so commonly accepted in our culture that have entered into us can now, by the discipline of forgiveness, either be removed or transformed to conform to the image of Christ.

Chapter Fourteen
Key #8: Follow the Leader

"And do not lead us into temptation"
(Matthew 6:13).

Before we deal with this line of prayer, we need to remember that temptation is not sin in itself. Temptation is the influence of an exiting hope or desire, exacted upon us when we are not in submission to the Will of God and do not conform to our God-given destiny. In temptation, we can be led into circles of influence that cause us to contemplate or do things just because we are in its sphere. Temptation is the urge to act contrary to our ideal, deriving either from self-delusion about fleeting pleasure or flattery from the enemy of our God-given destiny.

Does God Tempt?

We know that many things and persons can attempt to lead us astray and take us off the track of Divine good will. However, to insinuate, as this passage seems to do, that God can act to lead us into temptation will be met with holy indignation and sanctified fury from the lovers of God. In fact, even a biblical prophet vehemently opposes the idea that God can tempt a person:

> *Let no one say when he is tempted, "I am being tempted by God"; for God cannot be tempted by evil, and* **He Himself does not tempt anyone.** *But each one is tempted when he is carried away and enticed by his own lust. Then when lust has conceived, it gives birth to sin; and when sin is accomplished, it brings forth death. Do not be deceived, my beloved brethren.*
> (James 1:13 - 16, emphasis added)

So we know that God does not tempt us. What this passage is implying is that God can and does lead us to be tempted by the enemy so that we can be proved. *"Then was Jesus led up of the Spirit into the wilderness to be tempted of the devil"*

(Matthew 4:1). In Hebrews 2:18, we get an explanation for this temptation: *"For since He Himself was tempted in that which He has suffered, He is able to come to the aid of those who are tempted."* Reading further, we find:

> *For we do not have a high priest who cannot sympathize with our weaknesses, but One who has been tempted in all things as we are, yet without sin. Therefore let us draw near with confidence to the throne of grace, so that we may receive mercy and find grace to help in time of need.*
> (Hebrews 4:15–16)

In 1 Corinthians 10:13–14 we read:

> *No temptation has overtaken you but such as is common to man; and God is faithful, who will not allow you to be tempted beyond what you are able, but with the temptation will provide the way of escape also, so that you will be able to endure it. Therefore, my beloved, flee from idolatry.*

Could we cause God to lead us into temptation? Could it be that God leads us to be tempted but is not an active tempter, because there is no evil in Him? He leaves the tempting to Satan and his demonic cohorts who are habitations of evil.

Temptations does not just happen to us and cannot be separated from other aspects of our lives. According to James, temptations are outgrowths of our psychological landscape - our desires, moods and feelings are its launching pad. Though it is not evil in itself, it is for the tempted an important step to evil if not dealt with adequately. Victory can be achieved by accessing the power of Christ which He exercised over His own temptation. This is really a prayer to guard the heart in its innocence, so that it does not become the breeding ground for our own undoing. While temptations in themselves do not constitute production of evil, we should never underestimate the power temptation and its potential contribution to our spiritual distraction. However, an overemphasis on temptation can lead to spiritual and communal isolation, which keeps people from engaging the world with the power of God because of fear of falling.

This line of prayer points to the fact that God is not interested in veering us away from temptations which we think are too difficult for us, but to deliver us from its evil. When we see one that can overpower us, we cry, *"Lead us not into temptation."* We pray this also because some temptations can be distractions from what God has committed to us. Sometimes, in the *Authorized Version* of the Bible, the word "temptation" is used interchangeably with the idea of "trials." Of course, the temptation to sin is not from God. So, God does not lead us deliberately into temptation so that we might fall. This would go against the very character of God. We must make a distinction between temptation and trial for the purpose of clarifying the function and purpose of God from that of the enemy of our soul.

A Loving Father

Again, let us read:

> Let no one say when he is tempted, "I am tempted by God"; for God cannot be tempted by evil, nor does He Himself tempt anyone. But each one is tempted when he is drawn away by his own desires and enticed. Then, when desire has conceived, it gives birth to sin; and sin, when it is full-grown, brings forth death. Do not be deceived, my beloved brethren. Every good gift and every perfect gift is from above, and comes down from the Father of lights, with whom there is no variation or shadow of turning. Of His own will He brought us forth by the word of truth, that we might be a kind of firstfruits of His creatures.
> (James 1:13–18, NKJV)

According to this passage, God cannot be and does not desire to be the direct agent of our temptation by evil. But He does lead us into situations in which we are tested. The Greek word *ἀπείραστός* (akpeirazo, pronounced "ekpi-rad'-zo"), suggests a thorough test of the material of which our

> Temptation is the urge to act contrary to our ideal, deriving either from self-delusion about fleeting pleasure or flattery from the enemy of our God-given destiny.

character is made. It does not mean that God does not know our makeup. The Scripture insists that God proves our character by placing us in situations where we are tested and tried. God does this so we can see if we shall deal objectively with God's goodness and endeavor to keep faith with Him. Sure, this scrutinizing of our being may entice us to bring accusations against God, but it does not have to. For the purpose of God is to prove His glory in us, not to destroy us. This prayer is meant to keep us from avoiding the discipline of the Lord. Now, by discipline I do not mean the idea of punishment that has become attached to it. Rather, by discipline I mean the root idea of 'discipleship' in which the character of the Master is formed in us by lessons and tests on the way. God as Father "*disciplines us*" in the sense of a course of study in His eternal ways, which leads us "*as dear children*" to be "*imitators of God.*"

We are in school. So the trials of temptations that God allows to be put in our way are never intended to throw us into the hands of sin or evil, but to clarify for

> *Part of our inclination to sin is the false consciousness, which began in Adam, that assumes God deprives us unjustly of what we think is rightfully ours.*

us the lessons learned from the Father's heart. They are to affirm in our hearts the word we heard in the times we have spent with our Lord. "*Lead us not into temptation*" does not mean remove this trial from us; it means keep us from falling headlong into the trap of the enemy when our lessons are tested by life's circumstances. It is interesting that James inserts the phrase "*Every good thing given and every perfect gift is from above, coming down from the Father of lights, with whom there is no variation or shifting shadow*" (James 1:17). In this way, it is shown that whenever God permits any trial, He does so to shine the light into our lives and to check the shadow of variations which may serve to short-circuit our manifestation of God's image and likeness. The examination, as it relates to our relationship with God as a means of proving our character, is evidenced in what God said was the purpose in putting Israel through such ordeals in the wilderness. We read in Exodus 16:4,

> *Then the Lord said to Moses, "Behold, I will rain bread from Heaven for you; and the people shall go out and gather a day's portion every day, that I may test them, whether or not they will walk in My instruction.*

Even the manifestation of God to them was a test as it is said in Exodus 20:20,

> *Moses said to the people, "Do not be afraid; for God has come in order to test you, and in order that the fear of Him may remain with you, so that you may not sin."*

In summarizing the journey of the Children of Israel, Deuteronomy 8:2 says,

> *You shall remember all the way which the Lord your God has led you in the wilderness these forty years, that He might humble you, testing you, to know what was in your heart, whether you would keep His commandments or not.*

Later on in the same chapter, Moses told the Israelites that God "*In the wilderness He fed you manna which your fathers did not know, that He might humble you and that He might test you, to do good for you in the end.*" (8:16, emphasis added). All the trouble of the people which God permitted is directed to whether our way will be consistent with what we know and say we believe about the Lord in our actual walk.

Our Response

Though the purpose of God is not to lead us into temptation, our response in the situation may lead us into temptation. We may respond to God with anger or become hot against God which may lead us to speak haughtily and try to force God to prove Himself to us rather submit our wills humbly in prayer to God as Lord. Since this tendency dwells inside of us, God then permits trial once, twice, yea thrice! We read that Jesus was led into the wilderness by the Spirit to be tempted by the devil. This also means that God can and does intentionally take us to circumstances, atmospheres, people, and environments by which we are tested. When we look at Jesus, the goal of God was to initiate Him into the struggle of humanity and to hone His skills for human war against the enemy.

However, the devil's temptation was to undo the character of Jesus and make Him unusable by God. When our lives begin to grow, our fame is heard in the spiritual realm and our concern for the name of the LORD is recognized, then the devil takes permission to test us and to prove us through some hard questions of life.

But here is the heart of the issue in being led by God into a place where we can be tried. God never send us alone but send us with the help of the Heavenly City. With us come a great company of Heaven, the spices of the Word, the golden nuggets of Heaven's abundant mercies and doors of escape marked with precious stones of Heaven - as long as we continue to commune with Him with all our hearts. Furthermore, God leads us to the place of our trial to show us whom we will justify. If we justify ourselves in our time of trial, we have not learned the lessons of our Father very well. If we justify ourselves, then we set ourselves to fall into condemnation. But if in the trial we justify God and maintain the perfection of His praise, then we shall be proven to be His. David knew this so he cried in Psalms 26:2, "*Examine me, O LORD, and prove me; try my reins and my heart.*"

Prove All Things

If God's intention is to prove us, then the prayer "*lead us not into temptation*" does not focus on making sure we avoid all trouble (as some modern preaches tend to propose). Rather, it focuses on conforming us to the image of the Son and the transformative renewal of our mind. In another place we read, "*that you may prove what is that good, and acceptable, and perfect, will of God*" (Romans 12:2). How do we prove the sincerity of our love in the face of human forwardness? Is it not the ability to maintain that love in the face of continuous onslaught by the opposing side? Self-examination is not enough, for in it we may even delude ourselves into thinking we are what we are not. We need objective examination to see if we are truly in the faith. This is not to prove something to God but to prove to our own selves. This is how we come to truly know our own selves that Jesus Christ is in us, and that we are not reprobates. Every one of us is constantly working for God or for ourselves. The proof of our work is whether it ends in bearing joyful fruits to the glory of God or seeds of praise for ourselves. Testing our work has a certain sense of being alone. It is not temptation in which another person seeks to glory over us by our fall, but the test of what we own as ours in the presence of God. In 1 Thessalonians 5:21 we read, *"Prove all things; hold fast that which is good."* Test separates the true from the false, the viable from the non-viable, so that we might be able to hold onto the good and discard the evil.

In dealing with the issue of being led into temptation, this prayer to our Father is directed toward dealing with our desires and enticements and our bent to sin and death. Part of our inclination to sin is the false consciousness, which began in Adam, that assumes God deprives us unjustly of what we think is rightfully ours. He causes us to wait for a time while we, on the other hand, must have it now. So, instead of devoting ourselves to prayer, we let Satan use our lack of self control as an instrument of seduction, enticing us to go astray from right relations with the Father. That which has the quality to seduce us is truly given that it might qualify us for that which God holds back for a short time.

Tempting God

The prayer, in a sense, may also be directed to our tendency to tempt God. One of the temptations we are praying not be to be led into is that which was so common to the children of Israel in the wilderness - the temptation to tempt God. In Exodus 17:2 (NKJV) we read,

> *Therefore the people contended with Moses, and said, "Give us water, that we may drink." So Moses said to them, "Why do you contend with me? Why do you tempt the LORD?"*

In Deuteronomy 6:16, we are explicitly commanded, *"You shall not tempt the LORD your God as you tempted Him in Massah."*

Other Scriptures tell us this about temptation:

> *So now we call the proud blessed, For those who do wickedness are raised up; They even tempt God and go free.*
> (Malachi 3:15)

> *Jesus said to him, "It is written again, 'You shall not tempt the LORD your God.'"*
> (Matthew 4:7)

And Jesus answered and said to him, "It has been said, 'You shall not tempt the LORD your God.'"
(Luke 4:12)

Nor let us tempt Christ, as some of them also tempted, and were destroyed by serpents;
(1 Corinthians 10:9)

Leadership of God is mentioned here in a negative sense so that we would understand we must seek positive guidance form the Lord. There are, it seems to me, several types of leadership. Speaking in Psalm 23:2–3 (NKJV) the psalmist says, "*He leads me beside the still waters....He leads me in the paths of righteousness for His name's sake.*" The word "lead" may be directed to the good or to the bad.

> *The phenomena of temptation, when experienced and overcome, create a quantum leap into a higher plane of spiritual consciousness.*

The Four T's

There is no doubt in my mind that we often come into the sphere of temptation by our desire and intentions, but also that God sends us into an atmosphere of trials, even temptations (Deuteronomy 8). It would be a convenient denial to say that God is not involved at all in our trials, or that the devil is the main architect of our temptations, trials, tests, and tribulations (the "four T's").

Let us understand these terms better. There is a fine distinction to be made among the four T's.

1. **Temptation** finds its basis in human desire and is meant to make people meet their needs by avoiding Divine process.

2. **Tests** are mental processes having to do with the application of the knowledge we have gleaned in our experiences with the Lord and aims to extract the pearls of wisdom and nuggets of knowledge we have received in our walk.

3. **Trials** are directed at our physical endurance; sometimes they are directed at the body's capacity to endure hardship. Paul speaks of trials in his narrative of experience for the Gospel.

4. **Tribulations** have to do with when nature, God and other external circumstances conspire to thwart our very best movement and intentions, causing us suffering for which there is logical explanation. It is not the result of personal desires leading to failure which has

folded back upon itself to hurt us; nor is it the test of our acquired knowledge and presumed wisdom in the things of God or even the trial of physical strength which tests of our endurance. In fact, tribulations seem pointless, designed to strip us of all genuine desire for good, knowledge, strength, and perspective. It is case where the innocent suffer as though they were guilty. This what led the Greeks to speak of 'fate' and the Hindus to speak of 'karma'. This is what Job went through. Tribulation has led many believers to argue that Christians will not go through it. The intensity of tribulation can open one for temptation and a desire to curse God. It seems to reach beyond human capacity to bear.

I have chosen to deal mainly with temptation in this section because the word appears clearly in the Lord's Prayer.

> *This complete trust in God means we have come to know that Divine leadership will always leads us into victory.*

The phenomena of temptation, when experienced and overcome, create a quantum leap into a higher plane of spiritual consciousness. Until we move into a different stage or phase of our knowledge and relationship with God, we tend not to see this positive side of these four T's. Consciousness of temptation should not be mainly from the perspective of the possibility of falling, but also as containing the seed possibility of a quantum rise or leap to a deeper or higher experience of Heaven's purpose. The experience of Jesus Christ our Lord seems to suggest that its structures contain a God-driven stream leading to clarification of values, deeper wisdom, greater spiritual awareness, and even humility. In Hebrews we read, "He learnt obedience by the things He suffered." This is grounds for knowing that you and I can overcome temptations, tests, trials, and tribulations, because you and I possess the quality of the Divine consciousness and awareness. God's nature is always accessible to us in the midst of any of the four T's: temptations, tests, trials and tribulations.

Now, I have said that God does not lead us into temptation. However, can God lead us into a place where the purpose is for us to me tempted but He does not Himself engage in the act of tempting? The exception it would seem is in the case of Abraham: "*Now it came about that after these things that God tested Abraham*" (Genesis 22:1). I see no reason why we as believer should not allow God the right to try us and to prove us. However, God does not test with evil intention or bad will. When God tests, it seems to be dome with our good in mind, though it be at the cost of something dear to us. We consider there tests evil because of our attachment to temporal things and relationship and partiality of our perspective.

SPIRITUAL COMPOSITION OF TEMPTATION

What the are the spiritual compositions of temptation? What are their physical or mental structures? However one enters, the surface of temptation is never firm. But no matter what it feels like, it is compressed and composed with possibilities of star birth or star death. In the absence of temptation, if that is ever possible in this body, we should not read the favor of God but examine the atmosphere to see that we have not made an uncertain destructive peace with the enemy of our soul - our comfort zone. Whether temptation is limited to human beings is not the issue. The issue is that human beings are subject to temptations and trials for the Divine purposes.

When we speak of God's leadership, we must remember that if we pray not to be led into temptation, we are also saying that we are willing to follow the guidance which God provides. We are indeed saying that we will obey Divine guidance and follow God's leadership wherever it takes us. It is saying we are willing to let go of our own vision of what is best for us and trust God. This complete trust in God means we have come to know that Divine leadership will always leads us into victory. We understand that Divine leadership will always leads us unto clarity of thought and vision in the end. It will lead us into conformity with the life and action of Jesus Christ. Submission to this leadership entails openness to the ever-present companionship of God's precious Holy Spirit.

You Will Have Trouble

However, it does not mean a life without pressure or wars. While we are to pray "*lead us not into temptation,*" we should not become so morbidly preoccupied with fear of being led or falling into temptation that we cease to pray for the positive. We ought to pray for positive guidance and be willing to follow that guidance for ourselves and for others. "*Satan has desired to sift you,*" Jesus tells Peter (Luke 22:31). Yet in the next breath He says, "*I have prayed for you.*" Even though we must pay attention to the possibility of being thrown into an atmosphere of temptation, we need to hold fast to the idea, clearly written in Scripture and clearly exemplified by many faithful men and women, that God does lead and guide the beloved positively in all areas of life. "*Lead me O Lord in thy righteousness,*" says the psalmist in Psalm 5:8. Further along he says, "*Lead me in your trut*h" (Psalm 25:5). In Psalm 27:11 he says, "*Lead me in a smooth path.*" And again in Psalm 31:3, "*Lead me and guide me.*" Divine leading is a key reason for this prayer. Through this one and only 'negative' line in the Lord's Prayer, Jesus summarizes all the positive statements about Divine guidance.

There are five spectral flows of prayer dealing with the human ordeal as it relates to guidance: the spirit, the heart, the soul, the mind, and physical strength. Guidance proceeds in steps. Since spiritual guidance is our goal in praying this prayer, it calls for fluidity, flexibility, and willingness to see any experience of the moment as temporal and draw the courage to look beyond it based on our view of eternity. Says Paul, *"For I consider that the sufferings of this present time are not worthy to be compared with the glory that is to be revealed to us"* (Romans 8:18). Divine guidance and leadership means that we become aware of the impermanence of the present world.

Experiences are seen as markers on the way to knowing God more. We are ready to let go, release and demystify any experience for the purpose of following freely after God. Any analysis of Divine leading will have to deal with the presence of the unknown and the trials that accompany it. If we do not allow that Divine guidance to contain a "dark" uncomfortable dimension, then we tend to stumble when certain difficulties arise in paths we believe we took based on clear Divine leadership. Many of us have encountered problems with Divine leadership because of the dark night of our soul, the body, the mind, the ears, and the eyes. Questions arise: *"Is this really God's leadership? Did I really hear God right? If I hear God, why do I have all these obstacles?"* Simply saying that, *"If one is suffering, it must not have been of God,"* cannot solve the problem of Divine leadership.

Taking the view that God is causing us to be born into a different dimension, in which we take hold of the beauty, glory and wonder of our Father in a greater way, will help many of us deal with the shaking of turmoil that comes from following God's leadership. This birth like any other birth has its pangs, blood, sweat, and tears. God structured the world in such a way that because of sin we have to go through four T's to attain the glory prepared for us. The solution to the problem is not to run away or to conclude we're not being led, but to insist on following God and continuously breathe prayers for Divine guidance.

The Cloud of Unknowing

When we are being led by God, who is the Spirit, many aspects of what we may seem to know in the natural are up for grabs. The purity of Divine leading points to the yet unmanifested, unformed, unattained dimension in our lives. The truth is that usually where God lead us, no eye has seen, ears have heard, no mind has conceived, neither has it been grasped by anyone's heart, including ours. So the leadership keeps us in a state of fluid openness to the Divine. In the four T's, we are being melted, liquefied for reformation. There is a stripping of our carnality and psychic orientation in order to reformat, realign, and realize us spiritually. This cloud of unknowing leads us to where God is all and we literally "*no longer live but Christ lives in us.*" This life we begin to live is lived not by the power of ourselves, but by the grace of the Son of God who has loved us and given Himself a ransom for us. The opposite of being led to temptation is being led to what is good and right, to rest in God. There is no separation between our openness to the Spirit and the guidance we receive.

Divine leadership first leads us into the terrain of our own soul. By praying the line "*lead us not,*" we will discover where our resistance to positive health exists or where we reject the very God whom we seek. This leadership directionally flows through the stream of the inner structures we have developed. Thus, we may say that Divine leadership takes us where our hearts have already gone. Therefore, if we follow James, the prayer is not so much directed at God as it is directed to the structuring of our inner desire and consciousness.

> *But each one is tempted when he is carried away and enticed by his own lust. Then when lust has conceived, it gives birth to sin; and when sin is accomplished, it brings forth death.*
> (James 1:14–15)

Revealing What Is Hidden

Temptation is not 'out there'. The tempter is not external to us; we are often the tempter and the tempted in the most cases. Thus, maybe this is a prayer in which we ask God not to allow us to be drawn away by our own lust and be enticed by it, so that we cannot extricate ourselves from the tangled web we have woven. Just as temptation is not an external phenomenon, separated from the inward structures and landscapes of my being, so neither can the leadership of God be completely separated from the landscape of my interior and my willingness to be led by God into the unknown.

Temptation is simply the pursuit of our own shadow from which we seek to flee or hide. There reality of temptation is that it is *my temptation* - not God's temptation, nor the world's temptation. It is my own hidden desire, pressuring me and calling for acknowledgment. When I do not acknowledge and deal with it, these desires take on their own personality, which then torments me. God did not lead me into it. However, since God must bring me to the place of testing, so that I may know my heart truly before God, this alter persona of mine shows up so that I can deal with it and relate to God authentically. This persona which is my temptation is not in the image of God. It is the creation of my unacknowledged and, therefore, my unconfessed negative desires and devisions which take me captive. They are legitimately my offspring but illegitimately as relates to God.

My temptation is my projected self - my objectified self which I refuse to give to God, or which God will not take, because I give it to Him by way of "the lie" not "the truth". What is the lie? The lie is that I refuse to acknowledge the negative phenomena honestly as mine and let them be seen in light of the person of Jesus Christ, so that its repugnance in the sight of God may become ever so clear to me. Jesus says, *"Because you say that you have no sin, your guilts remains."* At another place John tells us:

> but if we walk in the Light as He Himself is in the Light, we have fellowship with one another, and the blood of Jesus His Son cleanses us from all sin. If we say that we have no sin, we are deceiving ourselves and the truth is not in us. If we confess our sins, He is faithful and righteous to forgive us our sins and to cleanse us from all unrighteousness. If we say that we have not sinned, we make Him a liar and His word is not in us.
> (1 John 1:7–10)

Therefore the Divine leadership that tests the material of our making pulls us vertically, horizontally, interiorly, exteriorly to show us what our hearts, souls and spirits clings to frantically in opposition to God. Every aspect of Divine guidance is made up of God's instructions and our willingness to follow.

Our Response

Temptation then is not what God does to us, but a matter of our total conformity to the goodwill of God. As the leadership of God is a spiritual action, which calls us to subordinate our baser and grosser personality traits to the purpose and glory of God, temptation allowed by God can also be seen as performing its purpose in this way. Every trial, every temptation, every test, or tribulation, whatever we call it, serves as a mirror to what is truly important to us. In our lives, temptation appears and performs the role of, as the old song goes, "consuming our dross and refining our gall."[17] In other words, no matter where we end up, whether we believe that God is behind the trial, temptation, test, or tribulation, the bottom line is how we act in them. This depicts for us where we are in our commitment to God and His purpose for our lives.

Temptation, trial, tests, tribulations and our overcoming of them is a significant measure of the weight of glory that will be upon us in life and ministry. Our victory is measured by the depth of or grasp of the passion of the Lord Jesus Christ, who endured all these and yet came out of them faithful to the One who sent Him into the world. It constitutes the catalyst for our 'Christilation'. Through it we pass from one stage to another; from one level of intimacy to another. It carries with it the seed of our transformation to higher, or if you prefer deeper, levels of experience with the Divine.

This then means that all temptation is transitory and very temporal. Because it is fleeting, we can rise above it and we can outlive temptation. In the process we become increasingly competent about how we deal with it if we pay attention and follow the example of Jesus Christ our Lord. There is always an antidote to temptation. There is always something disempowering in its venom, though in our blindness and sometimes frantic reaction we may not see it. If the temptation is in the area of thought, I have learned that another simple thought can displace it. If it is a word, I have learned that a word spoken fittingly can overcome. The key is that one makes sure that what displaces the temptation proceeds from a better place - Heaven. Remember, there are spiritual dimensions, emotional dimensions, psychic (soulish) dimensions and physical dimensions to temptations. There are certain vehicles for the manifestations of God in our lives contained in the Lord's Prayer. Above and beyond, remember in the Divine design, temptations' main aim is to reveal the splendor of our King in our lives.

Social-Relational Interactions and Divine Leadership

To deal more deeply with "*lead us not into temptation,*" we need to continue our excursion into Divine leading. God leads us in order to elevate us to the rock that is higher than "I," above the systems of this world and to conform us to the new nature, which has been given to us in the new creation. God's leading, even though intended to raise and transport us to the Heavenly places, must take us through the rough terrain of the Earth on which we live.

God Revealed In Us

The leadership of God is separated from our concrete humanity with its embeddedness in our social-relational interactions. The function of Divine leadership is to integrate in us the image and likeness of His Son. It is leadership to the place of Divine self-manifestation through us. The end of Divine leading is God as God revealed in us. The leadership of God manifests through all aspects of our lives. In these leadings, there are particular markers which point the way and God's presence is ever flowing to carry us if we will let God.

First of all, there is an aspect which comes intuitively by virtue of being created in the image of God. The residue of that first imprint remains even while we are sinners.

Then there is that which has grown from instinct which is the quest for spiritual survival, not just physical well-being. This instinct grows out of the baser, grosser animal nature which is directed by fear, while intuition raises us a notch higher than instinct and into the low dimension of the soul. From that point, God guides us through direct impact on our soul-psychic sphere, but all that is ties us to unrefined emotion and feelings which flow unchecked into our ego. The Bible clearly warns us not to be like the horse and mule, led by brittle and harness.

Everyone needs Divine leadership: Divine leadership is a fundamental good. We need this leadership not only away from temptation and its consequences, but so that we may set aright our services to God. Whether one can be led by God, where one can be led by God, how one can be led by God depends on the depth of the commitment of the human will to God. The one who submits to the leadership of God develops a spiritual mindset devoid of inner dissatisfaction and hastiness. What does a person gain by submitting to Divine leadership? The advantage of being led by God is that it opens us up to infinite arrays of Divine possibilities and moves us quicker, though not easier, through the spiritual stages of life. As we experience this leadership and are moved within it, we are effectively and affectively transformed into God's visional purpose for us in His Son Jesus Christ.

The result of being led is that our thoughts and affections begin to conform to the image of God. To be led by God brings us to a state of devotion that encompasses our heart, soul, mind, spirit and body. Divine leading is a very personal relationship of intimacy with God. As we grow in our acceptance of Divine leadership, we will experience an incredible capacity to harness the power of God and evoke that power, consciously using it to affect our atmosphere far beyond our immediate comprehension. This leadership when followed puts us in direct confrontation against the systems of the sinful world. It puts the God-image-likeness in the forefront and makes it accessible to others who may be struggling in their lives with direction.

Divine leadership means an unfolding of Divine direction and purpose. In Divine leadership, God works with the structures of our inner landscape to show us what we are truly made of. So the complex process of being led by the Spirit to the wilderness to be tempted by Satan, not by God, takes place partly in response to our own inner fears, degree of faith and hope, and even our attachments. So the temptation cannot be a complete description of God's leadership, for God leads to provision as He led Abraham to the ram in the thicket. He leads to victory as He led Joshua and the Children of Israel. He does lead by His righteousness, though He may lead through the valley of the shadow of death. Being in Divine leadership creates a sense of worth, identity and focus *"as many as are led by the Spirit, they are the sons of God"* (Romans 8:14).

Since Adam, man has spent most of his time away from the garden asserting the autonomy of his pitiful will. In this state, speaking of being led by God or by man is an affront to that sense of false independence. How Adam can be led and yet remain independent is precisely the question. Divine leadership means that one comes to define their identity and purpose totally in relation to God's Spirit. This leadership means that Adam must let go and that Adam must integrally become a manifestation of the Divinity from whom he has sought so much to be independent.

SUBMISSION TO DIVINE WILL

The nature of Divine leadership means that God takes the lead absolutely and relationally. Our participation in this is that of being led and it is not that of suggesting an alternative to God's Will. We are to conform to God's Will. The seven million dollar question is: How do we know that we are being led by God? It may sometimes be quite formidable to find the exact flow of Divine Will. However, to follow it when it is made known, and to empty our selves into it, is the Heavenly million answer. Divine leadership is not the mere maintenance of our comfort, equilibrium or status quo. Rather, it is the shaking up of comfort zones, the dynamic revolution or our spiritual geography.

Myths About God's Leading

But there are certain myths about Divine leadership (and hence of temptation) that keep us from having victory and receiving the benefits that flow from our experience with the four T's:

1. God leads objectively, without our inner subjective soul and sound.
2. Divine leadership means the absence of rational tension and untroubled harmony at every state and stage.
3. Evil, as we know it momentarily, cannot be used by God deliberately to achieve God's own end.
4. Leading into temptation and allowing temptation is the same thing.

Like Christ

After Jesus was tempted, gates were open for angels to come and minister to Him. He showed that He was able to handle power. There is so much power available to us, but the gates to them must remain closed, because we are not mature enough to handle them. Even though Jesus was God's Son and had received the approval of Heaven, yet the powers of Heaven were not at His disposal until He proved He could handle the negative forces of the human personality.

Jesus was tempted, tested, and tried and put into tribulation many times by His humanity. These were always a way for Him to bring forth a revelation of the Word of God. After His trial on the cross, He opened up the door of resurrection and life to all people. Trial, test, temptation, and tribulation are geared toward the big leap into other dimensions. Each of them is directly related to one of the four dimensions of the foursquare City of God.

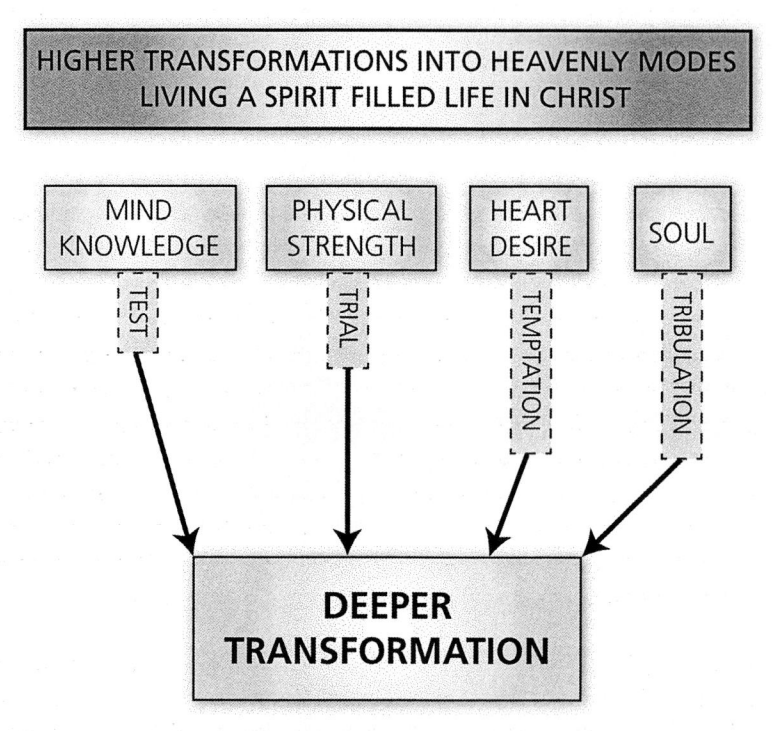

HIGHER TRANSFORMATIONS INTO HEAVENLY MODES LIVING A SPIRIT FILLED LIFE IN CHRIST

MIND KNOWLEDGE	PHYSICAL STRENGTH	HEART DESIRE	SOUL
TEST	TRIAL	TEMPTATION	TRIBULATION

DEEPER TRANSFORMATION

It is interesting that the phrase does not say "*Lead us not into tribulation*" or into "*trials*"; it refers to temptation. It points us to the commitment that places the agony of spiritual rebirth in us.

We as persons who believe in Jesus Christ cannot be separated from the profundity of inner truth that fascinates and forms us. In the four T's, especially in temptation, our spiritual agony is forced to the top of our lives as the self is plunged toward conformity with the life of the Master. Our life story must become intertwined with that of the Master; we must take up the Cross. It is our cross, but in a real sense, it is the cross of the Master. Our cross makes no sense apart from His. If in our inner self we recognize our deepest need of the mystery of His being - His incarnation, His life, death, burial, resurrection, ascension, and continual advocacy - our life story will be told in the flow of greatness. We tap into the supernatural, miracles, signs and wonders. Knowing Him, the mystery of His passion and the mystical power of His resurrection, moves us to trust Him at the depth that often may be too difficult to justify in psychological and religious terms.

God Leads From Love

Divine leadership has a salvific and transformative effect. God leads us so as to change our existential situation as well as our inner landscape. In this leadership, God acts in every moment to break the cycle of bondage to any time, place and tradition that blocks our view of Him and makes our prayer ineffective. The idea of God's leadership is putting together the broken and spiritual pieces caused by our blind flight into the wall of sin.

God leads in love, never in anger. In fact, this part of Divine leadership calls us to be aware of the presence of God and distinguish it from the fragmentation and possible misleading of our ego - or even by the demonic. God's leadership, because it is based on love, gives full affirmation of who we are. This means that God is fully connected to us in whatever space or act and He leads us: "*Even though I walk through the valley of the shadow of death, I fear no evil, for You are with me; Your rod and Your staff, they comfort me.*" (Psalm 23:4). This love is the manifest presence of God's Holy Spirit, creating an inner awareness of the Divine confidence and assurance that God's purpose in our lives will ultimately be actualized if we hold on to the end of the temptation, trial, test, or tribulation. This love leads us to conquer every wall, every foe, every principality, and every power. This love does not mean that we will not face the foe but it keeps us ahead in the fight.

God's leadership is kind. God's leadership is patient. God's leadership is tolerant of the weakness of our immaturity. God's leadership is not easily disappointed. God's leadership exhibits other concern. God's leadership rejoices in righteousness. God's leadership is easily appeased. Ultimately, where God leads us to, we cannot fail if we focus on His love, for love never fails. Where anger, resentment, negative criticisms, fault-finding, and intolerance abound, temptation rules easily and leadership of God has no sway. When we are led by God, the love of God, for God and for others so radiates from us that it overwhelms the self-worship at the heart of so much temptation.

In His loving leadership, God does not deny our imperfection but seeks, by the presence of temptation, to draw us intimately into Himself so that we might be changed from glory to glory. This loves sets the guideline for our capacity to trust and grow until we, by intimacy, recover the lost image and likeness. His leading love evokes trust in us. Trusting God's leading helps us, in that it keeps our hearts from releasing the venom of unbelief that ends up poisoning us and becomes the cause of judgment as we fall headlong into temptations. Without taking hold of this love, temptation creates perplexity which paralyzes our spiritual effectiveness. But this love gives us a larger interpretive perspective of life which keeps us from over-exaggerating the assumed destructive impact of our temptation-sphere or act. By holding and focusing on the love of God, there is made accessible to us the truth about God, ourselves and the situation. It will bring our natural body and psyche to be raised with the supernatural body and spirit. By this, I do not mean the mere transmutation of our carnal desire from one level to another, but the entrance of a new species of desire which has its genesis in God's nature.

Choosing God

Temptation is an ethical phenomenon, in the sense that it comes to the whole human person and demands a choice between self and God. The choice is between the tendency toward self-deification and openness to the voice of God.

Every temptation is about loyalty for the believer. Josiah Royce, the American philosopher, made loyalty the key ethical principle of his system of thought. It raises the question as to our willingness to completely commit ourselves to what we say and believe. Though often looked at mainly from a spiritual perspective, temptation is highly practical and material in a sense in that it presents an opportunity to choose God beyond roused emotions. In it our will is being trained to control and self-restrain its carnality. We, as disciples, cannot be separated from the profundity of the inner truths that fascinate and form us. All our spiritual agony or joy is to force to the top the truth that lies hidden in our deepest psyche. In fact, as we plunge ourselves into the Master's total life, this becomes more clear until we are formed completely into His true reflection.

Our life story must become intertwined with the Master's. As He said, we must take up our cross and follow Him. We are moved to trust Him at a depth that often seems too difficult to justify. The temptation, the trials, the tests are all meant to bring us there. But that is only if we learn how to deal with them and ultimately overcome them.

References

17 John Keith, "How Firm a Foundation" (Gospel Trumpet Company, 1911).

Chapter Fifteen

Key #9: Call for Backup - Deliverance

"But deliver us from evil"
(Matthew 6:13)

We all need the key for deliverance from evil in our lives. The question is: What is evil? I define evil as anything that does not conform to the eternal purpose of God for our lives. In that sense, evil is inclusive of personal as well as communal.

Some translations read *"deliver us from the evil one."* It is true that evil includes a personal aspect, but the idea of "the evil one" does not appear in many important manuscripts. It is usually supplied by implication. In this passage, there is a strong suggestion that evil is personal, something that we need a power larger and far more capable than ourselves to deal with. This is based on the fact that it follows the request *"lead us not into temptation."* If we are led into temptation, there is a possibility that we may become bound by ontological and existential, spiritual and material evil in thought and action. The progression of this is not hard to find in Scripture. It is a common assumption of both Judaism and Christianity that God created Adam and Eve as good. The declaration at the conclusion of the Genesis Creation story *"and God saw that it was very good"* supports this. The progression into evil tendency and evil action begins with Satan tempting man to do what God forbade. The result of this was the invasion of evil into the human soul. Humans became evil. Because of this, the Bible sees the devil as the primordial root of all of these dimensions of evil.

It Is God Who Delivers

The word *"deliver"* as used in the OT derives from the Hebrew נָצַל (naw-tsal', meaning "root"), because we have what may be called a root need for disentanglement from evil to which we have become intertwined. As human beings, we are caught like prey in the web of the enemy, so we need someone to snatch us away from this snare of his activities.

In a positive sense, it means that we are being delivered into the hands of God for safekeeping. In a negative sense, we are being delivered from the hands of our captor. As Deliverer, the Lord puts Himself at our disposal as the means of our escape. Without failure, the God to whom this prayer is directed, will pluck us from the hands of the enemy. He is able to preserve us for Himself if we stay with Him. Deliverance also entails the rescue not just of our souls from its captor, but the recovery of our God-given gifts that have been usurped by the enemy or discarded by our carelessness.

In deliverance, the Lord spoils the camp of the enemy and strips him of his power to hold us captive. Another word used in the Scripture usually translated *"deliver"* is shuwb (pronounced, "shoob"). In this case, it is the turning back of the enemy - God does not allow him or his army to transition into our territory. The deliverance is done before the enemy gets into our camp. Here God goes to battle and literally and figuratively turns the enemies' plan upon its head at its starting point. This deliverance does not give the enemy the opportunity to retreat but discomforts him at the point of his intention. This deliverance means that the enemy is broken at the very point where they have dug the ditch so that they are incapable of carrying out their evil design. At the very place of their strategy, they feed on their tears and lay down - their counsel for war becomes their gravesite. In such deliverance, God makes His people rejoice and sends weeping through the camp of the enemy. God answers again and again. All that is averse to the submission of our lives into Divine intention for us is pushed back as we direct our spiritual antenna homeward. Simply calling to mind, God can carry us beyond the stronghold.

Rescue, Restoration, Retrieval, Return and Reversal

Deliverance is not the cessation of troubles or even demonic attack. Certainly evil comes our way continually, but deliverance is always available. If we ask and accept deliverance from the Father, He will not deny us or draw back from us. Instead, He hastens to fetch us home again. Bringing us back to home, that is the heart of God and as He keeps us from being tossed to and fro by a demonic restlessness. The idea of deliverance as bringing one back again to a Divine center reminds us that, though deliverance is always spiritual, it may also be directed at the pull of our sinful self away from God. Often it is the recovery of something lost and the entrance of holistic refreshment and relief from the Lord Jesus Christ. Rescue, restoration, retrieval, return and, when possible, reversal and sending back problems into nothing are the aim of this call for deliverance. The OT uses the word *na-than* (naw-than') as a deep spiritual need of humanity to receive that which is given, with the greatest openness of heart possible - knowing that in such receipt from God's love lies the deliverance from many evils.

In calling on God for deliverance, we are in a sense assigning God the task of being the avenger and healer who bestows what is due to all whom we meet. The work of deliverance means that we are also in the process of bringing forth into the light that which is hidden or held captive by the enemy. But in many cases this bringing forth cannot happen unless there is casting out. In this casting out, we must seek the cause of the hindrance to the Divine manifestation and take charge in the Spirit of Christ, using His name to come against it. To do this, we must commit our own being completely to the deliverance that the Lord Himself offers. When we consider the cry for deliverance that comes from so much of humanity, we cannot ignore the fact that God has called us to distribute this deliverance as we preach the Gospel.

Without doubt, God is a God of deliverance - which we all do experience at some time in our lives. We all can and will experience it. The notion of deliverance implies that we all struggle with things or beings whose sole aim is to hinder, bind, constrict, and sway us from the purpose of God for our lives. From the fall of Adam, the struggle against evil has been constant. Even now we are engaged in this battle against evil and we search for meaningful ways to deal with evil. Philosophers and theologians theorize and pontificate about the nature of evil and the reason for its existence. Though its nature and source may be important, it is irrelevant to the one caught up in evil. What is vital and relevant is at the heart of this simple prayer taught by the Lord: "*deliver us from evil.*" No amount of politicizing is going to make evil go away. No amount of theological discussion is going to send evil packing from the life in which it is entangled.

> *The one deliverance minister is Christ, not man, for it is He who gave us His life and still makes available that life for security in the light.*

Deliverance Ministry

Deliverance is the answer, but not the way most so-called deliverance ministers think of it. These modern preachers I must say spread fear and anxiety, not faith and confidence in the finish work of Jesus Christ on the Cross. I must say again deliverance from evil is not summarizing, naming and casting out demons. Casting out demons is merely an infinitesimal part of the idea of deliverance. So dealing with demons is part of a wider and deeper problem that man faces and he and his progenies are caught in the web of evil.

The problem of evil is so deep in the world that it often implicates God in the mind of the sufferer. If you have a problem with this, look at the problem of Job. In deliverance, we must deal with evil as personal, social, spiritual, based in material deprivation, economic, political, relational, and a violation of human destiny. Evil may work itself from any of these places and infect the whole being. And evil does not always mean sin, though there is always sin in every evil context. However, evil always has a spiritual basis and from there it works itself out into the material dimension personally and globally. The possibility of evil begins with being led into temptation. When we are led into temptation, then the content of the heart is revealed in goodness or evil. When we are led and we succumb, then our will, the safety valve against the evil of others, is pacified and laid dormant until we are bound. The process or act of deliverance has a spiritual basis, as evil does. We can deal with it by tracing the process by which our being became bound by the evil and bring it to light. That light is God, and Christ also. For the same one who said, "*I am the Light of the world*" said with the same breath, "*You are the light of the world.*"

There is an interesting passage in 1 Corinthians which commands the church to "deliver" the perpetrator over to Satan that his soul might be rescued. What does it mean? At least in this sense it means that deliverance is used in various ways in Scripture. To deliver one to Satan so that the flesh of sin may be destroyed is based squarely on the work of Jesus Christ on the Cross - He came into the world to destroy the work of the devil. It is by being in the spirit that we stay delivered from the day-to-day attack which comes from our sinful self, as well as from the influence of demonic powers. Our everyday life must be likened to the Day of the Lord, so that our flesh is saved from its constraint with darkness. The one deliverance minister is Christ, not man, for it is He who gave us His life and still makes available that life for security in the light. Christ is He "*who delivered us from so great a peril of death, and will deliver us, He on whom we have set our hope. And He will yet deliver us,*"

> The impact of evil as social is both the temporal now as well as timeless space. When you pray this prayer, you in that moment touch the generations that will come out of your loins.

According to Galatians 1:4, it is He "*who gave Himself for our sins so that He might rescue us from this present evil age, according to the will of our God and Father,*" And there is a promise from God written by the hand of the Apostle Paul to Timothy in 2 Timothy 4:18 which states, "*The Lord will rescue me from every evil deed, and will bring me safely to His Heavenly kingdom; to Him be the glory forever and ever. Amen.*" In other words, deliverance is not my work but the work of God accomplished through my Lord Jesus Christ. On this side of the Cross, we are simply not asking to be delivered from evil. According to the passages cited above, our deliverance has been accomplished. It is a fait accompli. Like everything which has been accomplished in Christ for us, it can only be activated by faith and by consistent affirmation of its reality.

For it was fitting for Him, for whom are all things, and through whom

> are all things, in bringing many sons to glory, to perfect the author of
> their salvation through sufferings. [11] For both He who sanctifies and
> those who are sanctified are all from one Father; for which reason He
> is not ashamed to call them brethren, saying, "I will proclaim Thy name
> to My brethren, In the midst of the congregation I will sing Thy praise."
> And again, "I will put My trust in Him." And again, "Behold, I and the
> children whom God has given Me." Since the children share in flesh and
> blood, He Himself likewise also partook of the same, that through death
> He might render powerless him who had the power of death, that is, the
> devil, and might deliver those who through fear of death were subject to
> slavery all their lives. For assuredly He does not give help to angels, but
> He gives help to the descendant of Abraham. Therefore, He had to be
> made like His brethren in all things, so that He might become a merciful
> and faithful high priest in things pertaining to God, to make propitiation
> for the sins of the people. For since He Himself was tempted in that
> which He has suffered, He is able to come to the aid of those who are
> tempted.
> (Hebrews 2:10–18, NASB, emphasis added).

When all is said and done, believers know that the God whom they call Father has the necessary knowledge and ability to deliver us out of temptations and preserve those who cry to Him daily for deliverance. This is of course meant to remove the spirit of fear and cause the power and love of God to infuse the mind and saturate the spirit and to silence shame. It is to the testimony of the Lord that prisoners are set free and that we become partakers, not only of the afflictions of the Gospel, but we become the habitation of the power of God as was manifested in the Lord Jesus Christ. He intends to save us and sustain us so we arrive at the objective for which He has called us with that holy calling. Deliverance, as we see in prayer, is not by our works but according to God's purposeful grace which was given to us in Christ Jesus before the foundation of the universe. Deliverance from all evil is the continuous manifestation or outflow of the life of our Saviour Jesus Christ. It is simply the result of the fact that He has abolished the principle of death and has brought life and immortality to light through the Gospel in our lives!

Physical Healing

The Greek word used here for "evil" is the word **πονηροῦ** (pronounced, "ponhrou"). According to the lexical definitions, it could mean a physical state of being in poor health that is painful, virulent and causes one serious discomfort. It is then a call for us to be delivered from sickness. We can see this in the fact that Jesus went about healing the sick. Sickness is evil. In fact, in the Great Commission, one of the marks of the Kingdom message is that it deals directly with the evil of sickness. That which attacks a person's physical being is anything that makes this body unable to carry out the work assigned to it. So when we pray to deliver us from evil, we are opening up for the healing of the body from the evil of sickness which came upon it as a result of the fall.

Jesus healed the sick as a way of displaying this principle of deliverance. In healing human beings, He delivered them from physical evil. In healing sickness, Jesus confronted the presence of evil in illness and disease. By overcoming the illness and its symptoms, He proved it is God's will to deliver human beings from its evil clutches. It was a conquest over physical evil manifesting personally in the life of man. If Jesus *"appeared to destroy the devil's work,"* as 1 John 3:8 says, then the assault on human sickness, illness and disease was meant to deliver people from the infection of satanic power of over creation. The prayer *"deliver us from evil"* is a cry for participation in the victory of Jesus over Satan's power in the physical life of man. *"Deliver us from evil"* activates the healing of all our body's systems and restores our body's healthy function. It is in a sense a reclamation and recovery of wholeness for the physical body. Having proved that though Satan had tempted us and led us to be shackled with evil, God can still plunder the prison house and snatch us from his hands.

When we pray *"deliver us from evil"*, we call forth the healing that was so essential to the ministry of our Lord Jesus Christ. The deliverance is anticipated by the line in the Lord's Prayer that speaks of forgiveness. The ultimate activation of this aspect of deliverance is the physical impalement of the body of our Lord on the cross. His personal resurrection forecasts the deliverance and complete restoration of the human body in the eschatological reign of Christ. Jesus delivered the human body from the evil of leprosy, blindness, dumbness, deafness, epilepsy, lameness, general paralysis, hematological problem, fever, and death. Every healing and restoration signals deliverance from evil which has befallen the human body since the Fall (see Mark 2:1–12). *"Then Jesus said to her, "O woman, your faith is great; it shall be done for you as you wish." And her daughter was healed at once."* (Matthew 15:28).

Read also:

> *Then a demon-possessed man who was blind and mute was brought to Jesus, and He healed him, so that the mute man spoke and saw.*
> (Matthew 12:22)

> *When He went ashore, He saw a large crowd, and felt compassion for them and healed their sick.*
> (Matthew 14:14)

And large crowds came to Him, bringing with them those who were lame, crippled, blind, mute, and many others, and they laid them down at His feet; and He healed them.
(Matthew 15:30)

And the blind and the lame came to Him in the temple, and He healed them.
(Matthew 21:14)

Social Evil

In the social sense, deliverance signifies the sense of being disadvantaged and marginal. Usually women, foreigners and children were subjected to social evil even to the point of enslavement. Though Jesus never engaged in a physical fight to free those who were under the evil of slavery, His interaction with those who were social outcasts exemplified the intent of this line of prayer. In this sense, evil is personified in human beings who use their powers to subjugate others in the social sphere.

Social evil is not concentrated on the question of what is good for society, but in seeing evil in terms of social acceptance and its negative effect on God's purpose for human beings. It hinders the human experience of wholeness in the social sphere. Thus, when we pray *"deliver us from evil,"* we activate our Father's power to deal with social structures that deprives certain human beings of *"the good"* (This is the *good* which God saw in the beginning when it is said, *"and God saw that it was very good."*)

> He needs deliverance from the evil of his own nature. "Deliver us from evil" is meant to extract man from himself and move him to the realm of the one we call Father.

One consequence of evil as social involves the processes that human beings put in place to deny the legitimacy of the existence, survival, freedom, dignity, and destiny of other human beings. In the Bible, these social evils are continuously attacked by the prophet and spiritual leaders. Evil as social can take on a life of its own. It becomes so pervasive that human beings become active and dynamic participants. Human beings, meaning well, become "righteous agents" of it propagation.

This line of prayer introduces into our consciousness Divine themes of alternative reality which bear the seeds of transformation. It moves evil from an academic discipline into the realm of concrete action, needing to be dealt with by concrete action. But this prayer does not say, *"Help us to deliver ourselves from evil."* Rather, it directs itself beyond the person. The prayer beckons the Father to deliver us from the evil of social conformism which deadens our conscience to the wickedness of the society to which we belong. Second, it directs itself to the realm whereby we fall into hands of a social machinery of evil patterns that we cannot escape. We ask for deliverance from being victims of such evil and then also deliverance from participating in it. One cannot pray this line truthfully and deny his own participation in evil as social phenomenon. Note the plural referent of this deliverance. Not deliver 'me', but *"deliver us."* Every evil I experience or participate in catches others in its web. If it is sickness, it catches others in a web of pain and suffering. In its social setting, it touches not just us who are engaged in it or those who are its immediate target, but it can reach into the realm of generational possibility, poisoning the springhead from which the human consciousness emerges. If this bothers you, think of how we participate in the sins of Adam.

> *Whatever sinful habit that has enwrapped our souls, this prayer is directed to God for deliverance from it. The Scripture lists so many sins to which man is prone, that it is hard to list them all. However, in one fell swoop, we ask God to be delivered from all of them.*

In order to understand this prayer, it is important to remember that you as human being are caught up in a web of temporal and eternal relationships. Thus, the impact of evil as social is both the temporal now as well as timeless space. When you pray this prayer, you in that moment touch the generations that will come out of your loins. To pray it is to lock on the ever-present fact of evil which is intertwined with human social interaction. In saying *"Our Father, ...deliver us from evil,"* you reach for the possibility of the dissolution of the serpent's coil around the fabric of social consciousness of man. In it, our Lord gives us the words for releasing man from enslavement to the merely material aspect of the universe. By it, you are not trying to escape the world, but rather keep yourself and others grounded authentically *"in the world"* and freed from the poisonous tentacles *"of the world"*.

Again, this line of prayer *"deliver us,"* defends people against the usurpation of social forces which threaten to take over our souls. It also defends your God-given right to be here on Earth. At the same time, it opens one up to plunge headlong into the goodness of the Lord in the social sphere. It is about us, not just about me.

Political Evil

It would seem to me that some of the evils for which David received deliverance were social and political evils. For example, Psalm 7:1–2 states, *"A Shiggaion of David, which he sang to the Lord concerning Cush, a Benjamite. O Lord my God, in You I have taken refuge; Save me from all those who pursue me, and deliver me, Or he will tear my soul like a lion, Dragging me away, while there is none to deliver."*

In Psalm 27:12 we read, "*Do not deliver me over to the desire of my adversaries, For false witnesses have risen against me, And such as breathe out violence.*" All of these are violence sanctioned by the socio-political climate in which David found himself. When such is the case, one has no other place to turn to except God. It is even clearer in Psalm 43:1, "*Vindicate me, O God, and plead my case against an ungodly nation; O deliver me from the deceitful and unjust man!*" One of the most telling examples of deliverance from evil in the social realm comes from the story of the woman who washed Christ's feet.

Political evil involves giving legitimate voice and providing legal structures for evil to express itself. When political evil expresses itself, it takes voice and will away from the people who have been impacted by social evil. There may be many examples of this but the greatest still remains the record of the Children of Israel in Egypt. It begins in Exodus 1:8–22. This is a clear case of political structure giving voice and structure to social unease. It begins with social jealousy and fear arousing unnecessary suspicion:

> "*He said to his people, "Behold, the people of the sons of Israel are more and mightier than we. Come, let us deal wisely with them, or else they will multiply and in the event of war, they will also join themselves to those who hate us, and fight against us and depart from the land."*
> (Exodus 1:9–10)

It was common social perception among Egyptians that the people of Israel were taking what belonged to the Egyptians even though they lived in the ghetto of Egypt. The Israelites could not transact business freely. They lived in Goshen because their lifestyle and trade were deemed abominable by the Egyptians. According to extra-biblical sources, the Children of Israel fought for the army of Egypt, yet the Egyptians persisted in their social evil. From this social evil, the evil of political structures was set up to impose on the Israelites. Structures of forced labor were set up and when that did not work, political structures were set up for genocide.

> *Then the king of Egypt spoke to the Hebrew midwives, one of whom was named Shiphrah and the other was named Puah; and he said, "When you are helping the Hebrew women to give birth and see them upon the birthstool, if it is a son, then you shall put him to death; but if it is a daughter, then she shall live."*
> (Exodus 1:15)

Later in Chapter 3 we read:

> *The Lord said, "I have surely seen the affliction of My people who are in Egypt, and have given heed to their cry because of their taskmasters, for*

I am aware of their sufferings. ⁸ So I have come down to deliver them from the power of the Egyptians, and to bring them up to a good and spacious land, to a land flowing with milk and honey..."
(Exodus 3:7–8)

The cry *"Deliver us from evil"* set in motion the deliverance of the Children of Israel from the social and political evil to which they have fallen. When we ignore this line of prayer which our Lord taught us, there arises a tendency to underrate and overlook the political evil which is visited upon other people. One cannot truly pray this prayer and condone oppression. When we pray this prayer, we move the heart of the Lord for the poor.

SIN AS EVIL IN HUMAN BEINGS

The first kind of evil from which we need deliverance is the one that lurks beneath our own skin. The Scripture calls it sin. It is something within us that rebels against righteousness and pushes us as human beings into destructive behaviors. It is a nature that lives in the soul of the saintliest man and woman who have not yet met Christ. This is a cry for salvation in that sense. *"Deliver us from evil,"* for those who are not yet spirit born, is a cry for salvation. When we pray this as believers, we include in it all those who need salvation. Evil, in this sense, is not an act which we commit, have committed or will commit. It is part and parcel of who we are. In one sense, it is a cry to be delivered from ourselves. There are too many passages in Scripture that deal with the evil of human nature to bear any argument. However, since there are those who will argue that fact, we will give several quotations.

Human Nature

When we speak of evil here, we do not speak of it as an act, but as human nature. This does not mean that people cannot do good. Rather, it concerns the fact that, when it comes to matters of the eternal value of a person's soul, he or she is wholly bent on their own destruction. Here humanity is deprived of good at the very basic level. This is what corrupts his entire activity, even those considered by him to be his most sublime achievements. He needs deliverance from the evil of his own nature. *"Deliver us from evil"* is meant to extract man from himself and move him to the realm of the one we call Father.

Evil is also an act as much as it is an existence. Here, evil is human beings' defiance of God and their quest to act independent of God's moral requirements. Evil, in this sense, is the subjective and objective opposition of man's thought and action, meant to break the relationship between him and his God. In this, evil consists of the fact that man confronted with freedom chooses chaos, bondage and hubris. Since evil in this sense is intricately tied to man's being, he positions his activities vis à vis the good as an outsider. His choice creates a sense of the impossibility of the good. The good scandalizes him, righteousness offends him, peace disturbs him, and love is perceived as weakness. This is so much so, that every good becomes even for him the necessary guise of evil. As Paul puts it in Romans 7:14–24, "*I am flesh sold to sin,*" "*I am not practicing what I like to do but I am doing the very thing I hate,*" "*for I know that nothing good dwells in me,*" and "*I practice the very that I do not wish.*" In verse 20, we see these words "*But if I am doing the very thing I do not want, I am no longer the one doing it, but sin which dwells in me.*" At the end of the passage, Paul cries out, "*Wretched man that I am! Who will set me free from the body of this death?*"

It is to that cry which is within every man that the Lord directed this prayer line, "*Our Father which art in Heaven...deliver us from evil.*" When we pray "*deliver us from evil,*" we ask also for deliverance from sinful behavior and action. The Father can, and desires to, deliver me from wickedness, from all acts that sabotage purpose and destiny. Whatever sinful habit that has enwrapped our souls, this prayer is directed to God for deliverance from it. The Scripture lists so many sins to which man is prone, that it is hard to list them all. However, in one fell swoop, we ask God to be delivered from all of them.

> "Deliver us from evil" is inclusive of all the aspects and manifestation of evil in the world. Jesus is teaching us this prayer to give us the key for dealing with all dimensions of evil.

JUDGEMENT OF GOD

In a natural sense, this conveys the tragedy that often befalls man. In the natural realm, evil befalls human beings. Earthquakes, hurricane, tornadoes, volcanoes, and tsunamis are all common experiences which may be termed evil because they cause human suffering. The convulsion of nature against the pitiful strength of man is evil and may in fact lead man to the evil of denying God. Many people have used the horror of natural disaster as a reason to curse God and turn against God's children. I believe that Jesus taught this prayer because He believed that God is able to deliver us from natural disasters. He affects nature Himself in the stilling of the storm. In the Old Testament, prophets are often called to pray to help stop natural disasters or the people are called to repentance in order to avert natural disaster.

In the Old Testament, evil can denote the judgment of God upon a people or person. We find in Scripture people asking to be delivered from God's judgment, which is seen as evil because of the pain and destruction it can wreak on humanity. So when we pray this prayer, we are also praying for general deliverance that might come upon us and the world because of God's anger regarding human wickedness.

We also find in the Bible deliverance from devils and demonic possessions and attacks. This is obvious in the way Jesus dealt with demonic activities in the life of those He met. "*Deliver us from evil*" is inclusive of all the aspects and manifestation of evil in the world. Jesus is teaching us this prayer to give us the key for dealing with all dimensions of evil.

First of all, it forces upon us the realization of the reality and impact of evil upon our world. In this awareness, we are able to ask for strength to overcome it. Secondly, it activates within us knowledge of how the Father sees evil and, by this activated inner knowledge, we over-place ourselves in the place of deliverance. As it is written, "*Through knowledge the righteous will be delivered*" (Proverbs 11:9). Thirdly, this also allows us to submit ourselves to God in such a way that we can resist the devil and evil which he brings into our contexts. As it is written, "*Submit yourselves, then, to God. Resist the devil, and he will flee from you.*" (James 4:7, NIV)

CHAPTER SIXTEEN
KEY #10: RELEASE ALL TO THE ALL

"For yours is the kingdom, and the power, and the glory, for ever"
(Matthew 6:13)

THE KINGDOM POSSESSION

Two things are mentioned twice in this prayer: Heaven and Kingdom. The Kingdom of God is the main content of the Lord's Prayer and is the integrative principle of prayer. Its aspects are infinite. It is the single point at which all Divine purpose come together. In prayer, there is a one-to-one relation with the whole, for there the integrated soul of the believers, unified by his supernatural birth, communes with and participates in the Kingdom. If the Kingdom is the main content, then the Kingdom needs definition and its aspects need clarification. What is the Kingdom? Whose is the Kingdom? How is the Kingdom structured? Where is the location?

When we considered the first mention of the Kingdom in the Lord's Prayer, we considered how we prophetically announce it in all our contexts. The fact that it is mentioned twice shows its importance. The Kingdom is the place from which all emanates and to which believers must turn in prayer.

God Is King

What is the Kingdom as it relates to this aspect of prayer? In order to understand the significance of the Kingdom, we must first grasp its source and the role of the Father to whom the prayer is addressed. Of course, God is the supreme King of the Kingdom from whom all its content flows. In Him the Kingdom is formed, created and manifested. So then a prayer, having the Kingdom as its matrix, has the Father as its focus. Prayer follows the flow of this kingdom as it moves from His inner being of God to the created world. Until prayer is Kingdom-saturated, it misses its purpose and merely involves carnal wishes. When we pray in and through the Kingdom, we are actually interacting in the levels of God's nature and its effect upon the created world. Kingdom prayer traverses the spiritual domain in which various beings may be encountered. For the Kingdom is not what we see; rather, the most important agents are not seen and can only be tapped and revealed by Kingdom-saturated prayer. Prayer links us with the Kingdom's supernatural providence. We are citizens of this Kingdom and are open to it, flowing its wealth, thought, memory, love, mercy, life, and holiness into this world in which we live. Kingdom as the content of prayer works through the name of the King, manifesting through humans, seraphim, cherubim, princes, powers, and angelic hierarchies, hosts, and yes, even beasts of the fields.

Kingdom is the environment, the matrix if you may, which founds the existential universe. Authentic power flow from it. Kingdom is a tool meant to effect intentional change in the various spheres of existence. The Kingdom of God is the tool by which God intentionally effects change in the universe - and it is within Himself. The Lord's prayer states it thusly, *"on Earth as it is in Heaven."* That is why I see the Kingdom as a doorway, a portal to power and to glory. Kingdom, as we can see in the parables of the Master, inspires imagination and instigates an intellectual quest which will not rest until it finds the pearl of great price or the one lost sheep. The Kingdom is the seeing of everything in interrelatedness and every act in its eternal relation.

All Is Yours

Paul tells us, *"for the kingdom of God is not eating and drinking, but righteousness and peace and joy in the Holy Spirit."* (Romans 14:17). If the Kingdom is yours, then all is yours. The Kingdom is the summary of and embodiment of what God is lacking nothing - since all that it seems to lack in any era is within its creative potential. It is an inner awareness which influences the ebb and flow of that which it comes into contact with just by intending it so - by a faithful trust in God who is not just the owner of the Kingdom but is the Kingdom. If God be the kingdom, then we are in it and it is in us. We are intimately connected and touched by the visible and invisible realms of this Kingdom. It is a free-flowing process of our spirit in the Spirit of God who is the context. In the Kingdom, the world is seen in its Christocentric movement in which God continuously manifests into human form. This also means the world is being seen in spiritual ways because the move from God to man suggests that the world is not as ironclad as we sometimes would like to believe. This God becoming man, this all becoming one, this infinite becoming finite, this eternal becoming temporal suggests that at the deepest level, the Kingdom of God is indeed not meat and drink but spirit of flowing freely without limitation.

The Kingdom is God being released into new forms and realities for our sake and for our ability to use it as a ladder toward our creativity and salvation. This *"yours is the kingdom"* points to God as the spiritual matrix in whom we move and in which our lives have being. This is the activating possibility of inward change and world transformation. The Kingdom is the essence of Divine alchemy, in which God becomes man and man becomes God. In

Prayer links us with the Kingdom's supernatural providence. We are citizens of this Kingdom and are open to it, flowing its wealth, thought, memory, love, mercy, life, and holiness into this world in which as live.

this Kingdom, there appears a Christocentric functionality that is radical for those who are in it, so that "nothing, absolutely, nothing is impossible." What Christ means for the world is precisely this: By being connected to the Kingdom, with God as the spiritual matrix of all things, we can change from sinners to saints, from sick to healthy, from hate to love, from lies to truth, from mortality to immortality. The Kingdom opens us up to the very fabric of the universe and thrust us into dimensions of compassion and transformation that were previously unknown.

Sensitive Seekers

The Kingdom is deeper, higher, wider, and more expansive than anything we can imagine. In it is the very seed of eternity and life. What the Master meant when He said (Matthew 4:17), *"Repent, for the kingdom of Heaven is at hand"* points to two things: first, the Kingdom is so close we can reach out and touch it; second, our mindset is in the way. For us then to touch the Kingdom, or to let it through, we need to restructure the birth canal of our mind. We must think from a different dimension, see from a different vantage point and create a new kind of consciousness - Christocentric consciousness. The Kingdom, which is God's, through our submitted human will does distill the dew of life and Heaven's spectral light into the assumed concreteness of everyday life. The cry *"come, Kingdom,"* carries with it a fundamental dissatisfaction with the present situation. It makes those who are in touch to be 'seekers' - not so much in pursuit of knowledge, but of the life of God as it must be manifested in every dimension which they find themselves. Seeker is here a sense of the tapping into the expansive nature of the Kingdom which is God Himself. A refusal to be satisfied with the way things are is not dissatisfaction with life, but dissatisfaction in the holding back of the Kingdom from its full manifestation in the moment. Here those who have tasted the Kingdom are not willing to accept anything less. It is communion with the spiritual essence of the universe - and they will eat not defiled bread.

The Kingdom is the mother of manifestations. It is the source of abundance and the free-flowing power to receive the universal good. It is the wholeness and fullness of the vital force free from fear and based on love. "*The inexorable march of history drums all to God, people will spend kingdoms emerge and vanish, thrones and dominion rise and fall. The honorable becomes dishonorable and dishonorable becomes honorable. Where is the rock on which men may stand? Therein is the fixed point from which we may obtain a steady picture of the world. Why do the nations rages as well like the stormy sea? Mankind - "from where has it come and where is it going?"* [18]

The Heart Of The Creator

While it is true, God, the world and His Kingdom vanish like the fleeting morning sun, the Kingdom of our God is an everlasting kingdom. We read in Isaiah 9:7 that "*the increase of His Kingdom shall have no end.*" So when the Lord's Prayer ends with "*yours is the kingdom,*" it points to the Kingdom as tied directly to the very nature of the God whose Kingdom it is. The possession of the Kingdom is not motioned or achieved by unanimity of human opinion or a convergence of the streams of human thoughts mechanically woven together. Rather, it is an unstoppable flow from the very heart of the Creator.

> *This "yours is the kingdom" points to God as the spiritual matrix in whom we move and in which our lives have being. This is the activating possibility of inward change and world transformation.*

The possession of the Kingdom compels us to revise our hasty impressions of who we are and why we are here. In it we are called to discard the splitting of identity and the world in which we really exist. The Kingdom is what resolves our conflicts with creation, because it is a clear manifestation of the Creator's mind. When we discover the Kingdom, know whose it is and discover God as the one who bequeaths it to us, we come to the understanding that we intimately connect to it emotionally, morally, aesthetically, and spiritually. Those who have come into the Kingdom in this sense are they who can pray "*yours is the kingdom.*" Praying this section of the Lord's Prayer helps us to develop an appreciative consciousness, which energizes us for positive redirection of the created sphere.

We must not be tempted to believe that we can through anything in us conjure up the Kingdom and thus make it ours. The Kingdom is God's. It comes from God. It is the eminent manifestation of God's essential personality. Indeed, His infinitude, the riches of this Kingdom, the immensity of all its time and space are at the disposal of those who grasp it and are willing to participate in the Kingdom.

If indeed the kingdom is the focal point of our freedom and our eternal establishments, then we must live in its liberating reality now. For this reason, we can never consider our present moment, not even our willed future, as being shut or closed in. The Kingdom is the future that is present with us, as God is with us.

The New Humanity

Being in the Kingdom is letting something significant and truly moving emerge from within us. It is being moved and being open to dimensions that are full of possibilities. The power of those who possess the Kingdom is measured by the capacity to sustain meaning in this life and in the life to come. Being a manifestation of God, it holds the potential of crystallizing meaning into our new and inexperienced contexts. The Kingdom, which is God's, needs no justification by the old systems of the world. Nor does the Kingdom seek its reason in the flux of the merit of human feeling. It is an intentional production of God's eternal being. *"Yours is the kingdom"* is a reference to God's ownership and points to the inward growth and uniqueness of its pattern. We who pray *"your kingdom come"* and end it with the phrase *"yours is the kingdom,"* accept that we are involved in Divine environments which form the matrix for the bursting forth of the new humanity. In possessing the Kingdom by the benevolence of its owner, we possess the possibility of a continuous experience which is nothing more than manifesting God in all aspects of the universe.

The key to the Kingdom is this: God has determined to be fully available to all strata of creation. There is a statement in Scripture which suggests that though the Kingdom belongs to God, He is willing to give it to us. Jesus said to the disciples, *"Do not be afraid, little flock, for your Father has chosen gladly to give you the kingdom."* (Luke 12:32). In this sense, the Kingdom is God's and ours. I find this intricate connection between Divine ownership and our ownership rather intriguing. *"Yours is the kingdom"* implies that if I am God's son, then the Kingdom is mine, too. So when we come to end of the Lord's Prayer, we come to a thorough conclusion of our place in the scheme of Divine things. It is therefore a prophetic pronunciation of our place in God and in all that God does.

God's, Christ's, Ours

The power of this prophetic pronunciation *"yours is the kingdom"* can only be understood if we look at the life, act, suffering, passion, death, burial, and resurrection of Jesus Christ. For after Christ, one cannot speak of the Kingdom as belonging to God without speaking of the Kingdom belong to Jesus, also whom God has brought into Himself as co-heir. Again, Jesus said, *"Fear not, little flock; for it is your Father's good pleasure to give you the kingdom."* This is said without reservation. If the purpose for creating man was to give him dominion and rule, then the Kingdom cannot be said to belong to God alone for God intended from the beginning to give it to man, even if that Man is the only Son of God.

The Kingdom of God, Jesus said, it's at your door, "*it is at hand.*" It is a Divine innovation. The nature of Divine innovation is seen in all clarity in the person of Christ, who is the God-Man. In Him, the reality of the Kingdom is embedded and uncovered. Through Him, we see into the nature of God's Kingdom. As I said before, if the Kingdom is God's and we are God's children, then the Kingdom is ours. If this is not acceptable, then consider that we who are believers are now in Christ and Christ is in God. In Him, through Him and with Him, we inherit the Kingdom. The implications of these statements are far-reaching. If we identify with Christ's life, passion, death, and resurrection and He is identified with us, then our identity is a God-identity.

In speaking to the children of Levi, God said, "*I am their inheritance.*" So the Kingdom is not only in us but among us, through us and for us. Now, by saying that the Kingdom belongs to everyone, we mean only everyone who is Christ's, though potentially we must admit it is for everyone. This said, we must still remember that possessing the Kingdom is not merely an ideal or an impersonal abstraction - it is an actual, relational, interconnection of your person and my person with God. Through Jesus, the "All" has become my "All." Mine too is the Kingdom, not as its originator but as its inheritor. My prayer, "Yours is the kingdom," is the prophetic announcement of my being embedded in the King and the Kingdom.

The Kingdom is mine now, although it is still waiting to be manifested. I live in it now, though I will live in it in the future. Herein is the mystery. That which is mine is still going to be mine. Why is this so? Because there are areas of my being that are still waiting to be awakened. These dimensions of my being shall not wake up until the last human being comes to consciousness. This completed, and yet to be completed, is the mystery of the King and the Kingdom. According to E. Stanley Jones, "*The kingdom is written in the Constitution of our being*" yet its mysteries are yet unfolding. It is God's bequeathal of Himself to us in His Son Jesus Christ.[19]

E. Stanley Jones states further that:

"*When we fling open the doors of our being and let the Kingdom invasion possess us, we are not letting something strange, something alien and sinister into our being but the benevolent God whose mercy endures forever. We are letting in the very Fact for which we are made. The Kingdom within us rises to meet the Kingdom without us and together they cast out the unnatural Kingdom of sin and evil. The coming of this invading kingdom has the feel of homecoming about it.*"[20]

God's To Share

"*Thine is the kingdom*" puts a check on every human arrogation of rulership and power. After we have spoken of dominion and rulership given to human beings, talked about potentials and possibilities, theologized and divinized to the nth degree, the truth remains that God rules all. "*The Earth is the Lord's and fullness thereof; the world and all who dwell in it.*"

The Kingdom is not man's search for God nor is it man's action on behalf of God. It cannot be said to be originated in man or to belong to man in an absolute sense. It can only be given to man - as in "*thy kingdom come.*" The Kingdom as God's sole possession, which God either

The Kingdom is the essence of Divine alchemy, in which God becomes man and man becomes God.

chooses to share or not to share with creatures, is absolutely and unequivocally God's. Because the Kingdom is God's, man cannot progressively attain it by changing his social or even moral order. The Kingdom being God's carries the value of God and becomes the ordering bases of all that it touches. It may be important to note that Jesus taught us to pray "*thy Kingdom come... on Earth as it is in Heaven*" - not thy kingdom come to Heaven as it is on Earth. There is no reversal of this statement in any part of Scripture. Nowhere is the Kingdom said to go to Heaven as conceived on Earth by men and women, no matter how righteous they may be. Rather, the Kingdom descends from Heaven, if you like the ladder model. It grows from God if agriculture is your thing. It flows from God if you are a scientist. It is energized by God, if you have been tinged by the new age energy language. It flows from God into the whole universe which is subject to God's sovereignty and potency. The Kingdom is God's because:

- God is its legitimate Ruler;
- God is its foundation and its capstone;
- God is its Creator, Sustainer and Redeemer;
- The Kingdom's vision flows from within the recesses of His being, affecting every created thing.

THE KINGDOM IS GOD'S BECAUSE GOD IS THE KINGDOM

Because God is without end, the Kingdom flows unceasingly until it's either realized in creatures or something in them gives and they cease. The Kingdom is the presentation of God as God to creation for the complete fulfillment of God-

> The Kingdom is the mother of manifestations. It is the source of abundance and the free-flowing power to receive the universal good.

self in all. When we apprehend "*thine is the Kingdom,*" then we have come to the possession of the final good. We have arrived at that which all religious systems have sought often without any success. The Kingdom as God's possession is the ultimate ideal and to come to the realization of this connection between the Kingdom and God is the ultimate ideal, the Holy Grail that all mystics seek. The power of Christianity is the affirmation that Jesus Christ is God in the flesh, thus, making Him the King and Kingdom brought to Earth. It is the ultimate affirmation that the Kingdom must come from above, not from below. This is the response to the request which interrupts the human claim to supremacy in any realm. God's Will is done on Earth because the Kingdom is yours. We are forgiven because the Kingdom is yours. We forgive each other because the Kingdom is yours. We receive provision - "*daily bread*" - because the Kingdom is yours. We are not led into temptation because the Kingdom is yours. We are delivered from evil because the Kingdom is yours.

THE POWER

"Yours is the... power"

Power is the active force for the creation of something out of nothing or recreation and reordering of all the things in creation to make them manifest their Divine form. It is God's strength and ability. In God, it is inherent, not borrowed, residing in Him by virtue of God's eternal nature. When God exerts and puts forth power for performing miracles or manifest moral excellence, He does so not by our influence but as a natural extension of Himself. The Bible attributes our ability to increase riches and power to get wealth to the reservoir of God our Father. Though there are innumerable powers flowing from Him consisting of myriads of armies, forces, hosts of angels and archangels and living creatures, power thrones, dominions, absolute power belongs to the LORD God alone.

Power Belongs To God

Power is the conductor of a person's motive for harm or help. God our Father makes His power available to us for good. You are God-born, filled with His might and an embodiment of His strength if you have come into the Kingdom. You are Excellency of God's dignity, but the Excellency of power is of God and not of you or me. Indeed, the purpose for which God has brought you forth and raised you up is that you might be a conduit of His power. His power is to be declared through us into all the

Earth. The psalmist is very clear about this in Psalm 62:11, "*Once God has spoken; Twice I have heard this: That power belongs to God.*"

> *In the right hand of the LORD is glorious power which serves as the intermediary between the Kingdom and the glory. This power which belongs to God can dash obstacles to pieces to bring into manifestation everything that has been narrated as the need of the children of God who pray "our Father"*
> (Exodus 15:6)

It is good that power belongs to God and not to man. Because power ultimately belongs to God our Father, it can break the pride of the assumed power of men. In the presence of God's power, the most powerful creatures stand drained and powerless. His enemies, which often times are also the enemies of His children, melt in the awesome display of His power. In Numbers 14:17 Moses prayed, "*And now, I pray, let the power of my LORD be great,*" and tied the greatness of this power to the mercy and gracious God.

Because the power is His, His name shall be hallowed upon the Earth. To God belongs the power. His Kingdom will come. It is because He possesses the power that His Will must ultimately be done on Earth as it is in Heaven. It is because the power is God's that provision will never fail those who are His. In fact, in this power, God feeds even the enemies. By this power, God forgives and cleanses the sinner's follies. By this power that is God's alone, the righteous people are led in the path they should go. By this power, the LORD delivers those who call upon Him. The power of our God is not just brute force that runs over people. It is grounded in God's nature as love and is never separated from love for His children. It is because God loved the fathers Abraham, Isaac and Jacob that their descendants were chosen after them and were brought out of Egypt with His presence and might. In Deuteronomy 8:17, we are warned against the arrogant assumption that we have any real power to deliver ourselves. When we are blessed, we are warned not to suppose that "*My power and the might of my hand have gained me this wealth.*" Whatever power we have is received. We must remember, "*(It is) the LORD your God, for **it is He who gives** you power to get wealth*" (Deuteronomy 8:18, NKJV, emphasis added).

God Judges From Love

When we attribute power to God, we declare that He alone as LORD has the ability and will to judge the people based on intrinsic Divine compassion. The power of God goes out to us not to condemn us but to help us when our resources are gone. This power is not meant to bring us into bondage but freedom. It is true that sometimes God's power, when displayed, can strike great terror even in those whom

God loves. Yet, we must not forget that our Father seldom shows all His power to us for our own protection. When we look behind us, behold, His power ascends and descends between Heaven and Earth. When we have no power to flee this way or that way, we turn back on the power of the One whose Source is power itself. Our LORD is a great God and has great power. In 2 Samuel 22:33, David is quoted as saying, "*God is my strength and power.*" In 1 Chronicles 29:11 (NKJV) we read:

> *Yours, O Lord, is the greatness, The power and the glory, The victory and the majesty; For all that is in Heaven and in Earth is Yours; Yours is the kingdom, O Lord, And You are exalted as head over all.*

The power of God involves avenues of both riches and honor. God's power is declared to God's people so as to create an atmosphere in which they may experience His works without hindrance. It is through the power of God that we as believers receive our heritage. In fact, our calling is to speak of the glory of the Kingdom and to talk of God's power. When we say, as the psalmist says in Psalm 147:5 (NIV), "*Great is our Lord, and mighty in power,*" we attribute power to God as is fitting and we create an atmosphere conductive for manifestation of signs and wonders.

When power becomes our goal or motive, and not a compassionate process, it is easily distorted. Much of the problem with human power is that it has been regarded as an end in itself, as a violation of something or someone else to gain what we want. To truly deal with power effectively it needs to be seen as a process - a means to an end, the motive, the idea, the thought, and desires which furnish power with its ingredients for working. Every thought, idea, feeling, imagination, desire produces the power on which they travel towards their realization. Power is the tendency toward outward expression or manifestation of the inner structure of being (Proverb 18:21). Thus, "*death and life are in the power of the tongue,*" not as its substance but as an environment forming mechanism for the manifestation of life or death.

Power Is Not Force

When we consider the use of power to oppress as it occurs in many instances, we notice that power serves mainly to create an atmosphere in which the freedom of persons is hindered by physical force. This must not be confused with power as an attribute of God. The attempt to act as if an atmosphere of power is the creation of man has long since been the problem of man. This prophetic sound "*yours is the power*" releases energies that make the atmosphere favorable for manifestation of the works of God. When we say "*yours is the kingdom,*" we make the atmosphere unfavorable for those who presume to use human power to thwart the cause of righteousness.

There is no greater temptation than to ascribe too much credit to the natural man and overestimate his power to lift himself. So long as we think of power as a series of phenomena tied inherently and connected to the use of force, we cannot conceive the essence of power as pure activity flowing from pure being and pure intention. We must see it when attributed to God as the principle that unites and regulates the complexities of passion, thought, idea, and action. When we state that "*power belongs to God and to God alone,*" we then open ourselves up as possible agents of that power as we come to share in its endless flow - from its compassion essence to loving activity. But the problem with many of us is that, in spite of our concession of this point in prayer, we still seek ways to assert human magical powers over the power of God. In doing so we get ourselves entangled in opposition to the power of God against which we cannot stand. The idea that we may participate or even be agents of this power presupposes that we are connected to God as Father and this connection affirms our being in His being.

God's Faithfulness To His Children

We need to understand that the experience of God's power is connected to love, compassion, faithfulness, and God's redemptive intent. It is important to observe how the Scripture narrates the experience of God's power by those whom God chooses. How this power may affect those who are not in alignment with God differs from how it affects those who call God Father and whom God calls sons and daughters. Some people of course deem this demarcation irrelevant. But to those who pray "*yours is the power,*" we know that by His power He keeps the commitment He has made to us. It is His power that can help us, but at the same time hinder the presumed power of those who are working contrary to the Divine purpose for our lives. His power is the key element in the battle we face on our way to keeping our commitment to living a godly life.

Like the potential of an electrical force, the power of God can be brought to bear on our welfare in a vast array of things which we encounter. This power can be destructive or constructive depending on how we connect to it. It can also be distorted by persons in relationships or channeled as creative illuminative flashes of genuine Divinity in any situation. This power functions as a reminder that we need not fear or feel unrelenting guilt or shame, or allow condemnation to grip us so tightly that we forget the promise of the Lord's mercy to us. Remembering that power belongs to God as Father can serve to free us from so many things, even the compulsion of our fallen nature. Remember this power can cause us to summon

> *The power of those who possess the Kingdom is measured by the capacity to sustain meaning in this life and in the life to come.*

courage in the face of danger, elevate bravery from our anxious and fearful breast, incite bold action in our timid heart, and inspire faith in the face of despair.

"*Yours is...the power*" means that God is in control and not in a clichéd way. God has power to, power with, power for, and power through and even power in. As such, this prayer with its inner recognition is a ground for openness to life and future. When I say "*yours is the power,*" I raise a theme that reassures me of the glorious fulfillment of the gracious promises made by "*our father who is in Heaven.*" Harmful use of power cannot be attributed to God. Instead, His power provides a positive ground for our continuous victory over the negative forces of our lives, even when it contradicts our seeming sense of moral right. Power belongs to God. The acceptance of this as a fundamental reality is integral to our faith and trust in God. The story of God's power in Scripture is seen in God's act of creation, continuous deliverance, sustenance, and judgment. His power is revealed in His love and faithfulness backed by the Word and confirmed by miracles, signs and wonders. To speak of God's power is ultimately to speak of the promise of our own protection and victory.

Sons Can Access The Power

This power, though belonging to God, is also given to us who have received God's gift of His incarnation. "*As many as received Him, to them He gave the right (power) to become sons of God*" (John 1:12, NKJV). Through this power, God abides with us and energizes us to change different aspects of our lives. So the power is not merely a verbal exercise; the power results in producing outcomes in which the sick are healed, the prisoners set free, the sorrowful drawn to joy, and the oppressed delivered. God's power is committed to us, but unlike His love, it is not committed unconditionally. It is committed to those who have been proven or those who are being tested.

> *We who pray "your kingdom come" and end it with the phrase "yours is the kingdom," accept that we are involved in Divine environments which form the matrix for the bursting forth of the new humanity.*

It is interesting that the Lord chooses to use the Greek word $\delta\upsilon\nu\alpha\mu\iota\varsigma$ (dunamis - "mighty / ability") in this verse and not the word $\varepsilon\xi o\upsilon\sigma\iota\alpha$ (exousia - "authority"). Physicists tell us that power is energy exerted for motion or performance of work. Power here is the exertion of energy for the continuous manifestation of the Kingdom. By power, the Bible does not intend to convey the idea of God as an agent exercising an 'ability to act'. Nor does it mean to convey the idea of coercive force. Rather, God is the embodiment of the governmental origination of control and greatness and the ultimate persuasive principle toward the good. God owes His power to no superior agent, spirit or being. He is force originated, applied and productive, without inward or outward pressure. The degree to which this power is mirrored in creation by God's children depends on the magnitude of their availability and openness to Him. "*Thine is the power*" denotes God's ability to put forth or exert sufficient strength, force or energy that is equal to any situation. God's power is its own argument. God's power has the ability to exercise all kinds of control, authority, influence and dominion if God so chooses. He cannot be circumvented. All true prayer must find the Kingdom as one point of the Divine triangle.

THE GLORY

"Glory" as used in the TNK (Torah-Law, Nebiim-prophets and Ketubin-writings) includes several words which convey the idea: 1. *Haddreth*, which is derived from an Assyrian root word meaning "great." 2. *Hodh*, which means "bightness" or "shining," as in a flash of lightning. 3. *Yeqara*, which has the connotation of some thing that is rare and, hence, costly or the result of much labor. 4. *Tipharath*, which means "beauty." 5. *Tsebe*, taken from a Babylonian term which means something desirable. 6. כָּבוֹד(*Kabod*), which means weightiness as in value, cost and ornamental worth.

The word כָּבוֹד(kabod) to me, as used in this prayer, is a combination of all the five expressions of the inner nature of God as well as the outer expression of His person. It expresses in one line the greatness, rarity, honor, beauty, and brightness of God's manifest presence. This glory, when it appears in physical forms, is often seen as brightness, fire, storm clouds and lightning expressed by the Presence of Yahweh. To say "*yours is the glory*" is to proclaim praise to God in the most exalted state without condition. The manifest glory of God is the result of the power moving in the Kingdom environment and stirring its potential so that its light is transferred from its hidden place to all creation. The glory of God can startle by its appearance. The kabod glory is the physical tangible presence of God. This kabod was seen in various forms in the TANAK and could be observed by the people (as I have noted before in the form of clouds, fire, lightning and even storms).

In the New Testament, the Greek word translated "glory" is $\delta o \xi \alpha$ (doxa). $\delta o \xi \alpha$ connotes honor, respect and beauty. When used of a person or deity, it is the flow of beauty of action in any location or process with apparent ease and real inner attractiveness. In another sense, it means to manifest authority with finesse and to do one's business with commanded poise. In my understanding, in its inner sense, glory is the weight of righteous conviction informed by the simplicity of the good that is God. In its outer sense, it is the radiating brightness of power with God as its reference point.

"*Yours is ... the glory*" speaks to the idea of God being honorable and the source of abundance, riches, honor, splendor, dignity, and reverence balancing justice and mercy. Glory rises from the subjective or hidden character of God and becomes the displayed dignity of His Kingship so that it can be seen. In a sense, this dignity of God as King can also be manifest in the subjects of His kingdom as honor, wealth, fullness of life. This is the sense in which it is used in reference to great men and women of God in the Bible.

Manifest Glory

When we contact the glory in prayer and it becomes manifest, the result can include the physical transfiguration of creation. This we see in the life of the Lord Jesus Christ in the story of the Transfiguration on the mountain (Luke 9:28).

First, we see that His physical appearance changed; even His clothing became as white as the sun.

Secondly, we see that time loses its normal barrier as Moses and Elijah appear in the midst of the glorified brightness.

Thirdly, there is a coming together of the revelational paradigms as Moses, the man to whom God spoke mouth to mouth, meets the prophets who spoke in visions and dreams and sounds, and both of them meet the Word made flesh.

Fourthly, there is clear communication of God's voice: "*this is.*"

Fifthly, the disciples saw and heard clearly. Wherever the glory is present, these five manifestations are basic.

Sixthly, it is this manifestation from which signs, miracles and wonders flow.

When Jesus says "*this sign shall follow them*", there is in my perspective the assumption that the glory is manifest in the lives of the disciples.

The second major result of the glory is the transformation of the inner landscape of human consciousness. This we find in Isaiah 6. In encountering the glory in its beautiful brightness, splendor and weight, Isaiah's soul, thought, feelings, imagination, and spirit are stirred - revolutionized. This inner transformation thrust Isaiah into a prophetic ministry that lasted many years and ultimately cost him his life.

The third major result of this encounter is that it often opens up the flow of Heavenly treasures and riches. It is said of Jacob after his encounter with the glory that he came up with all his glory - meaning his wealth. Our Father Abraham also encounters the glory in his vision and at the end of his life, we read, *"and the Lord blessed Abraham with everything."* The glory can make one great, refine one's life and cause it to shine in godly splendor. So when we pray *"yours is... the glory"*, we ask for the beauty of God our Father, especially the beauty of God's holiness to cover us. When we press into the glory in prayer, we become saturated with the glory and, thus, become desirable to the company of Heaven as we become truly the abode of the Shekinah.

As it relates to social life, the glory bestows material wealth and is meant to support the Kingdom as it manifests in various places. It is also the increase of our dignity and majesty in the world as we read of Eliakim in Isaiah 22:23. The glory is the key granted to us to open closed doors. In fact, the glory is the key to all the doors. There is not a door the glory can not open and allow us in. Our soul increases in power and beauty as the glory is allowed to manifest more and more.

> *The Kingdom is the presentation of God as God to creation for the complete fulfillment of God-self in all.*

Glory To God

As we have seen, glory is not just what is intrinsic to God but is something which men and women can give to God through praise, adoration, worship, and thanksgiving. This is the sense in which we use the idea of glorifying God. This is why an exaggerated judgment, opinion, estimates, whether good or bad, concerning someone's splendor, could be described as glorified (see Acts 22:11). But when we say *"yours is the glory"* as we see here, we speak of that manifest physical radiance of the hidden nature of God, the Shekinah of the Living God, which manifests itself where people seek, worship and focus on His nature. It is part of His being as God. Acknowledgment of the glory as belonging to God in prayer does not mean that we are able to bear or see the fullness of this glory. No matter how much of the glory we experience, we only experience it in part. But one of the goals of prayer is to tap into that glory. To say *"yours is the power"* is to announce with clarity that God, the Father in Heaven, inhabits an unapproachable beauty and splendor. For the Christian, it is to speak of what the Father shares with the Son Jesus Christ and the Holy Spirit. According to Jesus, *"glory"* is one of the bonding elements that hold divinity together. That is why Jesus prayed in John 17:5, *"Now, Father, glorify Me together with Yourself, with the glory which I had with You before the world was."*

There are several things which we may mean in prayer when we speak of the glory that belongs to God. By this phrase, we may speak of the magnificence, excellence, preeminence, and grace of God. This is the majesty that belongs to God, that Kingly majesty of God's person as the supreme Ruler of the universe. When we say *"yours is... the glory,"* we speak of God's majesty in the sense of the absolute perfection of God's nature which we cannot attain without Divine grace (Romans 1:23). This majesty of the Father He gives to the Messiah so that He might have absolutely perfect inward personal excellence. Christ reflects the true likeness of the hidden God and has given it to us so that radiance is our heritage (2 Corinthians 3:18; 4:4).

The Hope Of Glory

The Spirit of God carries with it everything about this glory. This glory made Moses so fully alive and radiant that the people could not bear to look at him for its brightness. Our inheritance in paradise is being made fully alive and saturated with the glory of God.

> It is said of Jacob after his encounter with the glory that he came up with all his glory - meaning his wealth. Our Father Abraham also encounters the glory in his vision and at the end of his life, we read, "and the Lord blessed Abraham with everything."

But now in this era, as we press through prayer to the כָּבוֹד (kabod), the glory of God is then extended to cover and clothe us so that signs and wonders occur in our midst. The glory is the garment of the wedding feast which covers our nakedness and shame. The goal of the Messianic era is for the glory to become our daily experience and that our inner reality radiates the Life of God. It can be said that part of the fragmentation of churches and division of believers from believers is found in the absence of the glory. If we press into the glory, we will not work so hard to cover up our nakedness. To us who are believers in Christ is the inner reality of כָּבוֹד. It is written that Christ in you is the hope of כָּבוֹד (kabod) glory. He is that indwelling presence of the glory that becomes the impetus for our progressive transformation. Without glory, there is no real revelation.

When we acknowledge the glory as belonging to God, we can then move from there to ask for its manifestation upon the Earth. Moses knew this, so he asked to be enveloped in the blaze of light and splendor - which is the essential expression of Yahweh's holy majesty. We know of course that God refused, insisting that Moses will die if such glory was to be manifested to him (Exodus 33:18 ff.). However, God did let Moses see part of the glory through a mask. This acknowledgment of the glory as being God's is an indirect way of asking for it to be manifested in our lives. God will impart this beauty, brightness, majesty, and wealth which belong to Him to us who are called by His name.

The glory is clearly a physical manifestation of God's presence. It can be seen to some extent - but here is the catch: It belongs to God, it is an indication of the presence of God but it is not God. Therefore, it must not be worshiped as God. Fire, cloud, sounds of thunder, lightning, miracles, signs, and wonders can be indicators of the presence, but they are not GOD. We will see more and more of this physical manifestation of the glory as we draw near to the return of the Ark to Israel. But we must remember in all prayers, *"Yours is the Kingdom, the power and the glory, forever."*

FOREVER

"Forever" simply means to all worlds, eternity, all ages. This puts all things which are in God beyond measurable time. As I pray this prayer, I tap into eternity. In my prayer, I am connecting worlds and transforming time. I open gateways to other Heavenly places, new vistas of life, joy, power, and experiences. So I pray "Our father who is in Heaven" and I lift my heart to another dimension. This I do through Him who came from Heaven and taught me to pray, even JESUS THE CHRIST.

References

18 Erich Sauer, "Introduction," The King of the Earth (Exeter, UK: Paternoster Press, 1981).

19 E. Stanley Jones, A Song of Ascents: A Spiritual Autobiography (Nashville: Abingdon Press, 1968), p. 208.

20 Ibid.

Chapter Seventeen

Amen

In every prayer, "*Amen*" is spoken by all who participate as an affirmation of the God of glory. Power and majesty of Lord God as the omega point of the entire request is invoked. Not only is this the affirmation of the truth and certainly of the request, it is an affirmation of the nature of the one to whom the prayer is made.

Amen is an acronym which stands for "Adonai, Melech, Elohim, Naaman."

A=ADNY, which is an affirmation of the universal Lordship of the God of Israel. Of course, the name Adonai is usually a substitute for YHVH, which is the name of God. Adonai is the name of Divine revelation, power, provision, protection, preservation, and peace. When we say it, we invoke the Lordship of YHVH over the four elements, over everything in the air, water, wind and earth. By using this word, God's people in one swoop put to silence the elemental demons of the ungodly. The God of Israel stands above all who bend the power of fire for ill, who structure the power of water for destruction, who pull on the air to annihilate men and who subvert the gifts of the Earth for the ill health of man - even those who supposedly use these elements for good, who prescribe honor of their virtues to anything other than the Supreme Being.

M= Melech, in the Hebrew stands for Kingship. This rulership of God over every circumstance is also affirmed when we say "Amen." He is the King of Kings. In speaking the word "amen," we proclaim God's authority and dominion over all.

E=Elohim, in the Hebrew stands for God. Since it is in the plural, it points to the plural majesty of the Lord. He is the God of all that is God. He rules over all that may be called gods in all worlds. In this one phrase, we silence all false claims to Divinity. We subject all principalities and power to Him and make way for the flight of our prayer Heavenward.

N=Naaman, which stands for truth. Truth has to do with the fact of the reality of

YHVH over all idols. They are not real truth; God is truth absolutely. Our God is the embodiment of what is ultimately real. Furthermore, in terms of communication, He will never lie, make any false promise or deceive those who trust in Him. His strength will not fail. Thus, it is written: *"they shall not be put to shame that put their trust in Him."* When I say *"Amen,"* I affirm all that God is and thus on the basis of His nature, I believe He will answer the prayers uttered. In "Naaman," the praying person also forgoes all argument with God.

In the Book of Revelation, Jesus refers to Himself as the Amen (3:14). In so doing, He makes Himself the end and veracity of all true prayer. He is the Lord, who is King and God in truth. Ultimately, we get our prayers answered in the eternal realm because we have been connected to the Messiah by faith. In the Christian context, when we say "Amen," we indeed invoke the whole life and experience of our Lord Jesus Christ.

AMEN

Bibliography

Armstrong, A. H., ed. Classical Mediterranean Spirituality: Egyptian, Greek, Roman. New York: Crossroad, 1986.

Augustine, Aurelius. "Confessions." In vol. 1 of The Necene and Post-Nicene Fathers. First series, edited by Philip Schaff. Grand Rapids: Eerdmans, 1979.

Böhme, Jakob, et al. Concerning the Three Principles of the Divine Essence. 2 vols. John Sparrow, translator. London: J. M. Watkins, 1910.

Bounds, Edward M. E. M. Bounds on Prayer. New Kensington: Whitaker House, 1997.

Brown, Colin. The New International Dictionary of New Testament Theology. Grand Rapids: Zondervan, 1976.

Duewel, Wesley L. Ablaze for God. Grand Rapids: Francis Asbury Press, 1989.

Epstein, Isidore, et al. "Tract Hagiya." Vol. 5 of The Babylonian Talmud. Michael L. Rodkinson, translator. Boston: The Talmud Society, 1918.

Fosdick, Harry Emerson. On Being a Real Person. New York: Harper, 1943.

Harkness, Georgia. Disciplines of the Christian Life. Richmond: John Knox Press, 1952.

Hertz, J. H., ed. Pentateuch and Haftorahs: Hebrew Text, English Translation and Commentary. London: Soncino Press, 5761, 2001.

The Holy Bible: King James Version. Iowa Falls: World Bible Publishers, 2001.

Jones, Rufus. "What Does Prayer Mean?" In Rufus Jones Speaks to Our Time, edited by Harry Emerson Fosdick. New York: Macmillan, 1951.

Keil, Carl F. "Pentateuch." In vol. 1 of Commentary on the Old Testament, edited by Carl F. Keil and Franz Delitzsch. Peabody: Hendrickson, 1996.

Lightfoot, John. A Commentary on the New Testament from the Talmud and Hebraica. 4 vols. Grand Rapids: Baker Book House, 1979.

The New American Standard Bible. La Habria: Lockman Foundation, 1977.

Ogbonnaya, A. O. Church Next: The Seven Rewards of the Overcoming Church. Lansing: Kohanim Press, 2005.

Origen. "On Prayer". In The Library of Christian Classics: Alexandrian Christianity, edited by Henry Chadwick. Philadelphia: Westminster Press, 1956.

Parker, J. I. Knowing God. Downers Grove: InterVarsity Press, 1973.

Plotinus. "The Six Enneads." In vol. 17 of Great Books of the Western World. Translated by Stephen MacKenna and B. S. Page. Chicago: William Benton, 1952.

Scholem, Gershom. Major Trends in Jewish Mysticism. New York: Schocken, 1974.

Wigglesworth, Smith. Smith Wigglesworth on Spirit Filled Living. New Kensington: Whitaker House, 1998.

Witherington III, Ben. Jesus the Seer: The Progress of Prophesy. Peabody: Hendrickson, 1999.

ABOUT THE AUTHOR

Adonijah Okechukwu Ogbonnaya (BA, MATS, MA, Ph.D) is the founder of AACTEV8 International, an Apostolic and Kingdom Ministry which works with the Body of Christ across the globe for Soul Winning, Discipleship, Training, and Equipping the saints in Kingdom mysteries and Kingdom living. Located in Venice, California, Dr. Ogbonnaya (also known as A. Okechukwu or "Dr. O") began preaching the Word of God in the 1970s in his teenage years. He has served as a missionary, church planter, pastor, and professor. Dr. Ogbonnaya has traveled and ministered in over 25 nations in Asia, Africa, Europe, and North and South America with the message of the Gospel of Jesus Christ. He has seen God perform various signs and wonders as He promised in Mark 16:1–17—the blind receive sight, the deaf hear, the lame walk, the dead are raised, the barren receive the fruit of the womb, lives are transformed and minds renewed. He has focused on helping believers engage the spiritual realities which have been opened up for them in the person of the Lord Jesus Christ. He is a Hebrew-born native of Nigeria, West Africa. He earned his Ph.D and Master's degree in theology and personality and his Master's in religion from Claremont School of Theology. He completed his M.A. in theological studies at Western Evangelical Seminary and his B.A. in religion at Hillcrest Christian College in Canada. He also holds a Ph.D in business publishing.

He is also the presenter of numerous teachings found at: www.aactev8.com.

Dr. Ogbonnaya is married to Pastor Benedicta and is blessed with four wonderful children and grandchildren.

SeraphCreative
Heaven's Heart for Earth

Seraph Creative is a collective of artists, writers, theologians & illustrators who desire to see the body of Christ grow into full maturity, walking in their inheritance as Sons Of God on the Earth.

Sign up to our newsletter to know about the release of the next book in the series, as well as other exciting releases.

Visit our website :
www.seraphcreative.org